SOUTHERN BIOGRAPHY SERIES

THOMAS MANN RANDOLPH

Titles in the
SOUTHERN BIOGRAPHY SERIES

Edited by Fred C. Cole and Wendell H. Stephenson

FELIX GRUNDY, *by Joseph Howard Parks*
THOMAS SPALDING OF SAPELO, *by E. Merton Coulter*
EDWARD LIVINGSTON, *by William B. Hatcher*
FIGHTIN' JOE WHEELER, *by John P. Dyer*
JOHN SHARP WILLIAMS, *by George Coleman Osborn*
GEORGE FITZHUGH, *by Harvey Wish*
PITCHFORK BEN TILLMAN, *by Francis Butler Simkins*
SEARGENT S. PRENTISS, *by Dallas C. Dickey*
ZACHARY TAYLOR, *by Brainerd Dyer*

Edited by T. Harry Williams

JOHN BELL OF TENNESSEE, *by Joseph Howard Parks*
JAMES HARROD OF KENTUCKY, *by Kathryn Harrod Mason*
ARTHUR PUE GORMAN, *by John R. Lambert*
GENERAL EDMUND KIRBY SMITH, *by Joseph Howard Parks*
WILLIAM BLOUNT, *by William H. Masterson*
P. G. T. BEAUREGARD, *by T. Harry Williams*
HOKE SMITH AND THE POLITICS OF THE NEW SOUTH, *by Dewey W. Grantham, Jr.*
GENERAL LEONIDAS POLK, C.S.A., *by Joseph Howard Parks*
MR. CRUMP OF MEMPHIS, *by William D. Miller*
GENERAL WILLIAM J. HARDEE, *by Nathaniel Cheairs Hughes, Jr.*
MONTAGUE OF VIRGINIA, *by William E. Larsen*
THOMAS MANN RANDOLPH, *by William H. Gaines, Jr.*

VIRGINIA HISTORICAL SOCIETY

Thomas Mann Randolph (1768–1828)

William H. Gaines, Jr.

THOMAS MANN RANDOLPH

Jefferson's Son-in-Law

LOUISIANA STATE UNIVERSITY PRESS

To

BERNARD MAYO

In Appreciation

Library of Congress Catalogue Card Number: 66-17579
Manufactured in the United States of America by
KINGSPORT PRESS, INC., KINGSPORT, TENNESSEE
Designed by JULES B. MCKEE

Preface

WHEN MARTHA JEFFERSON was only eleven years old, her recently widowered father first began to "consider her as possibly at the head of a little family of her own." After he had given thought to her matrimonial prospects, Thomas Jefferson drew up "a plan of reading" for the motherless little girl. "The chance that in marriage she will draw a blockhead," he wrote in 1783, "I calculate at about fourteen to one, and of course that the education of her family will probably rest on her own ideas and direction without assistance." [1]

Within less than seven years Martha Jefferson had been wooed and won. On February 23, 1790, with her father's ungrudging approval, she was married at Monticello to her cousin Thomas Mann Randolph, Jr., of Tuckahoe plantation. Young Randolph, then twenty-two years old, was hardly a blockhead. He came to his bride after four years of study at the University of Edinburgh, then one of the most esteemed institutions of learning in the western world, and his intellectual gifts, particularly in the field of science, were to win him the respect of such qualified contemporaries as the Portuguese savant, the Abbé Corrêa.

Ambitious as well as able, Randolph was active in the political life of his time, serving as a congressman, as a governor of his state, and as a member of the Virginia General Assembly. He also took part, during the second war against England, in Wilkinson's St. Lawrence

1 Thomas Jefferson to Francois, Marquis de Barbé-Marbois, December 5, 1783, in Julian P. Boyd (ed.), *The Papers of Thomas Jefferson* (Princeton, 1950–), VI, 373–74.

campaign of 1813, and in the defense of his native commonwealth. Yet in none of these fields of action did he make any significant contribution, and both his political and military careers were barren of positive achievement. A similar pattern characterized his personal life. He lived out his last years as a bankrupt, estranged from his wife and most other members of his family.

Thomas Mann Randolph, in many ways, was representative of the Virginia planter-politician of the post-Revolutionary generation. Like many other members of that generation, he made a desperate but unsuccessful struggle against indebtedness—a struggle made almost hopeless by the continuing decline of the tobacco economy on which the plantation society was based. His politics, like those of many of his contemporaries, followed the doctrines of states' rights and strict construction, particularly in the period which followed the War of 1812. He was thin skinned and sensitive to the point of violent contentiousness, inclined to the belief "that lead and even steel make very proper ingredients in serious quarrels." [2]

Randolph is interesting, however, not only because he shared the predicaments of the Virginia plantation aristocracy in the morning of its decline but also because of his relationship with one of the great men of his day. Soon after his marriage, he settled down at Edgehill plantation in Albemarle County, near Monticello. From that time on, his life was so closely interwoven with that of his father-in-law that he has been remembered, when he is remembered at all, as Jefferson's son-in-law. Randolph was not only the husband of Jefferson's daughter but also a staunch, if sometimes erratic, political disciple of her father. The younger man's experience thus reveals a great deal about the older not only as a father and father-in-law but also as a political leader and philosophical guide.

Finally, I hope, this account of one man's life will be found interesting in itself. Randolph, so typical of his time in so many ways, and so untypical of it in others, had a character and personality of his own. In his frustrations and in his failures, he is entitled to understanding and sympathy; in his strivings, he deserves both respect and, I believe, a degree of admiration.

This biographical study was begun as a doctoral dissertation at the University of Virginia and has been extensively rewritten since the original version was completed in 1950. While much of the basic

2 *Annals of Congress,* 9th Cong., 1st Sess., 1106, for Randolph's remarks of April 21, 1806.

research was done more than fifteen years ago, additional materials, which were previously unavailable or unknown to me, have been used in the revision. In the course of rewriting, I have had cause to reconsider some of my earlier conclusions about Randolph, and have, I believe, gained a deeper insight into his character and thereby a better understanding of his predicament.

It is a pleasure to acknowledge my obligations to the many friends and associates who have assisted me in the preparation of this work and encouraged me in its completion. I particularly wish to express my thanks to the Division of Rare Books and Manuscripts, Alderman Library, University of Virginia, most especially to my former colleagues in that division, and to the staff members of the Archives and Reference divisions of the Virginia State Library in Richmond. Appreciation is also due to the Division of Manuscripts, Library of Congress; the Southern Historical Collection, University of North Carolina Library, Chapel Hill; the Duke University Library, Durham, North Carolina; and the Virginia Historical Society, Richmond, and their staffs. The availability of microfilm copies of the Jefferson Papers in the Library of Congress and in the Massachusetts Historical Society made it possible to consult these sources at the Alderman Library at a most welcome saving in time and travel expenses.

For typing and retyping the various drafts and revisions of this work I am indebted to my sister-in-law, Mrs. McPherson W. Gaines, formerly of North Garden, Virginia, and now of Kaiserslautern, Germany; to Mrs. Joseph Adt and Miss Martha Hundley, both of Richmond; and, above all to my wife, who has also provided never-flagging inspiration and keen editorial criticism during the years since she first became acquainted with Thomas Mann Randolph.

For interest and encouragement, for suggestions as to sources which might otherwise have escaped me, and for deeds of friendship, which defy category, I wish also to express my gratitude to Alfred E. Bush, W. Edwin Hemphill, France and Howard Rice, Robert L. Scribner, and, above all, to Joseph H. Harrison, Jr. My deepest thanks are due to Professor Bernard Mayo of the University of Virginia, who supervised the dissertation on which the work is based and to whom, with admiration and affection, the biography is dedicated.

Contents

List of Illustrations

THOMAS MANN RANDOLPH

CHAPTER I

A Randolph of Tuckahoe

On October 1, 1768, at Tuckahoe, on the James River, a son was born to Thomas Mann Randolph and his wife Anne Cary Randolph. The child was christened less than a month later by the rector of St. James-Northam Parish and named for his father.[1] By birth and breeding, Thomas Mann Randolph, Jr., was a member of one of the most prominent and influential planter families of the colony.

The Randolphs claimed descent from Thomas Randolph, first Earl of Moray, who had fought with the Bruce at Bannockburn, but this connection was highly uncertain. Long after 1768 Thomas Jefferson, a Randolph on his mother's side, spoke somewhat derisively of the family's attempt to "trace their pedigree far back in England and Scotland," a point on which he was willing to "let every one ascribe the faith and merit he chooses."[2] The direct English ancestor of the Virginia Randolphs was Richard Randolph, a Warwickshire country squire who had sided with his King in the English Civil War. Richard's son William emigrated to the colony soon after the Restoration, established himself at Turkey Island on the lower James River, and founded the family fortune in the new land.[3] William Randolph was both ambitious and acquisitive, and by

1 William Macfarlane Jones (ed.), *The Douglas Register, being a Detailed Record of Births, Marriages and Deaths together with Other Interesting Notes, as Kept by the Rev. William Douglas* [rector of St. James-Northam Parish, Goochland County, Virginia], *from 1750 to 1797. . . .* (Richmond, 1928), 282.

2 Thomas Jefferson, "Autobiography," in Paul Leicester Ford (ed.), *The Writings of Thomas Jefferson* (New York, 1892–99), I, 2.

3 Mildred S. Ogden, "Those Other Randolphs" (M.A. thesis, University of Virginia, 1941), 3.

1704 he had made himself the master of more than eleven thousand acres of land along the lower James.[4] The emigrant's achievements enabled his descendants to play a far more prominent part in the Virginia colony than the Randolphs had ever done in England or Scotland.

After William's death in 1711, his lands were divided among his nine children, and some of them founded plantations of their own. Three generations later, the Randolphs were so numerous and divided into so many branches that they were "obliged, like the clans of Scotland, to be distinguished by their places of residence." [5] Thomas Randolph, William's second oldest son, established a plantation on Tuckahoe Creek in what was then the upper part of Henrico County. His estate took the name of the creek, and the branch of the family which he founded became identified by the same name. Thomas Mann Randolph, the child born at Tuckahoe on October 1, 1768, was the great-grandson of Thomas of Tuckahoe, and a great-great-grandson of William of Turkey Island.[6]

Thomas Randolph increased his holdings, so that by the time of his death he owned more than 8,300 acres on both sides of the river. He also took an active part in public affairs, and represented Henrico County in the House of Burgesses from 1720 to 1722. In 1728, when Goochland County was created from Henrico, with Tuckahoe Creek as the dividing line, he became presiding justice of the new county.[7]

Thomas died in 1730, and Tuckahoe and his other properties passed to his son William, then a youth of seventeen. Colonel William Byrd, who visited the plantation two years later, described his host as "a pretty young man" who had had "the misfortune to become his own master too soon." [8] William Randolph overcame this disadvantage, however, and became a leader both in Goochland

4 Rent-Rolls of Virginia, 1704–1705, in Thomas J. Wertenbaker, *Patrician and Plebian in Virginia* (New York, 1910), 185–93.

5 Thomas Anburey, *Travels through the Interior Parts of America* (London, 1789), II, 352.

6 Thomas J. Anderson, "Tuckahoe and the Tuckahoe Randolphs," *Annual Report of the Monticello Association* (Charlottesville, 1936), 9–12.

7 Notes by Charles E. Kemper to "Virginia Council Journals, 1726–1753," *Virginia Magazine of History and Biography*, XXXII (October, 1924), 392; Anderson, "Tuckahoe and the Tuckahoe Randolphs," 23–24.

8 William Byrd, "Progress to the Mines," in John Spencer Bassett (ed.), *Writings of Colonel William Byrd of Westover in Virginia Esq.* (New York, 1901), 338.

and in the new county of Albemarle which was formed from it in 1744. Also prominent in the establishment of Albemarle was Peter Jefferson, an enterprising planter and surveyor who had married William's cousin Jane Randolph of the Dungeness branch of the family. William sold Jefferson a tract of two hundred acres of Albemarle land in return for a bowl of arrack punch, and it is highly probable that the purchaser of the land helped the seller consume the liquid proceeds at the Williamsburg tavern where the punch was concocted.[9] Under such convivial circumstances began the long relationship between the Jeffersons and the Randolphs of Tuckahoe.

William died prematurely in 1745, and the care of his family, including the responsibility for the rearing of his son Thomas Mann Randolph, fell upon others. He named his friend Peter Jefferson and his brother-in-law William Stith as the four-year-old boy's guardians.[10] According to William's last wish, Peter Jefferson and his family moved from their home in Albemarle County late in 1745 or early in 1746 and settled at Tuckahoe to look after the affairs of the estate. The Jeffersons remained in residence for the next seven years, and their own son Thomas learned his first lessons there, with his Randolph kinsman, taught by tutor John Staples in the plantation schoolhouse.[11] The two lads developed so close a relationship that Thomas Jefferson in later years could refer to the "knot of friendship, as old as ourselves," that existed between them, with only a slight degree of exaggeration.[12]

William Randolph, although an alumnus of William and Mary, had included in his will a provision that his son be sent neither to the college at Williamsburg nor to any English university "on any account whatever." [13] Peter Jefferson carried out this parental wish, and Thomas Mann Randolph seems to have received no formal

9 Henry S. Randall, *The Life of Thomas Jefferson* (New York, 1858), I, 6–7; Marie Kimball, *Jefferson: The Road to Glory, 1743 to 1776* (New York, 1943), 18.

10 Will of William Randolph, March 2, 1742, with codicil dated July 20, 1745, in Goochland County Will and Deed Book No. 5, p. 73, Goochland County Clerk's Office, Goochland, Va.; microfilm in Virginia State Library, Richmond, Virginia.

11 Dumas Malone, *Jefferson the Virginian* (Boston, 1948), 22.

12 Jefferson to Thomas Mann Randolph, Sr., February 4, 1790, in Boyd (ed.), *The Papers of Thomas Jefferson,* XVI, 154–55.

13 Will of William Randolph, March 2, 1742, in Goochland County Will and Deed Book No. 5.

schooling. Perhaps because of this lack, Jefferson's ward later came to the conclusion that "a good education, with good morals," was "the *summum bonum* of all earthly things." [14]

The new master grew to young manhood at Tuckahoe, learning his books from his tutors and the practical science of plantation management from his guardian. In addition to his home estate, which consisted of about 1,950 acres, Thomas Mann had also inherited five other properties, with a total area of more than 5,000 acres. The most important of these were Dover, 1,100 acres in Goochland; Edgehill, 2,000 acres in Albemarle; and Varina, 950 acres in Henrico.[15] By 1751 all of these properties, except Edgehill, were in tobacco production, and in that year a total of more than 112,000 pounds of the leaf were grown on his farms.[16] He did not restrict his activities to the cultivation of tobacco and by the beginning of the Revolution he was also growing wheat and producing flour in the mill he had erected near Tuckahoe.[17]

Like his father and grandfather before him, he was active in public affairs. In 1763 he was named a vestryman of St. James–Northam Parish in Goochland,[18] and in the following year he was commissioned a justice of the peace for his county.[19] Four years later, in 1768, he was elected to the House of Burgesses from Goochland, and held his seat in that body without interruption until the Revolution.[20]

As a Randolph and a planter, it was fitting that he marry early and begin a family. When he was twenty he married Anne Cary, the daughter of Archibald Cary and Mary Randolph of Ampthill in Chesterfield County. Cary was a muscular, pugnacious man who once thrashed the proprietor of one of Williamsburg's principal

14 T. M. Randolph, Sr., to T. M. Randolph, Jr. October 10, 1784, in Edgehill-Randolph Papers, Alderman Library, University of Virginia, Charlottesville. This collection is hereinafter designated as Edgehill-Randolph Papers.

15 Albemarle, Goochland, and Henrico county, Land Tax Books, 1782 [the first year for which such records are available], in Archives Division, Virginia State Library.

16 Peter Jefferson Account Books, 1732–57, Huntington Library, San Marino, Calif.; photostats in Alderman Library, University of Virginia.

17 References to Randolph's mills are found in Anburey, *Travels*, 370, 404.

18 Jones (ed.), *Douglas Register*, 8.

19 "Justices of the Peace of Colonial Virginia, 1757–1776," Virginia State Library *Bulletin*, 1921, XIV (Richmond, 1922), 57.

20 John P. Kennedy (ed.), *Journal of the House of Burgesses, 1766–1769* (Richmond, 1896), 221.

taverns. He was interested in domestic industry and in scientific agriculture, and besides his flour mill at Warwick, another estate in Chesterfield, he also maintained a ropery, an iron furnace, and a foundry. The bride's mother was a daughter of Richard Randolph of Curles, and thus Anne Cary was her husband's second cousin.[21] The match was one of the early examples of the Randolph habit of marrying other Randolphs, and created a valuable alliance between two prominent landed families.

Anne Cary, in the eyes of some, was quick tempered like her father; her son's friend, William Fitzhugh Gordon, said she had a "rash humour." Through her maternal grandmother Jane Bolling, she was descended from Pocahontas, and Gordon thought she might have inherited her disposition from her Indian ancestors.[22] Gouverneur Morris, however, thought her "an amiable woman,"[23] and John Leslie, her children's Scottish tutor, declared she had "exalted" his "opinion of the whole sex."[24]

Like most marriages of the period, the union between Thomas Mann Randolph, Sr., and Anne Cary was a fruitful one; between 1761 and 1786, she bore him thirteen children, ten of whom grew to maturity. Besides his first son and namesake, there were seven girls, Mary, Elizabeth, Judith, Anne Cary, Jane Cary, Harriet, and Virginia, and two other boys, William and John.[25]

The center of this large family was the plantation house at Tuckahoe, which seemed to visitors to have been built "solely to answer the purposes of hospitality." It was a two-story frame structure, built in the shape of an H, one wing of which was occupied by the family, while the other was reserved for the accommodation of visitors. The central portion joining the wings was a high-ceilinged hall, open on all sides to receive every vagrant breeze, and was used both as a ballroom and as a refuge from "the scorching and sultry heat of the climate." Furnishings and decorations at "Tuckahoe" were handsome but not ornate, and the frieze

21 [Fairfax Harrison], *The Virginia Carys* (New York, 1919), 91–93.

22 William Fitzhugh Gordon to Mrs. Gordon, December 27, 1823, in Armistead C. Gordon, *William Fitzhugh Gordon* (New York, 1909), 70.

23 Gouverneur Morris to Alexander Hamilton, June 13, 1788, in Harold C. Syrett (ed.), *The Papers of Alexander Hamilton* (New York, 1961–), V, 7–8.

24 John Leslie to T. M. Randolph, Jr., June 29, 1789, in Carr–Cary Papers, Alderman Library, University of Virginia. This collection is hereinafter designated as Carr–Cary Papers.

25 Anderson, "Tuckahoe and the Tuckahoe Randolphs," 25–26.

paneling on the walls of the lower rooms and the intricate carving of the staircases were among the more distinctive features of its interior.[26]

There, the elder Thomas Mann Randolph followed pursuits which were typical of his class. He was one of the more active horse breeders in the colony, and imported fine blooded stock from England. His stallion Shakespeare lived in a specially-built stable which contained a sleeping cubicle for his Negro groom. Tuckahoe horses were also successful on the track, and one bay horse won a meet near Petersburg in 1766, where "the course was run swifter than ever before." [27]

The course of politics, also running swifter than ever before, was then hurrying the colony towards the final break with the mother country, but Randolph, like other members of the planting class, did not become a consistent supporter of the patriot cause until March, 1775. At that time, when the crisis of independence was almost at hand, he took his seat in St. John's Church in Richmond as a member of Virginia's first revolutionary convention.[28] When the convention reassembled in Williamsburg on July 17, Randolph was present, and on September 30 he accepted an appointment as county lieutenant of Goochland County.[29] On December 1 he was back in Richmond for the new session of the convention. As a fairly recent convert to the cause of resistance he contributed little more than his presence until the December session, when he sat on special committees dealing with Indian affairs and with the disposition of Tory prisoners.[30]

His services in the conventions did not satisfy some of the more zealous patriots in Goochland, some of whom suspected his steadfastness. On March 15, 1776, Thomas Underwood appeared before the Committee of Safety and accused Randolph of hoarding salt, by then a scarce commodity in the new Commonwealth. Underwood then went on to suggest to the committee that Randolph was "a

26 Anburey, *Travels,* II, 358–59; Thomas T. Waterman, *The Mansions of Virginia* (Chapel Hill, 1945), 86–91.

27 Anburey, *Travels,* II, 359–61; William G. Standard, "Racing in Colonial Virginia," *Virginia Magazine of History and Biography,* II (1895), 302–303.

28 *Proceedings of the Convention of delegates held at . . . Richmond . . . on . . . the 20th of March, 1775* (Richmond, 1816), 3.

29 "Notes from the Records of Goochland County," *Virginia Magazine of History and Biography,* XXII (July, 1914), 315.

30 *Proceedings of the Convention of delegates held at . . . Richmond . . . on . . . the 1st of December, 1775 . . .* (Richmond, 1816), 61, 64, 87, 90.

dangerous man," words which could have been intended only to raise doubts about the planter's loyalty. The committee, already overburdened with a multitude of duties, merely referred the charge to the county authorities, after which no more was heard of the matter.[31] Randolph, who apparently regained the confidence of his neighbors without difficulty, was present as a delegate when the next, and final, session of the convention convened on May 6, 1776, at Williamsburg.

He did not play a major part in the work of that body, and he does not seem to have been influential in its principal accomplishments—the formal declaration of independence or the framing of the Commonwealth's first constitution. He did support both measures, however, and he served on the important Committees of Privileges and Elections and of Propositions and Grievances. He was also a member of special committees dealing with such subjects as the disposition of Tory property and the election of militia officers; he submitted an "essay" on the "culture and management" of hemp and helped prepare an "ordinance to encourage woollens, linen, and other manufactures." [32] During the fall of 1776 elections were held for delegates to the General Assembly, and Randolph was chosen to represent the district composed of Goochland, Henrico, and Louisa counties in the newly-established Senate.[33]

The next two and a half years, eventful as they were elsewhere, were apparently quiet ones at Tuckahoe. Although Randolph supported the political break with Great Britain, he was not particularly pleased by the growing spirit of equalitarianism which the struggle for independence provoked. Throughout the Revolution this Virginia gentleman continued to entertain guests of his own choosing, even when they wore the scarlet uniform of the enemy.

Early in 1779 a large number of British and Hessian prisoners of war, taken at Saratoga, were interned in a camp set up for that purpose near Charlottesville. Several young British subalterns took advantage of the courteous military custom of the day and applied

31 H. W. Flournoy (ed.), "Journal of the Committee of Safety of Virginia," *Calendar of Virginia State Papers* (Richmond, 1875–93), VIII, 123–24.

32 *Proceedings of the Convention of delegates held at . . . Williamsburg . . . on . . . 6th of May, 1776* (Richmond, 1816), *passim.*

33 Earl G. Swem and John W. Williams (comps.), "A Register of the General Assembly of Virginia, 1776–1918, and of the Conventions," Virginia State Library, *Fourteenth Annual Report*, 1917 (Richmond, 1918), 2–5.

for paroles. During the late winter and early spring some of these officer-prisoners wandered down the valley of the James, and, in the course of their travels, came to Tuckahoe, where, as at other mansion houses along the river, they were hospitably received and entertained. One evening while they were there, so Lieutenant Thomas Anburey recalled later, three Goochland farmers arrived to talk to Randolph about the use of his mill. The farmers entered the parlor and, ignoring the British guests completely, "took themselves chairs, drew near the fire, began spitting, pulling off their country boots all over mud, and then opened their business." After his neighbors had departed, Randolph reflected bitterly on their demonstration of democratic discourtesy. "No doubt each of those men," he burst out, "conceives himself in every respect my equal." [34]

Randolph's hospitality to the British officers aroused resentment among some of his neighbors, and that spring certain of the more vociferous patriots of the county were threatening to burn his mill. Learning of this, the planter appeared at the county seat on the next court day and made "a very animated speech" to his fellow citizens. He stated that "no one had a right to scrutinize into his private concerns, that his public character was well known, and that no one could with more zeal and perseverence support the cause of the Americans than he had done." He concluded by offering a reward for "the discovery of those who had made use of those threats." [35] He might have added that Thomas Jefferson, then governor of Virginia, had shown a similar hospitality to both British and Hessian captive officers and had entertained them at Monticello.[36]

That September the justices of Goochland requested that Randolph be replaced as county lieutenant by John Woodson.[37] Local resentment of his social activities may have been responsible for his

34 Anburey, *Travels,* II, 370. Although large parts of this work are shown to have been plagiarized and the whole written several years after the Revolution (see Whitfield Bell, Jr., "Thomas Anburey's 'Travels through America': A Note on Eighteenth Century Plagiarism," *Papers of the Bibliographical Society of America,* XXXVII, 1943, pp. 23–36), there is no substantial doubt that this incident at Tuckahoe actually occurred and was observed, if not by Anburey, by some British officer who reported the circumstances to him.

35 Anburey, *Travels,* II, 404.

36 Malone, *Jefferson the Virginian,* 293–97.

37 Goochland County Order Book No. 13, p. 288, Goochland County Clerk's Office; John H. Gwathmey, *Historical Register of Virginians in the Revolution* (Richmond, 1938), 649.

removal, but events showed that he had not completely lost public confidence. By the spring of 1780 he had regained the favor of his neighbors and was elected to one of Goochland's seats in the House of Delegates.[38] Nonetheless, the events following the British visit must have intensified his distrust of the democratic tendencies of his times.

Within the next two years the course of the war brought larger and more dangerous groups of British soldiers to Virginia, and enemy troops came dangerously close to Tuckahoe at least twice. Late in 1780 the renegade Benedict Arnold, having seized possession of Richmond, sent Lieutenant Colonel John Simcoe with a detachment of cavalry to destroy the state magazine at Westham, west of the town. The raiders blew up the magazine and burned military stores there, and some of them may have ridden as far as Tuckahoe, only six miles upriver. However, having accomplished their objectives at Westham, Simcoe's troopers fell back on Richmond.[39] Arnold soon afterwards withdrew to his base at Portsmouth, and the upper James breathed more easily for a few months.

In the spring of 1781 Phillips and Arnold attacked from the east while Cornwallis marched into Virginia from the south, and on May 14 the General Assembly voted to adjourn to Charlottesville. Jefferson left Richmond the next day and stopped off at Tuckahoe on his way to the mountains.[40] The redcoats were already at Hanover Court House, and the family may have left their plantation to seek refuge in Albemarle with the Jeffersons. Randolph, however, was no longer a member of the House of Delegates and, since he lacked any official reason for following that body in its flight to the west, he and his family probably remained at home until the crisis had passed. The plantation, so far as is known, escaped damage from enemy action, but the alarms and excitement caused there by the proximity of the enemy must have strained the nerves of every member of the family, including twelve-year-old Thomas Mann, Jr., and the seeds of his life-long antipathy to Britain may have been sown in those anxious months of invasion.

Four short months later Cornwallis surrendered with all his forces at Yorktown, and the valley of the James was safe at last. By 1784 both peace and independence had been won, and the senior

38 Swem and Williams (comps.), "Register of the General Assembly," 11.
39 John Graves Simcoe, *Military Journal* (New York, 1844), 163.
40 Malone, *Jefferson the Virginian*, 350.

Randolph was able to give serious attention to the education of his sons. He had received no formal schooling himself, and he wanted them to have the advantages he lacked. His oldest boy was now almost sixteen; William was two years younger. They had learned all that the family tutor Thomas Elder, could teach them, and their father decided that it was time to continue their schooling elsewhere. He decided to send them, not to the nearby college in Williamsburg, but to the University of Edinburgh, which already counted several Virginians among its graduates. Late in June, therefore, Thomas and William, accompanied by their tutor and by Archie Randolph, their fifteen-year-old cousin from Dungeness, went down to Richmond, and there on the twenty-sixth the four of them went aboard the *Marlborough* for a voyage to London.[41]

Their ship must have been several days at sea when on July 5 the *Ceres* sailed from Boston, also eastward bound. Aboard were Thomas Jefferson, the newly appointed minister plenipotentiary of the United States in Europe, and his oldest daughter Martha.[42] The young Randolphs may have known of their distinguished relative's appointment to Paris, but it is not likely that any of them gave the matter much thought. As the *Marlborough* approached the British shore, Thomas' mind, when it was not occupied with memories of the quiet and pastoral existence he had left behind, must have been filled with excitement and anticipation.

41 T. M. Randolph, Sr., to T. M. Randolph, Jr., October 10, 1784, in Edgehill-Randolph Papers. The young Randolphs sailed aboard a ship commanded by Captain Dancer. Dancer's vessel, the *Marlborough*, sailed from Richmond for London sometime during the week preceding June 26, 1784 (*Virginia Gazette*, June 26, 1784).

42 Malone, *Jefferson the Virginian*, 422–23.

CHAPTER II

"A Good Education with Good Morals"

BY AUGUST 1, 1784, the three Randolph boys and their tutor had reached London. After five weeks of shipboard life and fare, they must have been glad enough to feel solid ground under their feet. They tarried in the bustling metropolis on the Thames long enough to write dutiful letters home, replenish their wardrobes, see some of the sights, and sample some of the amusements of the city of Boswell and Burke. Then they proceeded north through England to the Scottish capital, the end of their long journey from Goochland County.[1]

Sometime late in the summer of 1784 the Virginians arrived in the smoky and crowded old town on the Firth of Forth, even then noted for its historic buildings. Dominating Edinburgh was its ancient castle, frowning over the city from atop the craggy rock which the boys' alleged ancestor Sir Thomas Randolph and his wild Scots had climbed almost five hundred years before to seize the fortress from its English garrison. Not far from the castle was Holyrood House, ancient palace of the royal house of Scotland, where visitors could see portraits and relics of Scotia's kings and hear the sad history of Mary, last and unhappiest of its queens. Between castle and palace lay the narrow crooked *wynds* and alleys of the Old Town, where most of the poorer inhabitants lived, packed into multistory, unsanitary tenements.

1 T. M. Randolph, Sr., to William Randolph and T. M. Randolph, Jr., October 10, 1784, in Edgehill-Randolph Papers, refers to the boys' letters of August 1 and 2, 1784, from London, but no copies of these earlier letters have been seen.

Less historic but far cleaner and more prosperous was the New Town, which lay to the north of the Old. This fashionable section, which was distinguished by wide, spacious streets and squares and by handsome, luxuriously-appointed houses, had grown up within the preceding generation and was a symbol of the expanding industry of the age. Printed cottons and other textiles, iron, glass, starch, and Scotch whiskey had contributed to the wealth which made the New Town possible, and wealth had led to the development of a more cosmopolitan, if less godly, city than the one which the Covenanters had known.[2]

Critical observers of the day noted an alarming rise in drunkenness, bastardy, prostitution, and petty crime among the poor, and an increased addiction toward adultery, gambling, and impiety in the ranks of the rich. There had been a grievous falling-off in church attendance, and various forms of deism and agnosticism were finding an increasingly receptive audience among all classes. Men like publisher William Creech lamented that "the decency, dignity, and delicacy" of the past had given way to "looseness, dissipation, and licentiousness." [3]

Edinburgh, however, was also celebrated as a place of intellectual and scientific activity, and its university was respected throughout Europe. The spirit of inquiry and experimentation which its faculty stimulated gave it an international reputation as a center of learning. British economist Adam Smith, whose academic associations were with Oxford and Glasgow, recommended the university as being better provided with able professors than any other,[4] while Thomas Jefferson thought that its courses in natural science were the best "on earth." [5] The quality of instruction however, was not matched by equal excellence in accommodations. The University's principal building was then about two hundred years old, and its classrooms

2 William Thomson (Thomas Newte, pseud.), *Prospects and Observations on a Tour in England and Scotland* . . . (London, 1791), 303–308; 323–24; William Creech, "Letters . . . Respecting the Mode of Living, Arts, Commerce, Literature, and Manners of Edinburgh . . ." in Sir John Sinclair (ed.), *Statistical Account of Scotland* (Edinburgh, 1791–99), VI, 593–97.

3 Creech, "Letters," 608–14.

4 Adam Smith to James Monteath, February 22, 1785, in William Robert Smith, *Adam Smith as Student and Professor* (Glasgow, 1937), 292.

5 Jefferson to T. M. Randolph, Jr., August 27, 1786, in Boyd (ed.), *The Papers of Thomas Jefferson,* X, 305–309; see also, Jefferson to Dugald Stewart, June 21, 1789, *ibid.*, XV, 204–205.

had become "unfit to contain the number of students who resorted to this celebrated school of science and literature." [6]

Young Tom Randolph matriculated at Edinburgh with the intention of preparing himself for a career as a lawyer, but he spent his first session there in courses of a more general nature. "As yet I have entered on no pursuit immediately relating to my intended profession," he wrote in 1786, "being convinced that to begin at my time of life the investigation of intricate points of law, before a proper foundation had been laid to proceed on by an intimate acquaintance with history and mathematics would not only be fruitless but tend to create an unwillingness to prosecute farther a subject which exhibited at first view such apparently unsurmountable difficulties." [7] Despite tutor Elder's previous efforts, the youth had almost no knowledge of languages and mathematics, so he enrolled for classes in those subjects. By the end of his first year Tom had satisfactorily completed this phase of his preparation. He could now pursue courses more to his liking.

He remained in Edinburgh during the summer of 1785 in order to attend the lectures in natural history given by Dr. John Walker, a member of the faculty of medicine. Several of Randolph's kin had already shown an interest in this subject. His great-uncle Isham Randolph of Dungeness was a talented amateur botanist, and his cousin Thomas Jefferson was a keen student of various branches of natural science.[8] The youth from Tuckahoe had "all along felt a particular attachment" to the subject, and he was entranced by Walker's presentation of it, both because of "his extensive information with respect to this science" and "the enthusiastic pleasure which he [took] in propagating the knowledge of it."

He continued his studies during the fall and winter of 1785, when for the first time, he "tasted of the exquisite pleasure which the mind derives even from the first insight into philosophy." [9] This exposure to abstract thought led him to question the formal but comforting Anglican faith in which he had been reared and to adopt a skeptical attitude towards revealed religion. As a result of his studies at the university and of the intellectual atmosphere which prevailed there,

6 Creech, "Letters," 591.

7 T. M. Randolph, Jr., to Jefferson, August 16, 1786, in Boyd (ed.), *The Papers of Thomas Jefferson*, X, 260–61.

8 Malone, *Jefferson the Virginian*, 15–16, 376–77.

9 T. M. Randolph, Jr., to Jefferson, August 16, 1786, in Boyd (ed.), *The Papers of Thomas Jefferson*, X, 260–61.

he eventually forsook the church of his fathers and became a thoroughgoing deist.[10]

Tom was easily the most studious and industrious of the three Randolph boys. Cousin Archie was "a young man of an open, generous and candid turn of Mind," as Elder put it, but he seemed motivated more by "love of dress and of those accomplishments which are only exterior" than by "those real improvements of mind most worthy of pursuit." Tom's brother William, although "equal to the general run of boys" in ability, found it difficult "to fix his attention on any Subject for a due length of time." Tom himself was "becoming a Worthy and Virtuous Character," whose conduct already denoted "both the Scholar and the Gentleman," although he was barely seventeen. He was not as gregarious as William, and the younger lad was regarded by his fellow-students as "a good natured facetious fellow who studies mankind more than his brother."[11]

The two young Virginians, however, shared a trait that was troubling to their elders. By the beginning of their second year at Edinburgh, Tom and William had accumulated debts to various local creditors which exceeded £220. Lighthearted William had incurred his part of this deficit by his frequent trips to England, and studious, serious Tom seemed unable to keep money in his pocket. Their father, it is true, did not furnish them with a sufficient allowance. Like many of his fellow planters, he was contending with bad crops, high taxes, and general hard times, and he felt that he was already doing the best he could for his sons.[12] When he learned of their plight, however, he made arrangements for funds to be deposited to the boys' credit in London, and he promised that, whether his crops were good or bad, they would have enough money in the future to pay all their necessary expenses.[13] To fulfill this pledge and to meet other calls, a year later he was forced to mortgage his fine plantation Varina,[14] an obligation which gave considerable difficulty to his oldest son in the years which followed.

10 T. M. Randolph, Jr., to Joseph Carrington Cabell, August 5, 1820, and August 11, 1820, in Randolph Papers, Duke University Library, Durham, North Carolina; photostats, Alderman Library, University of Virginia.

11 Thomas Elder to Jefferson, October, 1785, in Boyd (ed.), *The Papers of Thomas Jefferson,* VIII, 687.

12 T. M. Randolph, Sr., to T. M. Randolph, Jr., November 29, 1785, in Edgehill-Randolph Papers.

13 Randolph, Sr., to Randolph, Jr., December 23, 1785, in Kean Deposit, Alderman Library, University of Virginia.

14 T. M. Randolph, Jr., to Jefferson, October 31, 1793, in Jefferson Papers, Massachusetts Historical Society, Boston.

More serious than the temporary shortage of funds was the state of Tom's health. He fell ill during the autumn of 1785, probably from some respiratory complaint, and he recuperated so slowly that his tutor began to fear that "the stamina of his constitution" was "not vigorous enough for those exertions necessary for making the most distinguished figure in life." He thought it best for the youth to leave the cold wet climate of Scotland for some warmer place on the Continent and to complete his schooling there.[15] Cousin Thomas Jefferson recommended that the Randolphs spend the winter at Rome, where "there is a genial climate like their native one" and "classical ground to tread upon . . . and lessons in painting, sculpture and architecture . . . which no other place can offer." [16]

Presumably because of an improvement in Tom's physical condition, the move to Italy was not carried out, and the young men remained in Edinburgh for another winter. By the summer of 1786 the patient was well enough to undertake another series of lectures in natural history under Dr. Walker. He had now decided to continue his studies for "the time which is generally thought sufficient . . . for the completion of an academical education." In August Tom wrote to Jefferson and outlined his plans for the coming session. "It is my intention to attend this winter the lectures on Natural philosophy and civil history, perhaps likewise on Anatomy, for I have a great desire to obtain some knowledge of the structure of the human body, but am uncertain whether it would not be more advantageous to defer it some time yet. Your advice not only on that particular but the whole course of my education would be extremely acceptable and shall be implicitly followed." [17]

Thomas Elder had returned to Virginia sometime in 1786, after repeated appeals by his employer to undertake the education of the younger children,[18] and the departure of his tutor may have caused Tom to turn for guidance to his distinguished and sympathetic

15 Thomas Elder to Jefferson, October, 1785, in Boyd (ed.), *The Papers of Thomas Jefferson*, VIII, 687. The exact nature of Randolph's illness is not given in the correspondence. His father, writing from Tuckahoe, thought it no more than a result of his over-rapid growth. See T. M. Randolph, Sr., to T. M. Randolph, Jr., November 29, 1785, in Edgehill-Randolph Papers.

16 Jefferson to Elder, November 25, 1785, in Boyd (ed.), *The Papers of Thomas Jefferson*, IX, 58–59; Jefferson to T. M. Randolph, Jr., November 25, 1785, *ibid.*, IX, 59–60.

17 T. M. Randolph, Jr., to Jefferson, August 16, 1786, *ibid.*, X, 260–61.

18 T. M. Randolph, Sr., to T. M. Randolph, Jr., December 23, 1785, in Kean Deposit, Alderman Library; Randolph, Sr., to Thomas Elder, March 16, 1786, in Edgehill-Randolph Papers.

kinsman in Paris. Jefferson, ever keenly interested in education of the younger generation, was even then carefully supervising the training of his daughter Martha, a student at the fashionable Paris convent school, the Abbaye Royale de Pentemont, and had previously given advice to other youths, including his nephew Peter Carr,[19] so he gladly undertook to provide similar guidance and inspiration for his cousin.

His interest stemmed partly from his regard for young Randolph's parents and partly from the favorable reports he had had of the youth's own "genius and good disposition." [20] Jefferson began by encouraging Tom's interest in scientific subjects, and he recommended the study of anatomy, natural history, astronomy, botany, chemistry, and natural philosophy. When Tom had completed his academic work in Edinburgh, Jefferson proposed that he then come to France and learn the language of Voltaire and Lafayette while he pored over Coke and Blackstone.[21]

Before this advice reached him, Tom was already pursuing courses in anatomy and natural history, and during the session of 1786–87 he attended lectures in astronomy, chemistry, natural philosophy, and natural history. He also became an active member of "a society instituted . . . for the encouragement of the study of natural history among the students." In February, 1787, he took "the liberty to procure the seat of an honorary member" in this organization for Jefferson.

By the spring of 1787 Tom was giving serious consideration to the choice of a field of study. "It was not without the greatest difficulty and agitation of mind," he wrote Jefferson in April, "that I could select one [subject] to be the object of my future and allmost sole pursuit. Indeed as on it my success in life hereafter must entirely depend, to determine a matter of such importance without a struggle could argue a stupid carelessness and insensibility." He was still enchanted "with the charms of Natural History" and he still felt that "it was the most rational and agreeable amusement in which hours of relaxation could be employed," but he had come to the conclusion that "it was too trivial to spend a whole life in the prosecution of." He was also attracted by natural philosophy, because of "the exalted nature of its objects, and the utility which

19 Malone, *Jefferson the Virginian*, 393.
20 Jefferson to T. M. Randolph, Jr., November 25, 1785, in Boyd (ed.), *The Papers of Thomas Jefferson*, IX, 59–60.
21 Jefferson to Randolph, Jr., August 27, 1786, *ibid.*, X, 305–306.

mankind in general derive from their investigation," and by mathematics, "that delightful tho abstract science." Ambition, however, kept him "from fixing on a knowledge of either of these as the sole end to which I would wish to attain." He had come, finally, to the conclusion that "politics was a science which would lead to the highest honours in a free state, and . . . would be of the greatest utility to the community in an infant one," and he therefore "resolved to apply chiefly to it. From this time Montesquieu and Hume have been my chief study."[22]

Jefferson cordially approved his young cousin's choice of a career in politics. "It will remain," he replied, "to those now coming on the stage of public affairs to perfect what has been so well begun by those going off it." He repeated his previous advice that Tom complete his education on the continent and recommended that he remain in France for two years, living in one of the villages near Paris, where he would learn the language while reading widely in history, politics, and rhetoric. Later, according to Jefferson's plan, he would make the Grand Tour, visiting various provinces of France and Italy. After that, the young Virginian would return to Virginia and pursue his legal studies under Jefferson's own former teacher George Wythe of Williamsburg, for the diplomat felt that a knowledge of the law was absolutely necessary to anyone who contemplated a legislative career.[23]

One obstacle to the realization of this ambitious project was the wish of Tom's father that the youth return to Virginia by the summer of 1788. Jefferson therefore wrote to Tuckahoe to explain his plan, and requested the father's consent.[24] As the latter had already found it necessary to mortgage Varina, the prospect of financing another three years of education for his son must have given him concern. On the other hand, he had received reports from several persons, among them probably Thomas Elder, that Tom was "a boy of good disposition and very studious," and he was probably flattered by Jefferson's interest in his son. So he accepted the new proposals gratefully, if not wholeheartedly, and told his kinsman in Paris to "pray do as you please with him."[25]

22 Randolph, Jr., to Jefferson, April 14, 1787, *ibid.*, XI, 291–93.
23 Jefferson to Randolph, Jr., July 6, 1787, *ibid.*, XI, 556–59; see note to Jefferson to Randolph, Sr., August 11, 1787, *ibid.*, XII, 22, for plans for the grand tour.
24 Jefferson to T. M. Randolph, Sr., August 11, 1787, *ibid.*, XII, 20–22.
25 Randolph, Sr., to Jefferson, November 19, 1787, *ibid.*, XII, 370–71. See also Anne Cary Randolph to Jefferson, November 3, 1787, *ibid.*, XV, 638–39.

While his elders were deliberating, Tom continued his studies in Scotland. He spent the summer of 1787 attending lectures in anatomy and in botany, supplementing the anatomy lectures with visits of observation to Edinburgh's charity hospital, the Royal Infirmary. After an expedition to one of the "close wards" of that institution, he caught a fever, and his sickness hung on throughout early fall, sapping his strength so much that his college friends became anxious about his recovery.[26] But he was well enough by the middle of the autumn to return to his studies.

About this time he acquired a new friend and advisor. John Leslie, the son of a cabinetmaker of Fifeshire and an alumnus of St. Andrew's University, had recently been appointed as a tutor in mathematics and natural philosophy at the university. The young Scot was a self-styled citizen of the world who proclaimed liberal political views and an admiration of America, but it was probably his informed enthusiasm for science which did most to draw him and the Virginian together.[27]

Instead of going to France late in 1787 as Jefferson and his father had expected, Tom remained in Edinburgh that fall and winter, studying mathematics under Leslie's supervision.[28] His neglect to notify Jefferson of this change in plans provoked an anxious inquiry from Paris the following February, but he apparently did not take the trouble to answer it. As 1788 drew to a close Jefferson was still uninformed concerning Tom's whereabouts.[29]

Perhaps he yet intended to go on to Paris when he had finished his studies under Leslie, but before he could do so, his brother William received a stern letter from Tuckahoe. Reports about William's poor academic progress had been carried back, first by Elder and then apparently by Cousin Archie, who had departed for Virginia in the fall of 1787, leaving in such a hurry that he had forgotten his

26 Josiah Wedgwood, Jr., to T. M. Randolph, Jr., November 9, 1787, in Jefferson Papers, Massachusetts Historical Society, with Randolph's note thereon. Thomson, *Prospects and Observations,* 342–43, identifies the hospital.

27 "Sir John Leslie," *Dictionary of National Biography* (London, 1885–1900), XXXIII, 105; William Hanna, *Memoirs of the Life and Writings of Thomas Chalmers . . .* (New York, 1850), I, 465.

28 T. M. Randolph, Jr., to T. M. Randolph, Sr., April –, 1789, in Edgehill–Randolph Papers.

29 Jefferson to T. M. Randolph, Jr., February 28, 1788, in Boyd (ed.), *The Papers of Thomas Jefferson,* XII, 631–32; Jefferson to James Currie, December 20, 1788, *ibid.*, XIV, 365.

"sea-stores." [30] As a result of these reports, the elder Randolph early in 1788 ordered the frivolous younger son to return home.

As soon as the highly sensitive Tom learned that his brother was being summoned home, he wrote his father for permission to return. At the same time he tried to explain his motives to his mother. He was not deliberately abandoning the plans for study in Paris, he said, and he was deeply grateful to Jefferson for the latter's interest in him. He felt, however, that he was now capable of completing his education by a course of reading alone. Furthermore, he found the very prospect of parting from William was exceedingly disagreeable, and he admitted that he was eager to see his home again.[31] While he did not mention the state of his health, it is probable that his illness of the previous fall influenced his decision.

When John Leslie learned of his pupil's intentions he did his best to dissuade him, urging him not to throw away all his efforts of the past three years, and cautioning against "the blind desire of revisiting your native clime," [32] for Leslie sensed that homesickness influenced this abrupt decision. Part of the Scot's anxiety seems to have been inspired by genuine friendship and by a sincere desire to see him complete his education. But it also stemmed from the fact that Leslie had abandoned his tutorial position at Edinburgh on the strength of Tom's offer of a similar position in Virginia, an offer which the latter's father had not yet confirmed.[33]

In addition to urging patience, the tutor suggested a tour of England and Scotland as a means of passing the time before the Virginian's departure. The proposed itinerary, which included visits to the lead mines of Derbyshire, the pottery works of Staffordshire, the Duke of Bridgewater's canal, the libraries and museums of Oxford and London, failed to excite or even to interest Randolph.[34] By the end of June he had left his lodgings at St. Patrick's Square in

30 Josiah Wedgwood, Jr., to T. M. Randolph, Jr., November 9, 1787, in Jefferson Papers, Massachusetts Historical Society.

31 T. M. Randolph, Jr., to Mrs. Thomas Mann (Anne Cary) Randolph, Sr., May 1, 1788, copy in Nicholas P. Trist Papers, University of North Carolina Library, Chapel Hill, North Carolina. The letter from Tuckahoe calling William home, and Tom's letter of explanation to his father have not been seen.

32 John Leslie to T. M. Randolph, Jr., May 12, 1788, in Carr–Cary Papers.

33 Leslie to Randolph, Jr., June 22, 1788, in Carr–Cary Papers. Reference to Tom's part in Leslie's hiring also appears in the former's letter to his father, April –, 1789, Edgehill–Randolph Papers.

34 Leslie to Randolph, Jr., May 12, 1788, in Carr–Cary Papers.

Edinburgh for a Glasgow lodging house, where he awaited passage home. Soon, Tom was back in Virginia, having completely abandoned Jefferson's plan for study on the continent and without even having completed his course at Edinburgh.[35] It was not the last time that he failed to finished what he had begun.

He did not forget his friend Leslie, and immediately on his return, he persuaded his father to engage the Scot as a tutor. The young scientist formally accepted the appointment and sailed for America sometime in August.[36] But within a few months he regretted the move and yearned for Scotland again. Leslie's discontent began when he fell in love with his student's sister Judith, then a girl of seventeen. Although the tutor felt "a burning affection tinctured with tender melancholy" for this young lady,[37] her affections were already centered on her cousin, Richard Randolph of Bizarre, whom she married later that year.[38] Nor did Leslie's previous declarations of admiration for American ideals stand the strain of exposure to American practice. Arguments over politics took place in which the Scot indulged the "native bluntness" of his tongue and in which Tom displayed the "turbulence of temper" that was becoming typical of him.[39]

The strain produced by these disputes was soon overshadowed by family tragedy. Early in March, 1789, Anne Cary Randolph died at the age of forty-four.[40] While he left no record of his sentiments, Tom had felt close enough to his mother to confide in her his

35 Leslie to Randolph, Jr., June 22, 1788, and August 2, 1788, *ibid*. Randolph's name does not appear in "The Register of Laureations in the University of Edinburgh, MDLXXXVII–MDCCC," as given in *A Catalogue of the University of Edinburgh*, 214–15. Randolph's movements for May–August, 1788, are taken from the addresses, including directions for forwarding, which appear on Leslie's letters to him in the Carr–Cary Papers.

36 Leslie to Randolph, Jr., August 2, 1788, in Carr–Cary Papers.

37 Leslie to Randolph, Jr., June 6, 1789, *ibid*.

38 Anne Cary Randolph to St. George Tucker, September 23, 1788, in Mary Haldane Coleman, *St. George Tucker, Citizen of No Mean City* (Richmond, 1938), 109–10. For the later history of Judith's marriage, see William Cabell Bruce, *John Randolph of Roanoke* (New York, 1922), I, 106–20. For a fictional account see Jay and Audrey Walz, *The Bizarre Sisters* (New York, 1950).

39 John Leslie to T. M. Randolph, Jr., June 6 and July 23, 1789, in Carr–Cary Papers.

40 Jones (ed.), *Douglas Register*, 93; for her illness, see Elder to Jefferson, October –, 1785, in Boyd (ed.), *The Papers of Thomas Jefferson*, VIII, 687, and Gouverneur Morris to Alexander Hamilton, June 13, 1788, in Syrett (ed.), *The Papers of Alexander Hamilton*, V, 7–8.

reasons for leaving Scotland, and he undoubtedly experienced a keen sense of loss at her passing. His bereavement, and, perhaps, his tutor's determination to return to Scotland, made him restless, and in April, Tom and John began a botanical expedition to the Blue Ridge, the latter bearing the expenses of the trip.[41] After this the Scottish tutor departed for home. Despite their previous arguments, the two parted as friends, and in June, Leslie sent Tom a cordial message of farewell, accompanied by a gift of the works of Hume, Herodotus, and Hesiod.[42] For the next twenty years they kept up an intermittent correspondence, mostly on scientific subjects, but they never met again. Political developments, as well as time and distance, completed their separation.

Shortly after Leslie's departure, Tom announced a desire to visit New York where, he insisted, his time "would be much more profitably spent" than at home.[43] The capital of the nation was an excellent place for one who wanted "to be in the way of politics," [44] and he was soon on his way north. In New York he encountered his cousin Peter Carr, on vacation from the College of William and Mary. Carr found young Randolph "extremely intelligent and cleaver," and he listened respectfully when the former student at Edinburgh discoursed on the "surprising advantages" which could be gained from the study of modern languages, mathematics, and natural history.[45] Thomas, in his turn, was probably not unmoved by the fact that Peter's temporary guardian was James Madison, representative from Virginia and the administration's whip in the House.[46]

Tom returned to Virginia by the fall of 1789, but soon after his homecoming, he quarreled with his father. The cause of the son's rage was so obscure that the parent was completely baffled by the whole affair. Then, before tempers had cooled, Tom left home once more, "in a hurry & in bad weather" and rode upriver to Rock

41 T. M. Randolph, Jr., to T. M. Randolph, Sr., April –, 1789, in Edgehill-Randolph Papers.

42 John Leslie to T. M. Randolph, Jr., June 6, 1789, in Carr–Cary Papers.

43 T. M. Randolph, Jr., to T. M. Randolph, Sr., April –, 1789, in Edgehill-Randolph Papers.

44 T. M. Randolph, Sr., to Thomas Munford, May 15, 1789, in Hench Collection, Alderman Library, University of Virginia.

45 Peter Carr to Jefferson, May 29, 1789, in Boyd (ed.), *Papers of Thomas Jefferson*, XV, 155–57.

46 Irving Brant, *James Madison: Father of the Constitution, 1787–1800* (Indianapolis, 1950), Chapters 20–22; Madison to Jefferson, June 13, 1789, in Boyd (ed.), *The Papers of Thomas Jefferson*, XV, 180–81.

Castle, the seat of his Fleming cousins in western Goochland County. He was going there for the shooting season, he explained, but the master of Tuckahoe could not help feeling that his excitable son was "disgusted, not only with the world, but, I fear, with your father." [47]

While Tom was attempting to forget his discontent in the hunting field, kinsmen whom he had not seen for years were travelling from Norfolk to Richmond. Thomas Jefferson, accompanied by his daughters Martha and Mary (more often called Maria), was returning home to Albemarle County on leave of absence after more than five years in Paris.[48] Sometime during December young Randolph must have met them, either at the house of a mutual relation, or at Monticello, where he was a visitor just before the end of the year.[49] Undoubtedly, he talked with Jefferson about past studies and future plans, but he must have paid a great deal of attention to Jefferson's older daughter. A deep attraction developed between them and quickly flowered into love, although it was the first time they had seen each other since they were children.[50] Tom must have pressed his campaign ardently—before January ended, he had asked Martha to marry him, and she had agreed.[51]

47 T. M. Randolph, Sr., to T. M. Randolph, Jr., December 1, 1789, in Edgehill-Randolph Papers, with note by the recipient.

48 Malone, *Jefferson and the Rights of Man* (Boston, 1951), 243–46.

49 Jefferson to Madison, February 14, 1790, in Boyd (ed.), *The Papers of Thomas Jefferson,* XVI, 182–83, refers to Madison's visit to Monticello the previous December and speaks of the impending marriage between Martha and "the Mr. Randolph whom you saw here."

50 Various accounts hold that Randolph met and fell in love with Martha while on a trip to Paris during his Edinburgh days. See George Tucker, *The Life of Thomas Jefferson* (Philadelphia, 1837), I, 302; Randall, *The Life of Thomas Jefferson,* I, 558–59; and Sarah Nicholas Randolph, *The Domestic Life of Thomas Jefferson* (New York, 1871), 172, for indications of the hardihood of this legend. The extant correspondence for 1787–88 shows conclusively, however, that Randolph continually postponed and finally abandoned his plans to go to France. See note, Jefferson to Dr. Currie, December 20, 1788, in Boyd (ed.), *The Papers of Thomas Jefferson,* XIV, 365.

51 T. M. Randolph, Sr., to Jefferson, January 30, 1790, in Boyd (ed.), *The Papers of Thomas Jefferson,* XVI, 135, is the first reaction of the father of the groom on hearing the news. Obviously, Thomas Mann, Jr., had secured Martha's consent and her father's approval before informing his own parent, thus placing the date of the engagement sometime before the last week in January. Jefferson and his daughter, it is interesting to note, landed at Norfolk on November 23 and reached Monticello on December 23, while the marriage occurred on February 23.

CHAPTER III

"My Desire to Gratify Patsy"

ANNOUNCEMENTS OF THE wedding plans of Thomas Mann Randolph, Jr. and Martha Jefferson brought pleasure and satisfaction to both of their parents. The groom's father, although suffering so severely from gout that he doubted his ability to attend the ceremony, expressed "real and singular pleasure" when he learned of his son's intentions.[1] Jefferson was equally delighted. He was not only happy because the forthcoming marriage promised to tighten the bond of friendship which already existed between himself and his bosom friend at Tuckahoe, but he was also highly satisfied with the prospect of having Thomas as a son-in-law. He had "scrupulously suppressed" his own wishes and allowed his favorite daughter to "indulge her own sentiments freely," thus he was heartened and encouraged that her future husband was one whose "talents, disposition, connections & fortune" were such that he would have been Jefferson's "own first choice."[2]

Jefferson must have felt considerable relief that Martha had chosen as well as she had. His earlier fears that she would "draw a blockhead"—which had led him to provide her with a good education—seemed allayed, for Tom, so far as his academic qualifications were concerned, was far from being a blockhead.[3] He had

1 T. M. Randolph, Sr., to Jefferson, January 30, 1790, in Boyd (ed.), *The Papers of Thomas Jefferson*, XVI, 135.

2 Jefferson to Randolph, Sr., February 4, 1790, *ibid.*, XVI, 154–55; Jefferson to Madame de Corny, April 2, 1790, *ibid.*, XVI, 289–90; Jefferson to Doctor Richard Gem, April 4, 1790, *ibid.*, XVI, 297.

3 Jefferson to François, Marquis de Barbé-Marbois, December 5, 1783, *ibid.*, VI, 373–74.

given abundant proof of scholarly tastes and capabilities during his student days at Edinburgh, and the scope of his intellectual interests had already won Jefferson's respect and praise. Yet he had more to offer than his cultivated mind. Tall and sinewy, with black hair and a somewhat swarthy complexion, Tom was distinguished, if not handsome, in appearance. As became the son of a Virginia planter, he was a skilled horseman and a good athlete who could find pleasure in field sports as well as in his books.[4]

Tom's talents, as well as his fortunes and connections, were more than sufficient to win him the approbation of his future father-in-law and to overcome any doubts the latter may have had about the young man's disposition. The turbulent temper with which he had afflicted both Leslie and his father, and the overly-keen sensitivity which led him to do verbal battle over trifles may have been dismissed as mere youthful impatience which marriage and maturity would correct. His failure three years before to notify Jefferson of his change of plans and his abrupt return to Virginia indicated a certain irresponsibility and lack of consideration, but these youthful lapses seem to have been forgotten or overlooked in the first flush of paternal pleasure. Jefferson, after all, had encouraged Martha to make her own choice, and he was too much the devoted and indulgent father to voice reservations which he may have felt only subconsciously.

Martha apparently had no hesitation about accepting the proposal of a cousin whom she had known as an adult for only a few weeks. Then eighteen, "Patsy," as Jefferson called her, was tall and slender, with reddish hair and blue eyes—somewhat of a feminine counterpart of her father in physique and coloring. The miniature by Joseph Boze, made when she was seventeen,[5] shows her as a fashionable belle whose attractive, although not beautiful, features hold a surprising maturity. Contemporaries, however, considered her "rather homely," particularly when they compared her with her younger sister Maria.[6] Nearly everyone who knew her found her personality charming and her disposition sweet and cheerful.[7]

4 Randall, *The Life of Thomas Jefferson*, I, 558–59.

5 The miniature by Boze is reproduced in Boyd (ed.), *The Papers of Thomas Jefferson*, XIV, 361, with an explanatory and descriptive note on xli–xliii.

6 Margaret Bayard Smith, *The First Forty Years of Washington Society, Portrayed by the Family Letters of Mrs. Samuel Harrison Smith*, ed. Gaillard Hunt (New York, 1906), 384.

7 Martha was described as "modeste et aimable," along with her more

She brought to her marriage a degree of intellectual attainment equalled by few young women of her generation in America. Under her father's guidance she had read widely in "the graver sciences" and also had acquired skill in music, drawing, and other accomplishments more typical of the females of her day. She had also had the benefit of four years of instruction at the Abbaye Royale de Pentemont, the fashionable and academically respected convent school in Paris where she had brushed skirts with the daughters of nobility and the *haute bourgeoise.*

In such company she not only acquired social graces and accomplishments but was also influenced, at least briefly, by the worldly-wise social code of the French capital. Passing on a tidbit of Parisian gossip, she told her father about the gentleman who had "killed himself because he thought his wife did not love him," then added "that if every husband in Paris was to do as much, there would be nothing but widows left." [8] Jefferson in his reply refrained from commenting on the anecdote or his fourteen-year-old daughter's reactions to it; jests about marital matters never appealed to him.[9] By 1790 Martha herself had probably forgotten the story, and the thought that Virginia husbands might be upset by the failure of their wives' affections may never have occurred to her.

The Abbaye, besides being a place where sophisticated little girls chattered about the marital misfortunes of their elders, was also a religious institution conducted by nuns of the Roman Catholic faith. Martha took the sacraments there at Easter, hinting to her father's secretary in 1787 that she was resigned to an outward compliance with the requirements of an alien creed.[10] The papal nuncio at Paris found her more responsive, reporting to his superiors that she seemed "to have great tendencies toward the Catholic religion," although her father had "tried to distract her." [11] Nothing came of

---

physically attractive sister, by the Duc de La Rochefoucauld Liancourt, who visited Monticello in 1796. See François-Alexandre-Frédéric, Duc de La Rochefoucauld Liancourt, *Voyages dans les États-Unis d'Amérique . . . Fait en 1795, 1796, et 1797* (Paris, 1799), V, 32–33. Nathaniel Cutting praised her "happy serenity." Cutting to Martha Jefferson, March 30, 1790, in Boyd (ed.), *The Papers of Thomas Jefferson,* XVI, 207.

8 Martha Jefferson to Jefferson, April 9, 1787, in Boyd (ed.), *The Papers of Thomas Jefferson,* XI, 282.

9 Malone, *Jefferson and the Rights of Man,* 19.

10 William Short to Jefferson, March 26, 1787, in Boyd (ed.), *The Papers of Thomas Jefferson,* XI, 240.

11 Cardinal Dugnani to John Carroll, July 5, 1787, *ibid.,* XIV, 356. See also Malone, *Jefferson and the Rights of Man,* 207–208.

this gesture—undoubtedly the source of the family tradition that Martha actually considered entering the convent as a novice but was dissuaded by her father—but it indicated a more conventional attitude towards religion than that embraced by either her father or her fiance.[12]

As an institution of learning, the Abbaye gave everything to Martha that Jefferson could have expected. Although she was not unusually gifted, she acquired a love of music and a respect for intellectual attainment. These cultivated tastes and the polish gained from her social contacts there prepared her for an appreciation of Tom's abilities and interests.[13]

Yet, her preparation for the practical side of domestic life was not as good as that of most of her contemporaries. Her mother's death when Martha was ten and the long sojourn with her father in France had resulted in her reaching maturity without "learning . . . many things of the most useful in life." [14] Neither the Abbaye nor her father's books had provided the practical knowledge that she would have received under the tutelage of her mother or under the eye of one of her Eppes or Carr aunts.

In promising her hand to Thomas Mann Randolph, Jr., Martha did not by that token also give an undivided heart. Her father had been the principal object of her affection since childhood, and her love for him was returned in full measure. She was perfectly capable of scolding him when he failed to write her [15] or of hinting, with girlish impudence, that his journey to the south of France was "rather for your pleasure than your health," [16] but she constantly reiterated her love for him. "What I hold most precious is your satisfaction," she declared in 1787, "indeed I should be miserable without it." [17]

Differences in temperament and the possibility of conflicting loyalties were overlooked in the brief period of courtship. The circumstances of her upbringing had allowed Martha to know few young men during her girlhood, and Tom was almost certainly her

12 Randall, *The Life of Thomas Jefferson,* I, 538–39; Randolph, *Domestic Life,* 146.

13 Malone, *Jefferson and the Rights of Man,* 131–32.

14 Jefferson to Ellen Wayles Eppes, March 7, 1790, in Boyd (ed.), *The Papers of Thomas Jefferson,* XVI, 208.

15 Martha Jefferson to Jefferson, March 25, 1787, *ibid.,* XI, 238.

16 Martha Jefferson to Jefferson, March 8, 1787, *ibid.,* XI, 203.

17 Martha Jefferson to Jefferson, April 9, 1787, *ibid.,* XI, 282.

first serious suitor. She may have been unduly susceptible, therefore, to his wooing. Also she seems to have been somewhat less than eager to leave Paris for life on a Virginia plantation. Young Nathaniel Cutting, who sailed with her and her father from France to England late in 1789, noticed "some emotion of chagrin at the thought of being separated from the engaging circle" she had known in Paris. Tom, so soon back from the stimulating background of Edinburgh, may have seemed a potentially exciting compensation for "Rank and modish Refinement" to which she had become accustomed.[18]

Jefferson encouraged the young couple to set an early date for the ceremony. He had just accepted the post offered to him as Secretary of State in Washington's administration, and he felt that he should leave for the capital at New York by the first of March.[19] Naturally, he wished to see his daughter married before he left. It is not likely that either Tom or Martha objected to a short engagement, and all agreed on a simple ceremony in late February.

Their respective fathers combined to provide them with property. The senior Randolph deeded over Varina, his fertile Henrico County plantation which contained 950 acres of rich bottom land on the James below Richmond. With the estate went forty slaves, fourteen head of livestock, and two small dwellings. But it was burdened with a mortgage of nearly $2900.[20] Long afterward, the bridegroom recalled that his father-in-law had advised against acceptance of Varina, but Tom was grateful enough for the property when it was offered to him.[21] Jefferson, equally eager "to place them in security," gave the couple a thousand acres of his Bedford County plantation and twenty-seven of the Negroes living on the property.[22] Thomas Mann Randolph, Jr., on the eve of his marriage thus became the proprietor of two large farms totaling nearly two thousand acres.

He and Martha were married at Monticello on February 23, 1790. The Reverend Matthew Maury of the Episcopal church in Char-

18 Nathaniel Cutting to Martha Jefferson, March 30, 1790, *ibid.*, XVI, 207.

19 Jefferson to George Washington, February 14, 1790, *ibid.*, XVI, 184.

20 T. M. Randolph, Sr., to Jefferson, January 30, 1790, *ibid.*, XVI, 135; Marriage Settlement for Martha Jefferson, February 21, 1790, *ibid.*, XVI, 189–90. T. M. Randolph, Jr., to Jefferson, October 31, 1793, in Jefferson Papers, Massachusetts Historical Society, refers to the mortgage on the property.

21 Randolph to Francis Walker Gilmer, July 25, 1819, in Gilmer Papers, Alderman Library, University of Virginia.

22 Marriage Settlement for Martha Jefferson, February 21, 1790, in Boyd (ed.), *The Papers of Thomas Jefferson,* XVI, 189–90.

lottesville performed the ceremony, with the bride's father paying for the license and the clergyman's fees.[23] A week later Jefferson left for his duties at the capital, the newlyweds accompanying him as far as Richmond. Before they separated, Martha must have assured him of her contentment with the nuptial state, for his first letter to her from New York reflected his pleasure: "It is a circumstance of consolation," he wrote, "to know you are happier; and to see a prospect of its continuance in the prudence and even temper both of Mr. Randolph and yourself." He went on to give his daughter some pointed advice on the responsibilities she had assumed. "The happiness of your life depends now on the continuing to please a single person. To this all other objects must be secondary, even your love for me, were it possible that that could be an obstacle."[24]

Marriage also committed Tom to "please a single person," but he was equally concerned in the first weeks of their marriage in reaching a decision on his future occupation. The possession of Varina and the desirability of giving his attention to its cultivation naturally suggested an agricultural career, yet he hesitated to make farming his life's work. "To one as fond as I am of Physical research," he confided to Jefferson, "such an inclination might be dangerous; but however enticing the subject, however pleasing the employment, I am resolved it shall never seduce me from the study of the law, and the attempt to acquire Political knowledge."[25] He hoped, even then, to settle someday in Albemarle County near Monticello and, perhaps, to obtain part of Edgehill, the family plantation in that county,[26] but in the spring of 1790 there seemed to be no immediate prospect of realizing this wish.

Thus, after a round of visits to their mutual relatives along the

23 Randolph, *Domestic Life*, 172; Malone, *Jefferson and the Rights of Man*, 252. The officiating clergyman is identified in Edgar Woods, *Albemarle County in Virginia* (Charlottesville, 1901), 127, and in Jessie Thornley Grayson, "Old Christ Church, Charlottesville, Va., 1826–1895," Albemarle County Historical Society *Papers*, VIII (1947–48), 26–27.

24 Jefferson to Martha Jefferson Randolph, April 14, 1790, in Boyd (ed.), *The Papers of Thomas Jefferson*, XVI, 300.

25 T. M. Randolph, Jr., to Jefferson, April 23, 1790, *ibid.*, XVI, 370.

26 "Mr. Randolph's idea of settling near Monticello" is referred to in Jefferson to Martha Randolph, April 26, 1790, *ibid.*, XVI, 386–87. This letter, written before Jefferson had received any letters at New York from either Martha or her husband, indicates that the subject of removal had been discussed before the Secretary of State departed for the national capital.

lower James,[27] he and Martha decided "to settle immediately" at Varina, since they agreed that "the advantage of constant employment . . . will more than ballance the many inconveniences." There were two small houses on the property, "situated at a distance from each other," each one containing only two rooms each, but they were "resolved to suffer this disadvantage" until they could obtain a farm in Albemarle, rather than "incur the expense of removing or building." [28]

Martha privately opposed the plan for a temporary residence at Varina, but she did not openly reject her husband's proposal. "I am much averse to it myself," she confessed to her father in April, "but shall certainly comply if he thinks it necessary." At the same time the bride took the opportunity to assure Jefferson of her continued devotion. "I assure you My dear papa my happiness can never be compleat without your company. Mr. Randolph omits nothing that can in the least contribute to it. I have made it my study to please him in every *thing* and do consider all objects as secondary to that *except* my love for you." [29] Her husband was not only unaware of her opposition but believed that she was "impatient to encounter" the disadvantages of life in Henrico.

Accordingly, Martha remained with her cousins at Eppington while Tom went on alone to his farm to prepare the houses. He quickly discovered that the location was far from ideal. Although it was only May, he found the lowland heat excessive, and exposure to the sun brought on "Miliary eruptions," which kept him "for several days in excessive torture." Even an umbrella gave him no protection, and except for "an hour in the morning and a short time again in the Evening," he was "constantly confined" indoors. In his discomfort he was more convinced than before that "no situation in America" had "so many allurements" for him as did the hills of Albemarle.[30]

It had been Jefferson's hope that the couple would settle near him at the time of their marriage, and even before he knew of Martha's objection to Varina or of her husband's illness there, he recom-

27 T. M. Randolph, Jr., to Jefferson, April 23, 1790, *ibid.*, XVI, 370; Martha Randolph to Jefferson, April 25, 1790, *ibid.*, XVI, 384; Peter Carr to Jefferson, April 30, 1790, *ibid.*, XVI, 393.

28 T. M. Randolph, Jr., to Jefferson, May 25, 1790, *ibid.*, XVI, 441–42.

29 Martha Randolph to Jefferson, April 25, 1790, *ibid.*, XVI, 384–85.

30 T. M. Randolph, Jr., to Jefferson, May 25, 1790, *ibid.*, XVI, 441–42.

mended that Tom try to obtain Edgehill, which lay across the Rivanna River from Monticello.[31] This was the property which William Randolph acquired nearly fifty years before and which Peter Jefferson had cared for as part of his friend's estate. When Jefferson learned of his son-in-law's decision to move to Albemarle, he promised to do everything possible to help him carry out that plan and to assist in the procurement of part of Edgehill. Meanwhile he advised Martha "to take no measures for Varina which might be inconvenient." [32]

That same summer, however, Tom's father announced his decision to remarry. His intended bride was Gabriella Harvie, a granddaughter of John Harvie who had been Thomas Jefferson's guardian. She was still in her teens, her suitor barely fifty, and there was every prospect of more Randolph children at Tuckahoe. Furthermore, the senior Randolph announced his intention to sell six hundred of Edgehill's acres to John Harvie, Gabriella's father, and to retain the rest as a patrimony for his other children. This plan, if carried out, would block his son's plans to acquire the property. Thus the grounds for new disputes were laid.

Both Tom and Martha must have expressed their resentment, for Jefferson took immediate steps to soothe their anger. "Col. Randolph's marriage was to be expected," Jefferson reminded Martha. "All his amusements depending on society, he can not live alone." He cautioned that the forthcoming match should not "be the cause of any diminution of affection between him and Mr. Randolph, and yourself. . . . If the lady has any thing difficult in her disposition, avoid what is rough, and attach her good qualities to you. . . . None of us, no, not one, is perfect; and were we to love none who had imperfections, this world would be a desert for our love. . . . Be you, my dear, the link of love, union, and peace for the whole family." [33] Jefferson's appeal to Martha to play the role of peacemaker perhaps was inspired by his awareness of her high-tempered husband's incapacity for such a part, but that he addressed his plea for tolerance to Martha indicates that she too was not overly patient with the ways of others.

31 Jefferson to Martha Randolph, April 26, 1790, *ibid.*, XVI, 386–87.

32 Jefferson to T. M. Randolph, Jr., June 20, 1790, *ibid.*, XVI, 540–41; Jefferson to Martha Randolph, June 6, 1790, *ibid.*, XVI, 474–75.

33 Jefferson to Martha Randolph, July 17, 1790, in Randolph, *Domestic Life*, 187. The letters to which this was a reply have not been found.

News of the marriage plans gave Jefferson fresh reasons to handle the negotiations for Edgehill himself, and late in July he asked his old school fellow to sell the remaining part of the Albemarle estate to young Thomas Mann.[34] Upon his return to Virginia that fall the Secretary of State visited Tuckahoe with the draft of a deed for the property hoping to close the transaction with one conference. On behalf of his son-in-law, Jefferson made an offer of $1,700, to be paid in three installments; Randolph first asked for $2,000 on the same terms, but at last agreed to accept the other's price, and the matter appeared to have been settled.[35]

Thomas Mann, Sr., however, reconsidered his decision and, perhaps influenced by his newly acquired in-laws,[36] came to the conclusion that Jefferson had outmaneuvered him. When he saw his son again in late October, he renewed some of his former objections to Jefferson's proposal and finally declared that he would not fulfill the agreement unless "compelled." The son "took fire" at this statement and, without waiting to "hear another word," left Tuckahoe. The elder Randolph, perhaps hurt because his son had let another speak for him, could not resist a bitter gibe. "One half minute would have explained my use of 'compelled' . . . which I suppose you have sent to Mr. Jefferson." But he did not want a lasting quarrel. "I still wish," he wrote a few days after the fiery scene, "if you are not too much irritated, to speak 3 or 4 words to you . . . after that, your tempestuous temper may renounce your father forever, if it is your choice." In a final gesture of paternal capitulation, he made known his willingness to sell the sixteen hundred acres at Edgehill on the terms which he had proposed earlier to Jefferson.[37]

Tom meanwhile had grown calmer, and within a week he apologized to his father, explaining that his attempt to purchase Edgehill had been suggested by Jefferson and that he had consented both out of deference to his father-in-law's opinion and "my desire to gratify Patsy." [38] Because of the bad feelings which had risen on both sides, Tom had already decided to abandon his efforts to acquire the plantation and, after joining Jefferson at Monticello,

34 Jefferson to T. M. Randolph, Sr., July 25, 1790, in Edgehill–Randolph Papers.
35 Jefferson to Randolph, Sr., October 22, 1790, *ibid.*
36 T. M. Randolph, Jr., to T. M. Randolph, Sr., October [30], 1790, *ibid.*
37 T. M. Randolph, Sr., to T. M. Randolph, Jr., October 22, 1790, *ibid.*
38 T. M. Randolph, Jr., to T. M. Randolph, Sr., October [30], 1790, *ibid.*

began looking for some other suitable property in Albemarle County.[39] He and Martha were expecting their first child, and, on January 23, 1791, a daughter was born, whom they christened Anne Cary after Tom's mother.[40]

But Edgehill was never out of his mind, and his father continued to press him for a decision on it. The young man insisted that all he wanted was "a small tract, just sufficient to supply me with provisions." Martha agreed with this aim, he told Jefferson, "but we both wish to be guided by you."[41] Relations between the two Randolphs had improved since the preceding fall, and the son visited Henrico County during the summer of 1791 to aid his father's campaign for a seat in the state senate.[42] Later the two reached a final agreement. On January 1, 1792, the elder Randolph conveyed four hundred acres of that property, as he had earlier intended, to John Harvie, and the following month he gave his son a deed for the remaining 1,523 acres and for the Negro families living there. Tom agreed to pay $2,000, the same sum which his father had asked in 1790, finally coming into possession of the family property in Albemarle.[43] Thus was fulfilled Jefferson's desire that Martha and her husband would live near him, a desire which she fervently shared and which Tom, because of his own desire "to gratify Patsy," willingly accepted.

39 Jefferson to T. M. Randolph, Jr., October 22, 1790, *ibid.*

40 Anderson, "Tuckahoe and the Tuckahoe Randolphs," 26. The birth of Anne Cary and of Randolph's other children are recorded, with other family data, in Jefferson's *Prayer Book* (Oxford, 1752), the original of which is preserved in the Tracy W. McGregor Library, University of Virginia. A brochure, issued for the Bibliographical Society of America, *Thomas Jefferson's Prayer Book* (Meriden, Conn., 1952), includes facsimiles of the page on which the family memorandum was written, much of it in Jefferson's hand.

41 T. M. Randolph, Jr., to Jefferson, March 5, 1791, in Jefferson Papers, Library of Congress.

42 Randolph, Jr., to Jefferson, August 22, 1791, in Edgehill-Randolph Papers.

43 Martha Randolph to Jefferson, February 20, 1792, *ibid.* Deed, dated April 12, 1793, in Albemarle County Deed Book No. 23, p. 120, in Albemarle County Clerk's Office, Charlottesville, Virginia.

CHAPTER IV

"More His Son Than His Son-in-Law"

YOUNG THOMAS MANN RANDOLPH had become a familiar figure in Albemarle County even before he gained possession of Edgehill. Although he made occasional trips to Varina, he relied on his overseer Benjamin Hughes to look after the daily routine there. The rest of the time he spent with Martha at Monticello where, in his father-in-law's absence while at the capital, he supervised the management of the latter's estates. There were, indeed, overseers to look after routine operations at Monticello, at Shadwell, and at Jefferson's other farms. Tom only directed their activities, but this responsibility involved a variety of tasks. It was he who made sure that crops and trees were planted when and where his father-in-law wanted them; that tobacco and wheat were shipped to market at the proper time; that canals for drainage were dug; that the blacksmith shop, the sawmill, and the other domestic industries at Monticello functioned smoothly; and that construction on the outbuildings was carried forward.[1]

Thomas Mann undertook these tasks willingly and apparently did his best to see them carried out, for he felt a "Gratitude and Affection" for Jefferson which, he declared, almost equalled the esteem in which he held himself.[2] Despite his efforts the estates did

1 Letters between Randolph and Jefferson on agricultural matters are found in all the major Jefferson collections, particularly those in the Library of Congress, the Massachusetts Historical Society, and the University of Virginia. Many of these letters are quoted, in whole or in part, in Edward M. Betts (ed.), *Thomas Jefferson's Garden Book* (Philadelphia, 1944) and in Betts (ed.), *Thomas Jefferson's Farm Book* (Princeton, 1953).

2 T. M. Randolph, Jr., to Jefferson, February 20, 1793, in Jefferson Papers, Massachusetts Historical Society.

not prosper under his management, and when Jefferson resigned as Secretary of State in December, 1793, and returned to Monticello, he found "a degree of degradation far beyond" what he had expected.[3] He blamed this condition on his own prolonged absence rather than on his son-in-law, but he immediately reasserted personal control.

Despite the demands made on his time, young Randolph found the leisure to pursue his favorite study of natural history, discovering several subjects for investigation in the woods and fields near Monticello. In 1791 he began, with his father-in-law's encouragement, a study of the birth processes of the opposum, but the difficulties of finding the proper specimens prevented him from satisfactorily completing it. About the same time he succeeded in capturing a wolf and, after observing its habits and noting that it was "extremely fond of being caressed," sought to have it bred to a domestic dog. When unidentified insects attacked his crops in 1793, he collected various samples and, "having some little technical knowledge in Entymology," attempted to classify them according to Linnaean principles.[4]

He also tried to apply scientific methods to his agricultural practices and, shortly after he had acquired Edgehill, developed his own system of crop rotation for use there. His plan was based on two "coexistent" procedures, and for this purpose he laid out eight tracts of sixty acres each and six of ten acres each. He planted the larger tracts in wheat, corn, potatoes, rye, and peas, interrupting the cultivation of these with periods of fallowing and pasturing, and repeating this cycle after eight years. On the smaller lots he grew pumpkins, barley, turnips, and oats according to a six-year cycle, and used white clover as a restorative. Jefferson also used a system of crop rotation, and Tom argued the merits of his plan over that drawn up by his father-in-law. After exchanging views, each apparently continued to use his own system.[5] At this time, Tom

3 Jefferson to Washington, May 14, 1794, in Randolph, *Domestic Life,* 229.

4 T. M. Randolph, Jr., to Jefferson, April 30, 1791, in Jefferson Papers, Massachusetts Historical Society; Randolph, Jr., to Jefferson, March 14, 1791, in Jefferson Papers, Alderman Library, University of Virginia; Randolph, Jr., to Jefferson, June 13, 1793, in Jefferson Papers, Massachusetts Historical Society.

5 Randolph, Jr., to Jefferson, July 11, 1793, in Jefferson Papers, Massachusetts Historical Society; Randolph, Jr., to Jefferson, July 31, 1793, *ibid.* For Jefferson's plan of crop rotation, see Betts (ed.), *Thomas Jefferson's Farm Book,* 312.

began to experiment with horizontal plowing,[6] a practice which he succeeded in bringing to perfection some fifteen years later. Almost from the beginning he sought to improve his skill as a practical farmer and personally supervised the work in his fields, often getting "wet to the skin" in the process.[7]

Meanwhile, his family and his responsibilities were increasing; his second child and first son, Thomas Jefferson Randolph, was born on September 12, 1792.[8] The arrival of each grandchild filled Jefferson with an excited pleasure and intensified his desire to keep the Randolphs as near to him as possible. For Tom, each increase in the family meant extra efforts to see them properly reared and educated.

These efforts were plagued by difficulties, some of which were beyond his control. In 1792 his wheat crop at Varina fell below expectations, and his tobacco was damaged by rain on its way downriver to market.[9] And in the following year heavy spring rains and a prolonged drought that lasted most of the summer all but ruined his corn crop.[10] As early as the spring of 1792 Martha began to worry about the effect of these many misfortunes upon his prospects of achieving financial security for the family.[11]

Tom was forced to assume added burdens because of his father's failing health. In 1787 the elder Randolph had mortgaged Varina to Herman Leroy, a New York merchant, in an effort to pay the most pressing of his obligations and to raise money for his sons' educations in Scotland. He had discharged about half of this debt before Tom's marriage, but still nearly $2,900 was due, and his creditors were pressing for payment. His son decided that the best course was to pledge all the profits from Varina to the payment of the debt and to put up Edgehill as security, but first he consulted Jefferson.[12] The latter interceded with Leroy, who by this time was

6 T. M. Randolph, Jr., to Joseph C. Cabell, July 20, 1820, in Randolph Papers, Duke University Library, sketches the history of Randolph's development of the system.

7 T. M. Randolph, Jr., to Peter Carr, June 26, 1793, in Carr–Cary Papers.

8 Anderson, "Tuckahoe and the Tuckahoe Randolphs," 26; *Thomas Jefferson's Prayer Book.*

9 T. M. Randolph, Jr., to T. M. Randolph, Sr., February 26, 1792, in Edgehill–Randolph Papers; Randolph, Jr., to Jefferson, March 18, 1792, in Jefferson Papers, Massachusetts Historical Society.

10 T. M. Randolph, Jr., to Peter Carr, June 26, 1793, in Carr–Cary Papers.

11 Martha Randolph to Jefferson, May 7, 1792, in Jefferson Papers, Massachusetts Historical Society.

12 T. M. Randolph, Jr., to Jefferson, October 31, 1793, *ibid.* Part of the senior

established in Philadelphia, and suggested that he "couple" Dover plantation, in Goochland County, in the mortgage, so that it rather than Edgehill, would be sacrificed if a sale became unavoidable. Arrangements were also made for Randolph to sell all the wheat grown at Varina through Leroy and to market it in Philadelphia.[13] These expedients provided temporary relief, but the problem itself remained.

In November, 1793, Tom received "a melancholy summons" to the bedside of his father, who died on the 20th in Richmond,[14] after much suffering. Jefferson, in condolences to the son, declared anew his lifelong affection for the master of Tuckahoe. He recalled "the intimacy of brothers" which had existed between them, and he referred with sorrow to "the tormenting state of mind to which" his good friend "had been latterly reduced." [15]

Such was the torment of the dying man's mind and such was the weakness of his body that he had not been able to draw his own will, and that task had fallen on Gabriella's father John Harvie. Thomas Mann, Jr., and his brother William had been named executors, but Harvie himself was appointed guardian of the children at Tuckahoe, one of whom—the infant Thomas Mann Randolph III—was his own grandchild.[16] It was not an illogical arrangement, but the fact that Tom had not been entrusted with the care of his younger brothers and sisters filled him with mortification, and his sensitive nature led him to believe that this omission implied "the suspicion of inability." He even considered refusal of his appointment as executor, but finally accepted the responsibility.[17]

Jefferson returned to Virginia from Philadelphia early in 1794, and for most of the next three years he remained at Monticello,

---

Randolph's debt had been incurred prior to the Revolution as a result of his guaranteeing a debt of £20,000 owed by his father-in-law, Archibald Cary. See David J. Mays, *Edmund Pendleton, 1721–1803: A Biography* (Cambridge, Massachusetts, 1952), I, 213.

13 Jefferson to Herman Leroy, November 17, 1793, in Edgehill-Randolph Papers.

14 T. M. Randolph, Jr., to Jefferson, November 14, 1793, in Edgehill-Randolph Papers; *Virginia Gazette* (Richmond), November 27, 1793.

15 Jefferson to T. M. Randolph, Jr., December 8, 1793, in Jefferson Papers, Library of Congress.

16 Will of Thomas Mann Randolph, Sr., November 5, 1793, in Goochland County Deed and Will Book No. 16, p. 334, Goochland County Clerk's Office.

17 T. M. Randolph, Jr., to Jefferson, November 30, 1793, in Edgehill-Randolph Papers.

where the Randolphs spent much of their time with him. Although Tom's responsibilities in Henrico and Goochland counties continued to demand much of his time and attention, he had become, for all practical purposes, a resident of Albemarle, and in April, 1794, he was appointed a justice of the peace for his adopted county.[18] In spite of his "total ignorance of the military art," he applied to Governor Henry Lee for a captain's commission in the militia, and was duly appointed to the command of a troop of cavalry in the 88th Virginia Regiment, which was raised in the northern part of Albemarle.[19]

His activities during these years were greatly curtailed by a prolonged illness which struck him in 1794. To regain his health, he spent much of the next two years travelling to Boston, to New York, and to the various springs of western Virginia. Martha accompanied him on several of these trips, leaving her children at Monticello in the care of her father and his domestic staff.[20] But Tom's ailment persisted, producing a depressing effect on his disposition. Jefferson came to the conclusion that his son-in-law was suffering from gout, remembering that the young man's father had also been troubled by this disease, but the various doctors who were consulted confessed themselves mystified.[21] Whatever the cause of Randolph's illness, by the summer of 1796 his health began to improve.

Between trips in search of medical aid the Randolphs lived alternately at Varina and Monticello.[22] Relations between various members of the family were so harmonious that even strangers were impressed. In June, 1796, Jefferson received a visit from Francois-Alexandre-Frédéric, Duc de La Rochefoucauld Liancourt, the French philanthropist in exile, who was then touring the United

18 Register of Justices, 1780–1816, manuscript volume in Archives Division, Virginia State Library.

19 T. M. Randolph, Jr., to Governor Henry Lee, November 27, 1793, in Militia Papers, Archives Division, Virginia State Library; Woods, *Albemarle County*, 375. Randolph is listed as "Captain Randolph" in Albemarle Land Tax Book, 1795, Archives Division, Virginia State Library.

20 Jefferson to T. M. Randolph, Jr., August 7, 1794, in Jefferson Papers, Library of Congress; Jefferson to Randolph, Jr., October 27, 1794, *ibid.;* Jefferson to Randolph, Jr., August 11, 1795, *ibid.;* Jefferson to James Madison, September 21, 1795, in Madison Papers, Library of Congress.

21 Jefferson to T. M. Randolph, Jr., January 18, 1796, in Jefferson Papers, Library of Congress.

22 Jefferson to Martha Randolph, January 22, 1795, in Edgehill-Randolph Papers; Martha Randolph to Jefferson, January 1, 1796, *ibid.*

States. The Duke was impressed by his versatile host, and he also formed a most favorable opinion of the latter's family, who were spending the summer at Monticello. Martha and her sister Maria, he thought, were "handsome, modest, and amiable women," and he characterized the latter as "remarkably handsome." But he also noted the close relationship between Jefferson and Martha's husband. "He seems," noted the traveler, "to be more his son than his son-in-law." [23]

Nor was this display of affection a pose adopted for public consumption. A year later when Maria's betrothal to her cousin John Wayles Eppes was announced, Jefferson expressed his delight at the news. "After your happy establishment, which has given me an inestimable friend, to whom I can leave the care of everything I love," he wrote Martha, he was overjoyed that his younger daughter, had chosen equally well. "I now see our fireside formed into a group, no member of which has a fibre in their composition which can ever produce any jarring or jealousies among us." [24] One member of the Monticello circle, however, still put her affection for Jefferson above her feelings for all the rest and in 1798, after eight years of wedded life, Martha reiterated her devotion to her father and declared that no subsequent tie had been able to "weaken the first and best of nature." [25]

Early in the spring of 1797 Tom, who had by now recovered his health almost completely, made his first bid for elective office. Although he and Martha were then living at Varina, he decided to run for the House of Delegates from Albemarle County, a decision which his father-in-law, who had just been inaugurated as Vice-President of the United States, approved and encouraged.[26] When election day arrived at the courthouse in Charlottesville, where the poll was held Randolph failed to appear. His absence not only caused "much uneasiness and embarrassment" to his friends and to his

23 Duc de La Rochefoucauld Liancourt, *Voyages dans les États-Unis d'Amérique*, V, 32–33.

24 Jefferson to Martha Randolph, June 8, 1797, in Randolph, *Domestic Life*, 245.

25 Martha Randolph to Jefferson, June–, 1798, in Jefferson Papers, Massachusetts Historical Society; quoted in Malone, *Jefferson and the Rights of Man*, 253.

26 Jefferson to T. M. Randolph, Jr., March 23, 1797, in Jefferson Papers, Library of Congress; for residence at Varina, see Jefferson to Martha Randolph, March 27, 1797, in Edgehill–Randolph Papers.

father-in-law but it cost him the election. Wilson Cary Nicholas, later governor of Virginia, and Francis Walker, son of the explorer–physician Thomas Walker of Castle Hill, were chosen over the son-in-law of the Vice-President.[27]

Tom had remained at Varina to help nurse his children, who had just been inoculated against smallpox, but he left to Martha the task of explaining his absence.[28] Jefferson made the necessary apologies to the various militia captains of Albemarle and seemed satisfied that he had thus "set things to rights." As a father, Jefferson must have sympathized with his son-in-law's reason for remaining away, but he expressed regret that the explanation was not made sooner. He advised Tom to remember that it was better to "possess the affections of the people than . . . to make any use of them."[29] Thus ended the young man's first serious attempt to satisfy his ambition "to be in the way of politics."

Tom's disappointment at the polls was soon followed by a much more serious setback. In May, 1796, representatives of three British firms to which his father's estate was indebted had brought suit for recovery in the United States District Court at Richmond, and the cases, after successive postponements, were heard before that body in June, 1797. John Marshall, although a staunch Federalist and political opponent of Jefferson, appeared as the family's lawyer and acquitted himself well on his client's behalf. Marshall argued that the debt had already been paid in Virginia currency through the state's loan office and that this procedure had been sanctioned by a statute of the General Assembly, but the court refused to admit the validity of such payments, made in relatively worthless paper money under terms allowed by a revolutionary and inflation-minded legislature. Thomas and his brother were ordered to pay a sum of more than $27,000 to the estate of John Lidderdale of London and nearly $37,000 to representatives of two other firms, Farrell and Jones of Bristol, and John Bowman of Glasgow. Of the total of almost

27 Jefferson to T. M. Randolph, Jr., April 9, 1797, in Edgehill–Randolph Papers; for the victors, see Swem and Williams (comps.), "Register of the General Assembly," 48.

28 Martha Randolph to Jefferson, March 31, 1797, in Pierpont Morgan Library, New York City.

29 Jefferson to T. M. Randolph, Jr., April 9, 1797, in Edgehill–Randolph Papers; Jefferson's letter of explanation to the militia captains has not been located.

$65,000, approximately $42,000 was levied against the defendants' own property, and the remainder was charged against the estate under their administration.[30]

This judgment, although shared by his brother William, imposed a heavy burden on Thomas, who was already finding it difficult to support himself and his family. As if to counteract the effects of these frustrations, Tom sought comfort during the late 1790's in the writings of philosophers. From Francis Bacon he borrowed the thought that "tranquility is better than jollity to avoid or appease pain," and from the same author he drew a passage even more pertinent to his own situation: "Certain temperaments are little prone to passion: how fortunate are men of such constitutions! They are acquiring knowledge, while others are moderating their passions; they are running in the course of mental improvement, while others are preparing for the race."[31] Events were to prove that philosophy, in the long run, was not enough in his case, but his reading and his reflections thereon indicate he was aware that he himself was "prone to passion."

After the court made its decision against him, his life continued for a while in the old patterns. He and his family spent the summer of 1797 at Monticello and then moved to Belmont, a farm of John Harvie's near the present Albemarle County village of Keswick, remaining there until early in 1799, when they moved again to Monticello.[32] Jefferson's official duties as presiding officer of the Senate kept him in Philadelphia during the winters, and responsibility for operations at Monticello during his absences once more devolved on his son-in-law. Young Randolph made frequent trips of inspection to Jefferson's properties and let it be known to the overseers that he would "interpose with authority" whenever he thought it necessary.[33]

As a staunch Republican and an equally staunch Anglophobe, he was greatly disturbed by the increasing tension between the United States and the French Republic. Like his father-in-law, he was

30 All records in the case are in United States Circuit Court Records (Vol. 6F, pp. 126–72), in Archives Division, Virginia State Library.

31 These, and other literary quotations, are in Commonplace Book of Thomas Mann Randolph, Jr. Manuscript volume on deposit in Alderman Library, University of Virginia.

32 Cornelia Randolph, "Life of Maria and Martha Jefferson," Ms. in Edgehill-Randolph Papers. See also Randolph, *Domestic Life*, 248–49, 257.

33 T. M. Randolph, Jr., to Jefferson, January 19, 1799, in Edgehill-Randolph Papers.

dismayed by the anti-French reaction which the news of the "XYZ" affair aroused among his neighbors, but he was even more alarmed by the prospects of the "intimate union with the English monarchy" which a war with France would bring. Such a conflict, he declared, would destroy all his feelings of loyalty to the United States. Although he now held the rank of major in the militia, he had resolved to remain quietly at home, cultivating his own fields and letting events run their course, rather than fight in a war where redcoats would be his comrades-in-arms.[34] The dreaded war and the possible British alliance did not materialize, and the establishment of better relations with France after 1799 spared the fiery major from choosing between inactivity in a time of crisis and involvement in a cause he detested.

Devoted as he was to the cause of freedom abroad, there were limits to his democracy when he applied it to his own neighborhood. In December, 1799, William Woods, a personable Baptist clergyman, was elected to the state legislature as a delegate from Albemarle County to fill the vacancy created by the elevation of Wilson Cary Nicholas to the Senate of the United States.[35] Tom, like other members of the local gentry, disliked and distrusted "Baptist Billy," whose sermons seemed calculated to arouse the unpropertied members of his flock against their betters, "making the former take a pride in opposing the latter." He realized, nonetheless, that any attempt to deprive Woods of his seat would inflame this popular feeling "into downright hatred," and he therefore cautioned James Madison, then a member of the Assembly, against any effort by the delegates to oust Woods, even though "the just and most constitutional principle" against clergymen holding political office would sanction such action.[36] Woods, who had already resigned his pulpit, accordingly took his seat in the legislature without opposition.[37] Tom's attitude was colored by his personal dislike of Woods, but the sentiments which he expressed were reminiscent of the ideas which his father had expressed to Lieutenant Anburey twenty years

34 Randolph, Jr., to Jefferson, April 22, 1798, *ibid.*

35 Swem and Williams (comps.), "Register of the General Assembly," 52; Mary Rawlings, *The Albemarle of Other Days* (Charlottesville, 1925), 99–100.

36 T. M. Randolph, Jr., to Madison, December 28, 1799, in Madison Papers, Library of Congress.

37 *Journal of the House of Delegates of the Commonwealth of Virginia . . . 1799* (Richmond, 1800), contains no reference to any effort to unseat Woods. See also Woods, *Albemarle County*, 133.

before. For all of his Republican connections, he reacted to this particular demonstration of the voice of the people like a Randolph and an aristocrat.

Shortly after the Woods incident Thomas was once more faced with the prospect of losing Varina. In February, 1800, he had again fallen behind on the payments on the mortgage, and Leroy's Richmond agent George Pickett was pressing him strenuously. The young planter had held back his last tobacco crop in anticipation of a price rise that did not materialize, and he was short of ready cash when the demand was presented. There was not time enough to sell his crop, and Pickett refused to allow him any credit on it, so he was forced to borrow the requisite sum from George Jefferson, another Richmond merchant and a kinsman of Thomas Jefferson. This was only a very temporary loan, however, and Tom soon had to turn to his father-in-law for money to pay this newest creditor.[38] He advanced the necessary sum, taking his son-in-law's tobacco as security, and was able later to reimburse himself almost entirely from the proceeds of its sale.[39] Randolph was deeply grateful to Jefferson for this reprieve and severely critical of himself. He promised that he would "never be too late again in preparation for a demand," and he declared solemnly that he had had a lesson which he would never forget.[40]

Early in 1800 he and his family moved finally to Edgehill, two miles from Monticello, which then became their permanent residence. The house they occupied there was a small frame-covered structure of brick, two stories high, with a steep gabled roof and a gallery on one side.[41] Their children had by then increased to four. A daughter, christened Ellen Wayles, had been born in 1796; another, Cornelia, in 1799. Still another daughter, Virginia Jefferson, was born in 1801.[42] Their new home must have been cramped

38 T. M. Randolph, Jr., to Jefferson, February 22, 1800, in Jefferson Papers, Massachusetts Historical Society.

39 Randolph, Jr., to Jefferson, March 1, 1800, *ibid.;* Jefferson to Randolph, Jr., March 11, 1800, in Jefferson Papers, Library of Congress.

40 Randolph, Jr., to Jefferson, April 12, 1800, in Jefferson Papers, Massachusetts Historical Society.

41 The description of the house is based on observations made during a visit to Edgehill in 1950, when the property was in the possession of Mr. and Mrs. Edward Tayloe.

42 *Thomas Jefferson's Prayer Book;* Anderson, "Tuckahoe and the Tuckahoe Randolphs," 26–27. Another child, named Eleanor (or Ellen), was born August 30, 1794, but died July 26, 1795, *ibid.*

quarters for so large a family, and upon first occupying it, they found themselves "in the midst of mud, smoke, and the uncomfortableness of a cold house." [43] However, they soon made the place livable and comfortable.[44] They continued to spend their summers at Monticello with Jefferson, but when the latter departed for the capital, Tom, "preferring to reside on his own farm, took his family back." [45]

In 1800, the year in which he settled at Edgehill, he took part in the presidential election campaign in which his father-in-law was a leading candidate. In January Republican supporters of Jefferson met in Richmond where they set up a committee of correspondence for the whole state, and named similar committees for each Virginia county. Thomas Mann Randolph was one of those selected to membership on the committee for Albemarle.[46] He and his fellows probably did not have to exert themselves too strenuously, for the voters there and throughout the Commonwealth expressed a sweeping preference for the Republicans. When all returns were counted late in 1800, it was found that Jefferson had received the same number of electoral votes throughout the nation as had his running mate Aaron Burr. Some Republicans feared the consequences of the deadlock that resulted, since the final choice would fall upon the outgoing House of Representatives, still dominated by the Federalists.

Tom was confident that even if "the small band of Villains," as he described the extreme Federalists, sought to override the will of the people by choosing Burr, "the virtuous young citizens" would fall upon "Cataline" Hamilton and his followers and "give them the death that they deserve to meet in a more ignoble manner." [47] There even was talk during the early weeks in 1801 of raising a regiment of Republican volunteers in Albemarle, and Jefferson's son-in-law

43 Jefferson to Maria Eppes, February 12, 1800, in Randolph, *Domestic Life*, 263.

44 T. M. Randolph, Jr., to Jefferson, January 3, 1801, in Edgehill-Randolph Papers.

45 Jefferson to Catherine Church,—1799, in Randolph, *Domestic Life*, 252; Thomas Jefferson Randolph, "Reminiscences," Ms. in Edgehill-Randolph Papers.

46 H. W. Flournoy (ed.), *Calendar of Virginia State Papers, and Other Manuscripts* (Richmond, 1875–93), IX, 77.

47 T. M. Randolph, Jr., to Jefferson, January 10, 1801, in Edgehill-Randolph Papers.

composed a slogan to be embroidered on its banner: "No repose! but *on* the lap of Liberty or *in* the bosom of earth!" [48]

Republican leaders closer to the arena were also apprehensive of possible Federalist coups and took steps to forestall such moves. Governor James Monroe of Virginia feared that the "Anglican faction" might attempt to seize the arms and ammunition stored at the government arsenal at New London, and he sent Thomas Mann to investigate the situation. On February 9 the major left Edgehill to carry out this mission and reached his destination the following day, advertising that he was in the vicinity to inspect his lands in Bedford. First he called on the keeper of the magazine, obtaining what he believed to be an accurate count of the number of weapons on hand. After further investigation, he learned that the colonel of the local militia and four majors were Federalists but that the junior officers were "tolerably well affected." He therefore approached the "loyal" subalterns and urged them to keep a strict and vigilant watch on the arsenal in case the Federalists should attempt to seize the arms. He also discussed the subject with other citizens, but to these he spoke of a different danger. "A wicked Negro or a madman might blow them up in their sleep," he warned, unless the arsenal was carefully guarded. He returned to Albemarle on February 12, confident that he had accomplished his purpose without arousing suspicion, and submitted a detailed report on his mission to the Governor.[49] Five days later in Washington. Jefferson was finally elected President on the thirty-sixth ballot, and the crisis passed.

While his father-in-law was shaping the policies of the new administration, Tom continued in his accustomed routines at Edgehill. He had begun to lose some of his earlier zest for life in Albemarle, however, and in 1802, having become "allured by the immensely profitable culture of cotton," in the Mississippi Territory decided to emigrate there with his family.[50] When Jefferson learned of his son-in-law's plan he raised a number of objections—Mississippi was too remote and isolated, the climate was "unsafe," and the native Choctaw Indians were hostile. Furthermore, it seemed likely that

48 Entry under the heading "Enthusiasm," in Commonplace Book of T. M. Randolph, Jr.

49 T. M. Randolph, Jr., to James Monroe, February 14, 1801, in Monroe Papers, Library of Congress.

50 Jefferson to Maria Eppes, March 29, 1802, in Jefferson Papers, University of Virginia.

France, having recently acquired Louisiana by forced purchase from Spain, would soon occupy the lower Mississippi Valley. Jefferson was probably motivated in part by his unwillingness to see Martha and her children taken so far from Monticello, but the points he made were persuasive. Tom agreed to forget the "little helpless speck of a settlement" in the Southwest Territory and decided, on his father-in-law's advice, to seek his rich cotton lands in Georgia.[51]

But by fall a new obstacle had appeared—the South Carolina Assembly had prohibited the transportation of slaves across the state. Tom naturally intended to take his Negroes with him to the new land, but he realized that the cost of transporting them from Virginia by sea or of purchasing a new group of bondsmen in Georgia would be prohibitively expensive. He was forced to reconsider his proposed emigration, particularly after he learned through Jefferson that Governor John Drayton was unwilling to make any exceptions in the enforcement of the South Carolina law.[52]

By the end of 1802 most of the impetus back of the Georgia project had waned, and Tom finally abandoned it completely. He hoped, of course, that the move would improve his fortunes, but he also seems to have been animated—if only subconsciously—by a feeling of personal inadequacy and by an increasing sense of isolation from his domestic environment. Only six years earlier, visitors had commented with wonder on the filial relationship between him and his father-in-law; only five years before, Jefferson had expressed confidence that nothing could produce "any jarring or jealousies" which would disrupt the harmony of the group around his fireside. But by 1802, perhaps because his confidence in himself and in his own prospects had been so undermined by failure and frustration, perhaps because he had accomplished so little in his thirty-four years, he had come to feel out of place in the President's domestic group. Not even his father-in-law's assurances of regard and esteem were enough to undo his consciousness of the rift, existing in his own imagination if not in actuality, between himself and the others. Late in October, 1802, Jefferson had declared his

51 Jefferson to T. M. Randolph, Jr., March 12 and 21, 1802, in Jefferson Papers, Library of Congress; Jefferson to Maria Eppes, March 29, 1802, in Jefferson Papers, University of Virginia.

52 Jefferson to T. M. Randolph, Jr., November 25, 1802, in Jefferson Papers, Library of Congress.

willingness to do anything that would place their mutual fortunes on a stable basis. "I cannot serve my family more solidly," he wrote, "than by clearing the old debts hanging on us." [53]

Randolph seized upon his father-in-law's routine reference to "family" and to "us," with pathetic eagerness, but he expressed doubts that he really was worthy of being included "within the narrow circle" around the President. He was, he said, "so essentially and widely different from all within it, as to look like something extraneous, fallen in by accident and destroying the homogenity," and he compared himself to "the proverbially silly bird" who could not "feel at . . . ease among the swans." Having thus questioned his own worthiness, he went on to pay lavish tribute to his father-in-law, both as a man and as a statesman. "The sentiment of my mind when it contemplates yourself alone," he declared, "is one of the most lofty elevation and most unmixed delight," while his heart overflowed with "gratitude and affection . . . when I attempt to estimate the value to the whole human race . . . of the incredibly, inconceivably excellent political system which you created, developed, and, at last I think, permanently established." [54]

Nowhere in this anguished outburst did he mention his wife, and that omission, deliberate or otherwise, points to emotional tension within his own household. One cannot avoid the feeling that Martha, probably without so intending, had been responsible for his feeling of inadequacy and of isolation. Whether this was intentional or not, he most certainly felt that she did not consider him one of the swans of Monticello.

Jefferson found the praise Randolph bestowed upon him embarrassing, but he was much more disturbed by his son-in-law's declarations of self-abasement. "The shade into which you throw yourself," he chided, "neither your happiness nor mine will admit that you remain in. . . . In matter of interests, I know no difference between yours and mine. . . . I hold the virtues of your heart and the powers of your understanding in a far more exalted view than you place them in." [55]

This advice probably did little to improve the "mutual con-

53 Jefferson to Randolph, Jr., October 22, 1802, in Jefferson Papers, Massachusetts Historical Society.

54 T. M. Randolph, Jr., to Jefferson, October 29, 1802, *ibid.*

55 Jefferson to T. M. Randolph, Jr., November 2, 1802, in Jefferson Papers, Library of Congress.

sciousness of mutual esteem" which Jefferson considered so important or to make his son-in-law feel less "extraneous." Yet the President's consoling words may have encouraged him to make a fresh attempt to prove his abilities to himself and to others. He had indulged in little direct political activity since his marriage, but he had not forgotten his early ambition to seek "the highest honours in a free state." In March, 1803, at the age of thirty-four, he decided to find fulfillment of that ambition by seeking election from Albemarle to the House of Representatives.[56] If he still thought of himself as "a silly bird," he was willing to show his family that he could swim with the swans.

56 John Wayles Eppes to Jefferson, April 14, 1803, in Edgehill-Randolph Papers.

CHAPTER V

"As Little Useful As Any Member . . . of Congress"

NO FEDERALIST HAD the effrontery to offer himself as a congressional candidate from the Albemarle-Amherst-Fluvanna district in 1803, and the contest there was waged between two members of the Republican party. One candidate was the incumbent Samuel Jordan Cabell of Amherst, who had represented the district since 1795;[1] challenging him was Thomas Mann Randolph, who had never before held elective office. Cabell had supported Jefferson loyally and steadfastly during the hectic days of February, 1801, "lying two nights on a blanket to make him President," and he was more than a little chagrined to be opposed by his leader's son-in-law.[2] Tom had decided to make the race without consulting the President, and when Jefferson learned of his son-in-law's intentions, he tried to dissuade him and "to prepare him by calculation for failure." Tom, however, did not take the hint, and Jefferson thereafter carefully maintained a position of neutrality.[3]

Randolph barely defeated Cabell, winning by only 13 votes out of the 1,800 which had been cast.[4] Both candidates had received a number of "bad votes," and Cabell announced his intention to contest the election. Tom was not only pessimistic about the

1 "Samuel Jordan Cabell," *Dictionary of American Biography* (New York, 1928–37), III, 388–89.
2 John Wayles Eppes to Jefferson, April 14, 1803, in Edgehill-Randolph Papers.
3 Jefferson to Samuel J. Cabell, April 25, 1803, in Jefferson Papers, Library of Congress.
4 T. M. Randolph, Jr., to Jefferson, April 29, 1803, in Edgehill-Randolph Papers.

results of a recount, but the exceedingly narrow margin of his victory had left him writhing under "the consciousness of wanting the qualities . . . necessary for passing through with honour." [5] When friends and "indifferent persons" alike assured him that his poll would "bear the most rigid scrutiny," he abandoned his misgivings and then began to accuse his opponent of connivance at the irregularities which he had protested.[6]

He remained in Virginia throughout most of the summer, and that fall rode up to Washington to take his seat in the Eighth Congress, which convened on October 17. He led a bachelor's existence during his first season in the sprawling and unfinished governmental village on the Potomac, for Martha remained at home, where her sixth child Mary Jefferson Randolph was born on November 2, 1803.[7]

The new congressman was luckier in one respect than most of his fellow legislators, who were forced to accept the rude accommodations of noisy and unclean boarding houses where they lived "like bears, brutalized and stupified." [8] Randolph found quarters in the President's house at the far end of muddy Pennsylvania Avenue, as did his brother-in-law John Wayles Eppes, also a member of the Virginia delegation. The furnishings were "plain and simple to excess," but the President's steward and French cook kept the table well supplied, and "republican simplicity" was, in this respect at least, "united to Epicurean delicacy." [9] On the occasions when the President entertained, the two men had opportunity to meet and converse with cabinet officers, diplomats, and congressmen, as well as visitors from nearby Georgetown and Alexandria.

But such occasions were rare, and even Tom, for all of his love of solitude, must have found Washington a frustratingly dull place. There were, indeed, the resources of the Library of Congress, whose less than two thousand volumes furnished both information and amusement to gentlemen marooned in the "desert city" by the public interest.[10] One could hunt snipe and partridge a few yards

5 T. M. Randolph, Jr., to Jefferson, May 22, 1803, in Jefferson Papers, Library of Congress.

6 Randolph, Jr., to Jefferson, June 10, 1803, *ibid.*

7 *Jefferson's Prayer Book.*

8 Augustus John Foster, *Jeffersonian America: Notes on the United States of America Collected in the Years 1805–6–7 and 11–12,* ed. Richard Beale Davis (San Marino, California, 1954), 9.

9 Smith, *The First Forty Years,* 391–92.

10 William Plumer, *Memorandum of the Proceedings of the United States Senate, 1803–1807,* ed. Everett S. Brown (New York, 1925), 541.

away from Pennsylvania Avenue or "even under the wall of the Capitol;" [11] one could go to the horse races in nearby Maryland; one could play brag, that "most gambling of all games;" [12] and, of course, one could drink. The principal activity was politics, and life in Washington was centered around Congress and the President.

When Randolph arrived in Washington the south wing of the Capitol was still under construction, and the representatives were meeting in a temporary brick structure nearby, called "the Oven," [13] In addition to his brother-in-law John Eppes, another colleague was his cousin John Randolph of Roanoke. The latter, who had served in the House since 1799, was already famous as a redoutable and caustic debater, and was chairman of the important Committee on Ways and Means.[14] All were Republicans and planters, as were more than two-thirds of the delegation from Virginia, that "aristocratick State" whose "Gentlemen Jacobins" seemed to dominate Jefferson's party.[15] Randolph allied himself with this group from the beginning, and there were few occasions during his congressional service when he opposed them or the administration which they represented.

During most of his first term in Congress he took a very passive part in its proceedings, perhaps, because his status in that body remained uncertain until near the close of the session. On October 18, the day after the House convened, a memorial was received from Samuel J. Cabell, charging irregularities in Randolph's election and pleading that he not be seated. This document was referred to the Committee on Elections, of which William Findley, Republican of Pennsylvania, was chairman, and there it rested until the following March.[16] The committee received little assistance from Cabell in its investigation of the returns, the latter even ignoring an invitation to come to Washington to testify personally. Failing to find any substantial evidence that the President's son-in-law had not been legally elected, the committee recommended on March 9, 1804, that he retain his seat, and the House voted to uphold this finding.[17] By the time this decision was reached the session was almost over.

11 Foster, *Jeffersonian America*, 8.
12 *Ibid.*, 88. For a vivid description of the national capital in these years see Bernard Mayo, *Henry Clay, Spokesman of the New West* (Boston, 1937), Chap. 8.
13 Wilhelmus Bogart Bryant, *A History of the National Capital* (New York, 1914), I, 453.
14 Bruce, *John Randolph*, I, 155, 169.
15 Foster, *Jeffersonian America*, 153.
16 *Annals of the Congress of the United States*, 8th Cong., 1st Sess. 373.
17 *Ibid.*, 1128.

An incident occurring soon after the Eighth Congress convened may also have influenced Tom to play an inconspicuous role. John Eppes had offered a resolution calling on the Committee on Ways and Means "to inquire whether any, and, if any, what reductions may be made in the expenses of the different Departments of the Government," and on November 25 John Randolph had spoken in rebuttal, declaring that he would form his "opinion of every resolution that shall come before this House, *without reference to the quarter from which it shall proceed*." [18] This shaft, apparently directed at Eppes' personal connection with the President, was reported in somewhat garbled form in the newspapers, causing John Randolph to write to Jefferson, disclaiming any intention to label Eppes as an administration mouthpiece. Jefferson's letter in reply accepted the chairman's explanations and indicated an awareness of the problem inherent in the presence of two sons-in-law in the House: "In parts of the Union, and even with persons to whom Mr. Eppes and Mr. Randolph are unknown and myself little known, it will be presumed, from their connection, that what comes from them comes from me. No men on earth are more independent in their sentiments than they are . . . We rarely speak of politics, or of the proceedings of the House, but merely historically . . . ." [19] There the matter ended, and the undaunted Eppes continued to take an active part in debate and in the other work of the House. But Randolph, with his right to a Congressional seat already under investigation, may have been unduly affected by this demonstration that his actions and his votes might become objects of public scrutiny because of his relationship to Jefferson.

At any rate he was a silent member throughout most of his first congressional session. He was not idle, however, serving on several special committees appointed to examine private claims, and voting, although without comment, on most of the measures considered. On practically every issue he supported the administration, voting for the proposed twelfth amendment [20] and approving the various measures implementing the recent treaty with France for the purchase of Louisiana.[21] He privately thought, so he recalled later, that his father-in-law should have insisted on a definite boundary

18 *Ibid.*, 627–28.

19 Jefferson to John Randolph, December 1, 1803, in Paul L. Ford (ed.), *The Writings of Thomas Jefferson*, VIII, 281.

20 *Annals of the Congress*, 8th Cong., 1st Sess., 554, 584.

21 *Ibid.*, 488.

between Louisiana and Texas,[22] but he did not make an issue of his stand at the time. With some personal reservations, he backed the administration's bill for the government of the new territory.

Many Republicans from the northern and western states opposed this measure because it gave virtually complete control to presidentially-appointed officials in the Territory of Orleans, but Randolph had little patience with such arguments, which seemed to him "abstract" and "metaphysical." [23] He supported a provision in the bill which would have given exclusive legislative powers to the territorial governor,[24] but the House voted instead to establish a legislative council of thirteen of "the most discreet" citizens of the territory.[25] On the other hand, Randolph wished, so he claimed, to "tack a clause" to the bill which would "impower the people of the country to call for a representative government when they pleased" and which would pledge the United States "to grant it when called for." [26] He did not formally propose this measure, and the law as finally enacted contained no provisions for such a referendum.[27]

On only one major measure before the House that session did he disagree with the administration—this was the "Yazoo compromise," designed to settle the nine-year-old controversy involving the disposition of the Yazoo River lands on the east bank of the Mississippi. This region, then part of Georgia's western territory, had been granted to a group of four land companies in 1795 by a bribed and lobby-ridden legislature. This overly generous grant had been repudiated the following year, but three of the companies already had sold large tracts to unsuspecting third parties, who suddenly discovered themselves shorn of legal title to their new acquisitions. When Georgia ceded her western lands, including the Yazoo country, to the central government in 1802, these purchasers, many of them New Englanders, appealed for relief. Republicans from the states of the northeast and from the Ohio Valley supported

22 T. M. Randolph, Jr., to David Campbell, February 20, 1819, in David Campbell Papers, Duke University Library.

23 T. M. Randolph, Jr., to John Milledge, March 11, 1804, in Harriet M. Salley (ed.), *Correspondence of John Milledge, Governor of Georgia* (Columbia, S.C., 1949), 112–13.

24 *Annals of the Congress,* 8th Cong., 1st Sess., 1193.

25 *Ibid.,* 1294.

26 T. M. Randolph, Jr., to Milledge, March 11, 1804, in Salley (ed.), *Correspondence of John Milledge,* 112–13.

27 "An Act Erecting Louisiana into Two Territories," *Annals of the Congress,* 8th Cong., 1st Sess., 1293–1300.

their claims, and the Jefferson administration adopted their view that some compensation ought to be made. Southern strict-constructionists, sensitive of any federal action which might reflect upon a sovereign state's honor, refused to concede that the United States had assumed any responsibilities for the injured purchasers and opposed even token payments to them.[28]

The debate on the Yazoo compromise reached a climax on March 10, 1804, the day after the Committee on Elections had approved Thomas' election. John Randolph had proposed a set of resolutions affirming the right of the Georgia legislature to revoke the transaction and forbidding any appropriation of federal funds to compensate the claimants.[29] After he had spoken at great length and with great emotion on the subject, Thomas took the floor to make the first—and only major—speech of his congressional career.

He began with a spirited attack on all parties involved in the original transaction, but he reserved his choicest epithets for the speculators who had offered the bribes rather than for the bemused legislators who had taken them. Any compensation to such "bands of sharpers," he declared, would "cast a broad stain on the American character." In his view, the Yazoo transaction was "a fraud of unprecedented enormity," comparable only to John Law's Mississippi Bubble and the "South Sea cheat in England."

Unlike John, to whom all Yazoo purchasers were suspect, Thomas discriminated between those who had bought their lands in good faith and those who had bought knowing that the Georgia legislature had revoked the whole transaction. He was not opposed to compensation for persons in the former category, although he made clear his conviction that they should be paid off in the solid and honest currency of land and not in speculator's paper or banker's gold. Yet he wished to make sure that the guilty were not rewarded; therefore he demanded that every claim be given the most rigid and severe scrutiny. He proposed to judge the legitimacy of each claim by determining the date on which the purchaser might reasonably have been expected to have known of the Georgia rescinding act.

Although Thomas' proposals technically included some conces-

28 Irving Brant, *James Madison: Secretary of State, 1801–1809* (Indianapolis, 1953), 234–40; Thomas P. Abernethey, *The South in the New Nation, 1789–1819* (Baton Rouge, 1961), 136–68.

29 *Annals of the Congress*, 8th Cong., 1st Sess., 794.

sion to the compensators and were based on a desire to be fair to the innocent purchasers, they were not essentially different from those of John Randolph. His arguments followed the same states' rights pattern as did those of his eccentric and single-minded cousin, and like John, he viewed all proposals for unqualified compensation as a reflection upon Georgia's sovereign right to undo the misdeeds of her own servants.

Having devoted a large part of the speech to his proposal for dealing with the third parties, he concluded with a blazing attack on the original villains, the speculators of the Yazoo companies themselves: "They escaped the thunder of heaven, but they have not [escaped] the certain earthly punishment. Since that day, they have stood in the eyes of an indignant nation, riven, blasted, stripped of all the lovely foliage of reputation by the lightning of eloquence." [30]

With this bow to his cousin's oratory, and probably not too dissatisfied with his own, he took his seat. As he privately admitted, he had "unveiled more" of the transactions of 1795 than was desirable for American honor, but he felt his revelations were "absolutely necessary." [31] His speech attracted brief but complimentary attention from Thomas Ritchie, the influential editor of the Richmond *Enquirer*, who praised the speaker's "indignant eloquence" and, by way of encouragement, hailed the emergence of his "modest merit from the retirement in which it delighted too much to dwell." [32] Meanwhile, Tom had the further satisfaction of seeing action on the Yazoo bill postponed for the remainder of the session; fifteen members of the Virginia delegation, including Eppes and the two Randolphs, voted against the administration. The question continued to occupy the time and energies of succeeding Congresses until 1810 when the Supreme Court, in its decision in *Fletcher* v *Peck* invalidated the Georgia rescinding act and reopened the doors of litigation which the Randolphs had sought to close.[33]

When the Congress adjourned Tom returned to Albemarle County and resumed the life of a farmer and family man, little knowing that he had expended his eloquence in a losing cause. Not long after, his sister-in-law Maria Eppes became seriously ill, and

30 *Ibid.*, 1138–53.

31 T. M. Randolph, Jr., to Milledge, March 11, 1804, in Salley (ed.), *Correspondence of John Milledge*, 112–13.

32 Richmond *Enquirer*, March 12, 1804.

33 Brant, *James Madison: Secretary of State*, 338–40.

died on April 17. From then on, the grieving Jefferson was to cling more tightly to his surviving child Martha, and the bonds between Monticello and Edgehill were drawn closer than ever. Although Randolph gave no sign that he was deeply affected, Martha was unquestionably shaken by her sister's death. She was ill that spring of cramps which her husband diagnosed as "hysterics," but which she attributed to eating radishes and milk.[34]

In the summer Tom became involved in a public quarrel with an English workman he identified only as "Hope." [35] The two were engaged in a business conversation in the street of Milton, the port-village on the Rivanna where Tom owned some property. Proceedings passed the stage of peaceful discussion, with Hope calling the congressman a liar "in such round terms" that the latter "flew into a rage," and, picking up a stone from the street, threatened to "pound his skull for him if ever he did the like." The Englishman apologized quickly enough to save his skull, Tom dropped the rock, and the two proceeded to Hope's house to resume their conversation. Once they were inside, the workman renewed the battle with a stream of curses. Knowing that "Hope was not one of those who fight duels," Tom "dared him to come out into the street and fight with his fists," but the workman declined the challenge. Randolph departed at last, after which his antagonist "adopted the usual defense of cowards, the fabrication of malignant lies." As a result of these insinuations, some of which may have reflected on his near-defeat at the previous election, the congressman intimated to friends that he might not run for reelection.[36]

The rest of the summer passed uneventfully, and he returned to Washington, for the opening of the new session of Congress on November 5, 1804. During the next few months he conducted himself quietly, serving on a few special committees and supporting the administration on most issues. He voted for the articles of impeachment against Justice Samuel Chase,[37] this being a matter on

34 Martha Randolph to Jefferson, May 31, 1804, in Kean Deposit, Alderman Alderman Library, University of Virginia.

35 Jefferson Account Book, 1804–1809, in Jefferson Papers, New York Public Library. Randolph's antagonist was probably Michael Hope, who was employed by Jefferson between 1802 and 1805 in minor construction work at Monticello, but a Robert Hope was also present in the county at the time.

36 T. M. Randolph, Jr., to Peachy R. Gilmer, May 11, 1804, in Randolph–Gilmer Letters, Archives Division, Virginia State Library.

37 *Annals of the Congress*, 8th Cong., 2nd Sess., 749.

which all Republicans were agreed. On the Yazoo question, which was aired again that session, Randolph voted with the states' rights wing of his party.[38] He made no more speeches, however, on this or any other issue, apparently content to leave the oratory to others.

Returning home at the close of the session he found Martha seriously ill of a stomach complaint, and he may have shared Jefferson's fears for her life.[39] By late March, however, she was recovering, and he could turn his attention to other matters. He had intimated the previous year that he would not seek another term,[40] but had changed his mind by the spring of 1805. He was opposed this time by Walter Leake, who had just completed a term in the Virginia General Assembly as delegate from Albemarle.[41] When Randolph prepared to begin his campaign, he found that his friends were somewhat pessimistic about his changes of reelection. Leake was conducting a campaign of personal criticism, "instead of positively elevating himself." Thomas thereupon set out on his own "electioneering excursion" through the district "not only to counteract, but to retrovert such measures." [42] The excursion was thoroughly successful, and, supported by ex-Senator Wilson Cary Nicholas, he won a substantial victory, gaining 1,184 out of a total of 1,863 votes.[43] In the same election his father-in-law was reelected by an overwhelming margin. Despite Leake's campaign tactics, the victor later supported his appointment to a judgeship in the Mississippi Territory, paying tribute to the latter's "judgment and integrity." [44]

Thus assured of the continued confidence of his constituents, the congressman settled down with his family for the summer, but he enjoyed little surcease from his many responsibilities. His wheat

38 *Ibid.*, 754.

39 Jefferson to Mme. de Tessé, March 10, 1805, in Jefferson Papers, Missouri Historical Society, St. Louis, Missouri.

40 T. M. Randolph, Jr., to Peachy R. Gilmer, May 11, 1804, in Randolph–Gilmer Letters.

41 "Sketch of Gov. Walter Leake of Mississippi," *Virginia Magazine of History and Biography*, XI (1904), 417–19.

42 T. M. Randolph, Jr., to Wilson Cary Nicholas, March 30, 1805, in Edgehill–Randolph Papers.

43 Randolph, Jr., to Jefferson, April 27, 1805, in Kean Deposit, Alderman Library, University of Virginia.

44 Randolph, Jr., to Jefferson, February 20, 1807, in Clarence E. Carter (ed.), *Territorial Papers of the United States* (Washington, D.C., 1934–), V, 515.

crop was ruined by the ubiquitous Hessian fly in June, a blow which must have set back his hopes for financial recuperation even if it did not discourage him from "new agricultural projects." [45] He had been able to make a slight reduction in his debt to John Lidderdale and had secured his creditor's agreement to stay execution on the remainder (approximately £2600) for two and a half more years.[46] Nonetheless the tightening coil of financial uncertainty must have kept him under considerable constraint during the fall of 1805.

Late in November he turned his back on his domestic concerns and returned to Washington for the opening of the Ninth Congress on December 2.[47] Again he stayed with the President, and this time Martha, then far advanced in her eighth pregnancy, went with him. She could have demanded special social privileges as the President's daughter and as his official hostess, but she insisted on receiving and making visits on the same terms as other congressional wives.[48] When Mrs. Anthony Merry, the haughty spouse of the British minister, inquired whether Mrs. Randolph expected to receive the first call as the President's daughter or to make it as the wife of a Congressman, Martha did not hesitate. At Jefferson's suggestion, she replied that "she was in Washington as the wife of a Virginia gentleman and as such expected the first visit," [49] but Mrs. Merry refused to accept such terms, and there was no interchange of calls between the two ladies. The birth of James Madison Randolph took place at the executive mansion on January 17, 1806.[50]

Meanwhile, the Virginia gentleman was pursuing a quiet but busy course in the House. In this session he took a generally nationalistic stand, being one of the two Virginia congressmen to support the bill authorizing a survey for a national road between the Potomac and the Ohio rivers.[51] Since the proposed road would have neither benefited nor harmed his constituents, he was probably influenced by the fact that his father-in-law warmly supported the project. He

45 T. M. Randolph, Jr., to Jefferson, June 16, 1805, in Edgehill-Randolph Papers.

46 *Lidderdale* v. *Randolph* . . . in chancery, November 27, 1805, copy in Creed Taylor Papers, Alderman Library, University of Virginia.

47 *Annals of the Congress*, 9th Cong., 1st Sess., 253.

48 Smith, *First Forty Years*, 404.

49 Thomas Jefferson Randolph, "Reminiscences"; Smith, *First Forty Years*, 404–405.

50 *Jefferson's Prayer Book.*

51 *Annals of the Congress*, 9th Cong., 1st Sess., 840.

likewise served on a committee which drew up the bill establishing a national university at Washington, another project cherished by Jefferson.[52]

The Representative from Albemarle also supported presidential policy on West Florida, the area between the Mississippi and the Perdido rivers, retained by Spain after her relinquishment of Louisiana to France. Jefferson, having secured the nation's western flank by the purchase from Napoleon, now sought to extend the southern frontier to the Gulf of Mexico. Seeing no reason why the methods which had acquired Louisiana would not succeed again, the President asked for an appropriation of $2,000,000 to effect the purchase, and Congress met in secret session in January, 1806, to consider his proposal.[53] States' rights southerners, led by John Randolph, sided with the Federalists against the President's expensive scheme. It was generally known that Spain had become a Napoleonic satellite, and Randolph openly accused the administration or planning to bribe the French emperor to force the purchase.[54] This outburst did not deter the House from approving the appropriation, but only ten of Virginia's twenty-two representatives stood by the administration, Thomas Mann Randolph being one of them. He took no active part, however, in the debates on the purchase project, and said nothing at this time to rebut his cousin's charges of a policy based on international bribery.[55]

Late in the session he collided head-on with his rancorous kinsman on another matter of executive policy. Despite their earlier collaboration against the Yazoo compromise, Tom and his cousin had been moving in opposite political directions, and the breach was completed with John's open declaration of war on the administration, with his statement of April 7.[56] Tom's reaction, expressed in a private letter, was that John had brought final political ruin on himself with this reckless step.[57]

Then, on the night of April 21, as the Ninth Congress was preparing to adjourn, an open quarrel developed between the two

52 *Ibid.*, 880
53 *Ibid.*, 1117–44.
54 Henry Adams, *History of the United States of America during the Administrations of Thomas Jefferson and James Madison* (New York, 1889–91), III, 136–40; Bruce, *John Randolph*, I, 231–32.
55 *Annals of the Congress*, 9th Cong., 1st Sess., 1144, and *passim.*
56 Adams, *History*, III, 164; Bruce, *John Randolph*, 276–85.
57 T. M. Randolph, Jr., to Capt. Joel Franklin, April 17, 1806, in Grinnan Papers, Alderman Library, University of Virginia.

cousins as quickly as a grass-fire in a dry Virginia field. The House was considering John's bill to repeal the tax on salt. This levy, originally created to support the Barbary War, was now counted on by the administration to finance the purchase of Florida.[58] Congressional tempers were undoubtedly strained by four months of life in Washington, and William Findley of Pennsylvania, apparently made somewhat incautious by liquor,[59] charged in the course of a loud tirade that the purpose of the repeal bill was to embarrass the administration and frustrate its policy. When David R. Williams of South Carolina, one of John Randolph's allies, attempted to rebut this not inaccurate charge, he was quickly called to order by Thomas. John himself then took the floor to make a few conciliatory remarks, in the course of which he deplored the "contumely and hostility" which had been shown during the debate by some of his colleagues.[60]

He was almost certainly referring to Findley, who had spoken at length, rather than to Thomas, who had intervened only to silence Williams. Yet the man who had "taken fire" at his father's use of the word "compelled" during the negotiations for Edgehill seventeen years before, took equally quick offense at his cousin's use of "contumely," and he made a bitterly hostile retort. Declaring that John had "made more noise than had been useful" during the session then coming to an end, he accused his cousin of using language "behind the shield of the dignity of the house, which he would not venture to make use of elsewhere." Thomas went on to proclaim himself prepared to take the consequences of his remarks, declaring that he had "always thought . . . that lead and even steel make very proper ingredients in serious quarrels." He concluded with a few thrusts at his cousin's political habits, proclaimed John "bankrupt forever as a popular statesman," and then stalked out of the House chamber.[61]

John Randolph was outraged by this speech and immediately sent a message to his cousin, through Congressman James Mercer Garnett of Essex County, that he expected either an apology or a duel. Tom, in his turn, secured the services of Isaac A. Coles, the President's secretary, and the stage was set for a formal and possibly fatal

58 Adams, *History*, III, 182.

59 See Richmond *Enquirer*, July 4, 1806, for Findley's condition. See also *Annals of the Congress*, 9th Cong., 1st Sess., 1102, for his remarks.

60 *Annals of the Congress*, 9th Cong., 1st Sess., 1102–1103.

61 *Ibid.*, 1104–1106.

meeting. Both intermediaries, however, handled the negotiations discreetly. Garnett even went so far as to assure "Edgehill" through Coles that "Roanoke" had not directed his remarks concerning contumely at him but at Findley, while Coles was careful not to inform Thomas of John's ultimatum.[62] This assurance, coupled with the opinions of other members who were hastily consulted, persuaded Tom that he could withdraw his words with honor. He therefore returned to the floor of the House and, speaking in tones so low as to be almost inaudible,[63] acknowledged his error and apologized for his "very severe and harsh language." [64] "Roanoke," being informed of this, gratefully dismissed Garnett and sent word through Coles to "Edgehill" that he was perfectly satisfied.[65] There, everyone hoped, the matter had ended.

Journalistic interference, however, threatened to bring about a renewal of hostilities that June, after both principals had left Washington. A correspondent of the antiadministration *Aurora* interpreted the whole affair as a "conspiracy" against John Randolph.[66] The equally pro-Jefferson *National Intelligencer* opened a dispute on another level by intimating that Thomas Mann had made his public apology only after John had categorically disavowed any intention to wound him. The Richmond *Enquirer*, whose editor, Thomas Ritchie, usually supported the administration, countered with a defense of "Roanoke" and a charge that it was "Edgehill" who had been the first to back down.[67] Once the question was raised as to which Randolph had first pulled in his horns, the feud between them was revived. Peaceable Virginians like John Taylor of Caroline held their breaths, waiting for the two cousins to "cut each other's throats." Taylor, who despised "the pugnacious humor of false honor," begged Wilson Cary Nicholas, Thomas Randolph's neighbor, to prevent the clash he felt was almost certain.[68] Jefferson, after reading the newspapers, stepped in and appealed to his son-in-

62 James Mercer Garnett to editor, in Richmond *Enquirer,* July 1, 1806; Isaac Coles to editor, *ibid.*, June 24, 1806.

63 Coles to editor, *ibid.*, July 4, 1806.

64 *Annals of the Congress,* 9th Cong., 1st Sess., 1105–1106.

65 Isaac Coles to editor, in Richmond *Enquirer,* June 24, 1806.

66 Hugh A. Garland, *The Life of John Randolph of Roanoke* (New York, 1854), I, 242.

67 Richmond *Enquirer,* June 17, 1806.

68 John Taylor to W. C. Nicholas, June 26, 1806, in Jefferson Papers, Massachusetts Historical Society.

law to remember his family obligations.[69] He also asked James Ogilvie, the Charlottesville schoolmaster, to intercede and to recommend "a conduct, cool, candid and merely defensive." [70]

Tom may not have been sufficiently irritated to send a challenge at this point, but if he had not been soothed by the calming influence of Jefferson and Nicholas, his hair-trigger temper might have led him to provoke one. Although the two decided to keep the peace, and there was no further talk of a family duel, the two cousins maintained a cordial dislike for each other from that time on.

Meanwhile he had taken up his pen to defend Jefferson's West Florida purchase scheme. News of this proposal, discussed in the secret session, had gotten out and had aroused enough suspicion, even in the Virginia Piedmont, to make an explanation seem desirable. To allay these feelings and to counter the opposition's attacks on the government, he completed, late in April, a *Letter to His Constituents* which he first had published as a pamphlet, and later, in the columns of both the *National Intelligencer* at Washington and of the Richmond *Enquirer*.

The *Letter*, which may have been encouraged by the President, was devoted to a review of the West Florida boundary question and to a defense of the administration's purchase project. Tom tacitly admitted his cousin's charge that the two million dollars voted at the secret session would go into French rather than Spanish coffers, but he argued that Napoleon would eventually get the money, even were it paid first to Madrid. Ardent Republican though he was, he believed that the much criticized secret debates were necessitated by the exigencies of the situation and by "the naturally confidential character of diplomatic matters," and he lashed out at the talkative Congressmen and the prying editors who had exposed and frustrated the administration's intentions.[71]

His lengthy manifesto had little discernible effect upon that segment of public opinion to which it was addressed, and the policy

69 Jefferson to T. M. Randolph, Jr., June 23, 1806, in Edgehill-Randolph Papers.

70 Jefferson to James Ogilvie, June 23, 1806, in Jefferson Papers, Massachusetts Historical Society.

71 T. M. Randolph, Jr., *Letter to His Constituents . . .* (Washington, D.C., [1806]). This work also appeared serially in the *National Intelligencer* (Washington, D.C.), June 13–16, 1806, and in the Richmond *Enquirer*, June 20–24, 1806.

which he defended proved a failure. Spain refused to sell under any circumstances, and Napoleon made it clear that he had no interest in forcing her to do so. There the matter rested until four years later when the United States obtained West Florida by rebellion.[72]

Randolph made no effort to follow up this first effort at political pamphleteering, and through the summer and fall of 1806 he devoted himself to farming and to the supervision of his father-in-law's properties. In December he took leave of his family and returned to Washington for his fourth and last congressional session. Except for serving on a committee which drew up a bill forbidding the further importation of slaves into the United States after 1808,[73] he played a relatively inactive part in the proceedings of this second session of the Ninth Congress.

Martha again chose to remain in Albemarle with her family, and during the early part of the session Tom lived, as he had before, at the presidential mansion. There, sometime in February he quarreled with his brother-in-law John Eppes, who also had returned to the same quarters. Jefferson attempted always to treat them alike and to avoid any show of favoritism, but Eppes' very active life in Congress may have subtly influenced the President's attitude toward the two men. Contention also arose from the redistribution of Jefferson's property necessitated by Maria's death, and the two sons-in-law were at odds over Eppes' share of Poplar Forest.[74] At any rate, Tom was certain that Jefferson "felt a preference" for Eppes,[75] and when his brother-in-law was invited to join a party at the President's in which he was not included, he felt confirmed in his suspicion that he was being overlooked.

About this time he conceived the singular notion that someone had libelled him to the chief executive as a Federalist.[76] Earlier that year he had ventured to disagree with the President over General

72 The standard account is, I. J. Cox, *The West Florida Controversy, 1798–1813* (Baltimore, 1918). For a revisionist view see Irving Brant, *James Madison: The President, 1809–1812.* (Indianapolis, 1956).

73 *Annals of the Congress*, 9th Cong., 2nd Sess., 114. This bill was enacted in pursuance of the Constitutional provision prohibiting any Congressional interference with the slave trade until 1808.

74 Norma B. Cuthbert, "Poplar Forest: Jefferson's Legacy to his Grandson," in *Huntington Library Quarterly*, VI (1942), 333–38.

75 Jefferson to T. M. Randolph, Jr., February 18, 1807, in Jefferson Papers, Library of Congress.

76 Jefferson to Randolph, Jr., February 19, 1807, in Edgehill-Randolph Papers, alludes to Randolph's notion on this point.

James Wilkinson, lately involved in the Burr conspiracy, and had urged that the unsavory old intriguer be removed from command of the army.[77] Jefferson did not take the advice, but this apparently caused no serious split between them. These attacks on Wilkinson, if expressed to administration supporters in the House, may have been enough, however, to lead some to believe that the Virginia congressman had gone over to the Federalists.

It is also possible that the accusations of coat turning, in whatever form such charges were made or implied, were inspired by Tom's vote in the House that February on the suspension of habeas corpus. The congressman from Albemarle had voted in favor of the resolution offered on February 7, by Federalist James M. Broom of Delaware, which called "for further provision for securing the privileges of the writ . . . to persons in custody under or by color of the authority of the United States." [78] This resolution, although seemingly a proclamation of faith in one of the articles of the Republican creed, was offered by a member of the opposition in an effort to embarrass the administration in its handling of the Burr conspiracy. A motion for the indefinite postponement of Broom's resolution was narrowly passed (60–58) on February 19, with Eppes and most other administration supporters voting to table. Thomas, however, joined the Federalists in voting to continue discussion.[79] Whatever his reasons, his stand indicated a disagreement with the administration on the Burr case, a disagreement that was also reflected in his low opinion of the government's star witness General Wilkinson. Since the Federalists were making Burr's cause their vociferous own, anyone who tended to aid that cause, even by a ritual vote on the habeas corpus matter, might have laid himself open to charges of desertion.

Most distasteful of all Tom's concerns was his feeling that his father-in-law was not sufficiently attentive. Because of this and because of his jealous anger with Eppes, he let himself be overwhelmed by melancholy, and, without saying a word to anyone, left the President's mansion in mid-February, moving to Frost's and Quinn's boardinghouse at the other end of Pennsylvania Avenue.[80] There he remained, ignoring all of Jefferson's entreaties to

77 Plumer, *Memorandum*, 618–19, 623.
78 *Annals of the Congress*, 9th Cong., 2nd Sess., 472.
79 *Ibid.*, 590. John Randolph also voted against the administration.
80 Plumer, *Memorandum*, 622, states that on February 23 Randolph had been at the boardinghouse a week.

return and disregarding his assurances of affection and esteem.[81] He did continue to visit his father-in-law, thus counteracting the gossip that he had quarreled with Jefferson.[82]

Frost's and Quinn's was a quiet establishment, where the guests were served only a half-pint of spirits daily. Most of the boarders were Federalists. Also living there was Senator Henry Clay of Kentucky,[83] but the Virginian seems to have had little contact with the carefree and convivial "Harry of the West." Randolph kept to himself, preferring solitary meals in his own chamber to the company of other diners. He did, however, make friends with one of them, Senator William Plumer, a moderate Federalist from New Hampshire. Plumer was impressed by the new boarder, finding him "a pleasant agreeable companion," and "a man of study—much devoted to books." The Hampshireman was somewhat surprised, therefore, to discover that the reticent student kept a pair of pistols and a sword over his mantel.[84]

By the end of February Tom was so ill with a fever that it was feared he would not recover. Jefferson demonstrated great concern and tried to move him back to the presidential mansion where he could obtain better care and treatment,[85] but the sick man chose to remain at the boardinghouse. He rallied from his illness, but his recovery was slow and painful, and he was not completely well until the end of March.[86] As soon as he was able to travel, he returned to Albemarle. During his illness, he had decided not to run for reelection, and Jefferson called on Wilson Cary Nicholas to stand for the district in the coming congressional campaign.[87]

Thus ended Thomas Mann Randolph's active participation in national politics. His congressional record, as even his friends admitted, was not a particularly distinguished one. Except for his stands on the Yazoo compromise and on the Broom resolution, he

81 Jefferson to T. M. Randolph, Jr., February 18, 1807, in Jefferson Papers, Library of Congress; Jefferson to Randolph, Jr., February 19, 1807, in Edgehill-Randolph Papers.

82 Plumer, *Memorandum*, 622.

83 Mayo, *Henry Clay*, 291; see also Plumer, *Memorandum*, 608.

84 Plumer, *Memorandum*, 622–23, 642.

85 *Ibid.*, 642; Jefferson to T. M. Randolph, Jr., February 28, 1807, in Jefferson Papers, Library of Congress.

86 Jefferson to John Wayles Eppes, March 21, 1807, in Jefferson Papers, Alderman Library, University of Virginia.

87 Jefferson to W. C. Nicholas, February 28, 1807, in Jefferson Papers, Library of Congress.

had voted with the administration on every major issue. He had made only one real speech, he had not served on any of the more important committees, and he made little noticeable effort to influence other congressmen. He may have felt self-conscious about his close relationship to the President, but a similar bond did not hinder John Eppes from playing an active and vigorous role in the national legislature.[88] Although Tom's "zeal, intellect, and information," were recognized, some of his colleagues felt that he had been "as little useful as any member on the floor of Congress." [89] He had begun his congressional career conscious of the narrow margin of his election and fearful that he was "wanting the qualities necessary for passing through with honour." He had succeeded in "passing through," but he had done so without distinction.

88 "John Wayles Eppes," *Dictionary of American Biography*, VI, 170–71; James H. Bailey, "John Wayles Eppes, Planter and Politician" (M.A. thesis, University of Virginia, 1942), 25–65.

89 Isaac Coles to Joseph C. Cabell, December 23, 1809, in Cabell Papers, Alderman Library, University of Virginia.

CHAPTER VI

"A Practical Farmer of Industry & Reflexion"

ONCE TOM had recuperated from the illness which had led to his retirement from politics, he returned to the routine of plantation life. The President came to Monticello that August for his vacation, and the Randolphs, as was their custom, came from Edgehill to be with him. It was very much like other summers in Albemarle. Guests were likely to be left to their own devices during the day, for after breakfast "the president retired to his books, his daughter to give lessons to her children, her husband to his farms." [1] Not until evening did the busy members of the household emerge from their respective retreats, and then Jefferson, with spirited assistance from Martha, dominated the conversation. Randolph, at least when visitors were present, held himself aloof from the prolonged after-dinner discussions at Monticello.

This reticence reflected in part the ex-congressman's preoccupation with his own affairs and responsibilities, but his withdrawal in the summer of 1807 may have been inspired by another cause. One visitor to Monticello that season was Augustus John Foster, secretary of the British legation in Washington, and Tom was then in no mood to be cordial to any representative of George III. He had been stirred to anger by the encounter of June 22 between H.M.S. *Leopard* and the U.S.S. *Chesapeake*. The British warship, cruising off the Virginia capes in search of naval deserters, had fired on the American vessel, forced her to submit to a search, and carried off

1 Foster, *Jeffersonian America*, 147. See also Smith, *First Forty Years*, for an account of a visit to Monticello in the summer of 1809, when a similar pattern was observed.

four seamen. The incident had aroused indignation in calmer men than Randolph, and on July 6 a group of excited citizens held a meeting in Charlottesville to condemn the action and call for reprisals. Randolph was present at this gathering, at which an address to the President was prepared and a committee of correspondence was selected.[2]

He was eager to play an even more active role, and on July 12 he appealed to Governor William H. Cabell for authority to raise a company of riflemen in Albemarle and march them to Hampton Roads, where the *Leopard* still lingered. "In that kind of warfare with which we are threatened," he wrote, "light corps armed with rifles must be the most efficient troops." They could be used, he explained, "to repel descents made by light parties with marauding views" and might also "prove in an extraordinary degree effective as marines on board of gun boats or other vessels of war which it may be necessary to employ to drive the enemy from our waters." Confident that he possessed "some considerable portion of the esteem of the old and the confidence of the young men" in his neighborhood, he believed that he would have no difficulty in enlisting "one hundred chosen young men" who could be used as amphibious snipers, and he hoped only that his command of a contingent of infantry would "not be incompatible" with his "present post in the Cavalry of our state." [3] His patriotic offer was not accepted—Governor Cabell pointed out that a colonel of cavalry could not hold the rank "of Capt. of a Rifle company." [4]

Meanwhile, the administration was attempting to bring England to terms by means of an embargo on American shipping, and that fall President Jefferson called on his son-in-law to explain the purposes of this instrument of economic warfare to the people of Albemarle. "I must not be quoted," he wrote Randolph; "You will be free however to mention that these are your own opinions." [5] The believer in direct action probably did not make a very convincing case for the embargo, but his loyalty to his father-in-law must have impelled him to try. The measure, which deprived

2 Richmond *Enquirer*, July 17, 1807.

3 T. M. Randolph, Jr., to William H. Cabell, July 12, 1807, in Executive Papers, Archives Division, Virginia State Library.

4 William H. Cabell to Randolph, Jr., July 13, 1807, in Executive Letter Book, 1807–1808, Archives Division, Virginia State Library.

5 Jefferson to T. M. Randolph, Jr., October 26, 1807, in Jefferson Papers, Library of Congress.

southern planters and farmers of foreign outlets for their surplus produce, surely threatened Thomas' own hopes for financial recovery, a possibility he may not have been aware of at the time. By the following winter, however, the significance of the embargo was brought home to him. With all sources of imported cloth shut off, the production of homespun became necessary. Martha herself made nearly 160 yards of the stuff in the first five months after the measure went into effect, and all of her children were clothed in it.[6]

In spite of his decision of 1807, Tom had not abandoned all political desire and ambition. Late in 1809 he learned that Wilson Cary Nicholas, who had succeeded to his seat two years before, had decided not to seek reelection. Thereupon, Tom announced his candidacy. His friends, remembering "the disgust which he had so lately felt for public life," were surprised that he should come forward again,[7] and few of them supported him with enthusiasm. His opponent was David Shepherd Garland, a lawyer of Amherst County who had already served a term in the Virginia senate.[8] Garland had entered the race, so he told his supporters, to show Randolph and Nicholas that they could not monopolize the district's seat in Congress,[9] and he set out to convince the voters that it was time to send an ordinary citizen to Washington.

Perhaps Tom underestimated his disadvantages; probably he did not recognize the feeling held by Isaac Coles and others that he was "not popular."[10] Nor, on the other hand, does he seem to have shared the belief of the class-conscious John Hartwell Cocke that it was "effrontery" for a man like Garland "to stand forward, when our national affairs never stood in greater need."[11] Tom did not, however, wage a vigorous or an effective campaign, and he was decisively defeated, carrying only Albemarle County while Garland won handily in Amherst.[12]

After this failure he relinquished further congressional ambitions, although he did not thereby abandon all political aspirations. Early

6 Anne Cary Randolph to Jefferson, March 18, 1808, in Edgehill–Randolph Papers.

7 Isaac Coles to Joseph C. Cabell, December 23, 1809, in Cabell Papers.

8 *Biographical Directory of the American Congress,* (Washington, 1961), 930.

9 John Hartwell Cocke to Joseph C. Cabell, December 26, 1809, in Cabell Papers.

10 Isaac Coles to Joseph C. Cabell, December 23, 1809, *ibid.*

11 John Hartwell Cocke to Joseph C. Cabell, December 26, 1809, *ibid.*

12 William H. Cabell to Joseph C. Cabell, January 2, 1810, *ibid.*

in 1810 he considered running for the Virginia senate, but when Joseph C. Cabell entered the race in March, he withdrew and threw his support to the latter.[13] Cabell was elected, and Randolph turned once more to face his personal problems.

With the birth on July 16, 1808, of Benjamin Franklin Randolph, Tom and Martha's children numbered eight.[14] The older children were growing up, and their needs were becoming more complex and expensive. Tom's debts were still a source of harassing anxiety, despite his manful efforts to rid himself of the burden. In such circumstances, he must have turned with real relief to the routines of cultivation on his various farms and to the experimentation with new techniques which, he hoped, might increase their productivity. It was in the years after he left Congress that he finally perfected his system of horizontal plowing and introduced it to his neighbors.

His efforts in this direction were undertaken to check a condition that had existed in Albemarle County even before he had settled there. The land had been butchered by inefficient methods of plowing which left many hillside fields gashed by furrows running with the slope. When widened by the pelting Piedmont rains, these had developed into ruinous gullies which operated on the red clay soil like "ulcers do on animals." As a result, "farm after farm" had been "worn out, washed and gullied so that scarce an acre could be found . . . fit for cultivation."[15] Such were the circumstances in which Tom adapted his system of horizontal plowing to the needs of his county and perfected a plow capable of making effective furrows in its thick red soil. He prided himself that it had taken "a practical farmer of industry & reflexion, occupying a gullied hill-country farm, and possessing some little geometrical knowledge," to put the system into practice. Far from claiming to be the discoverer of the method, he freely admitted that the idea had occurred previously to others.[16]

A form of contour plowing had been known to farmers of the

13 John Harris to Joseph C. Cabell, March 2, 1810, *ibid.;* William H. Cabell to Joseph C. Cabell, March 24, 1810, *ibid.*

14 *Thomas Jefferson's Prayer Book.*

15 [W. S. Morton], "On Horizontal Plowing," *The Farmer's Register,* II (February, 1835), 558–59; and [John H. Craven], "System of Farming," *ibid.*, I (August, 1833), 150. The authors of these and other unsigned articles in *The Farmer's Register* have been identified by Earl Gregg Swem, "An Analysis of Ruffin's Farmer's Register . . . ," Virginia State Library *Bulletin,* XI (1918), 41–144.

16 T. M. Randolph, Jr., to Joseph C. Cabell, July 20, 1820, in Randolph Papers, Duke University Library.

early Roman Empire, and at least two Latin authors had mentioned the procedure in their writings. Pliny the Younger, in his *Natural History,* had advised in A.D. 77 that hilly ground be "ploughed only across the slope of the hill . . . with the share pointing now up hill and now down." [17] His contemporary, Lucius Junius Moderatus Columella, recommended in *Res Rustica* ("On Agriculture") that furrows be "run obliquely." [18] Similar methods had been recommended by the eighteenth-century British agriculturist Jethro Tull, in his influential *Horse-Hoeing Husbandry.* " 'Tis a better method to plow the *Ridges* across the Hill, almost *Horizontally,*" wrote Tull, since "the more *Horizontal* they [the furrows] are, the Sooner the Rain will run off the lands." [19] As a student of both of the classics and of natural history, Tom was probably familiar with these works at the time he began his own experiments. The works by Pliny and Columella were in his own library, while Jefferson owned a copy of Tull's book.[20]

By the end of the eighteenth century, men were practicing horizontal plowing as well as advocating it, and observation, in addition to reading, may have stimulated the young Virginia planter. During his student days abroad he might well have seen the system in operation in the hills and fields around Edinburgh, for the "ignorant highlanders" had long been employing a crude but effective form of the practice.[21] Before the end of the eighteenth century a few Virginians were experimenting with the practice, and James Madison was using horizontal drainage ditches at his estate in hilly Orange County.[22] Other minds earlier had accepted the "suggestion of curvilinear furrows, as opposed to rectilinear ones," [23] but he first put the suggestion to use in Albemarle County and in the Piedmont region of Virginia generally.

17 Gaius Plinius Secundus, *Natural History,* tr. H. Rackham (Cambridge, 1938), 178. These and other agricultural works which may have inspired Randolph are cited in [Nathaniel Francis Cabell], "Inquiry into the Origin of Horizontal Plowing," *Farmer's Register,* II (1835), 667–69.

18 Lucius Junius Moderatus Columella, *On Agriculture,* tr. Harrison B. Ash (Cambridge, Mass., 1941), I, 35.

19 Jethro Tull, *The Horse-Hoeing Husbandry, Or An Essay on the Principles of Tilling and Vegetation . . .* (London, 1733), 118.

20 Inventory of Thomas Mann Randolph's Estate, July 29, 1828, in Albemarle County Will Book No. 11, pp. 346–49, Albemarle County Clerk's Office; E. Millicent Sowerby (comp.), *Catalogue of the Library of Thomas Jefferson* (Washington, D.C., 1952–59), entry no. 701.

21 John Taylor, *Arator* (Georgetown, D.C., 1814), 172.

22 Brant, *James Madison, Father of the Constitution,* 323.

23 T. M. Randolph, Jr., to Joseph C. Cabell, July 20, 1820, in Randolph Papers, Duke University Library.

His system in its perfected stage involved several separate operations. First, he had guide lines, each about thirty yards apart, run horizontally across the field to be plowed, using a 10-foot rafter level for this purpose. After the lines were marked off and plowed, the intermediate furrows were cut parallel to them.[24] Tom's operation, however, demanded a heavier and more manueverable plow than was available at that time in Virginia. It was also necessary to the success of his system that every furrow be thrown in the same direction—downhill. The British agricultural writer Francis Forbes had written in 1778 of a "turnwrist or turn-ridge plow," having a "swing-plough in the mould-boards" which would be both "double and moveable." [25] By the fall of 1808 Tom had conceived the idea, possibly inspired by Forbes, of shifting the share from right to left, whenever the direction of the plow was changed. Jefferson applauded this notion as "the simplest that ever occurred, & indeed a happy one" and encouraged his son-in-law to continue the experiment.[26] For greater efficiency, he devised a double share, the two parts of which were welded together at right angles. This device was fixed to the plow on a movable bar or pivot, the horizontal part of the share cutting soil, while the vertical part served as a moldboard. The relative position and function of the two pieces was changed at the end of every furrow, by using the pivot, the shift being accomplished with "a single motion of the hand." [27] Practice soon proved that this plow, when pulled by a 2-horse team, was highly efficient in breaking the red clay soil of Albemarle County and in making furrows as deep as ten inches.[28]

Although Jefferson encouraged his son-in-law's experiments and by 1807 was instructing his overseer at Monticello to "plow horizontally as Mr. Randolph does," [29] some of the neighbors ridiculed the "novel and difficult practice." [30] It took a heavy winter rainstorm

24 Jefferson to Tristram Dalton, May 2, 1817, in Paul L. Ford (ed.), *The Writings of Thomas Jefferson*, X, 79–80.

25 [N. F. Cabell], "Inquiry into the Origin of Horizontal Plowing," *Farmer's Register*, II, 667.

26 Jefferson to T. M. Randolph, Jr., October 11, 1808, in Jefferson Papers, Massachusetts Historical Society.

27 Jefferson to Tristram Dalton, May 2, 1817, in Paul L. Ford (ed.), *The Writings of Thomas Jefferson*, X, 79–80.

28 T. M. Randolph, Jr., to Joseph C. Cabell, July 20, 1820, in Randolph Papers, Duke University Library.

29 Jefferson to Edmund Bacon, May 31, 1807, in Franklin Papers, Yale University Library; photostat copies in Alderman Library, University of Virginia.

30 [J. H. Craven], "System of Farming," 150.

to dramatize the superiority of the Edgehill system. In February, 1810, three inches poured down on Albemarle in an hour, and "every hollow of every hill presented a torrent which swept everything before it." But, Tom's furrows "arrested the water at every step till it was absorbed, or at least deposited the soil it had taken up," and his farm was the only one which did not suffer. Many owners decided thereupon to adopt the same system on their own farms, but tenants, with "no interest in the preservation of the soil," remained indifferent and uninterested.[31]

As became a Virginia gentleman, Randolph did little to advertise his achievement, but Jefferson, whose interest in Albemarle's agriculture equalled his interest in Martha's husband, gave credit to his son-in-law at every opportunity.[32] John Taylor, the political theorist and practical planter of Caroline County, was another who recognized Randolph's achievement. In his *Arator*, first published in 1813, Taylor recommended the practice of horizontal plowing to his readers and reported that "a gentleman of Albemarle" had adapted it to the particular needs of that locality.[33] And in 1822 the Agricultural Society of Albemarle, which Tom had helped to organize five years before, presented him with a silver plate, thereby demonstrating its "just estimation of the important benefits which the agricultural interests of our County have derived from the introduction . . . of the system of Horizontal Ploughing." [34]

Yet, despite the support of Jefferson and the applause of other gentlemen farmers, Randolph's innovation was not widely adopted, even in his own region. Within seven years after his death in 1828, his methods of laying hilly fields in horizontal beds had been replaced by "less scientific and accurate," but also less laborious, systems. It was discovered that the horizontal system required more consistent, elaborate care than the average hillside farmer was able or willing to give, and experience also showed that improperly cut furrows, by

31 Jefferson to William A. Burwell, February 25, 1810, in Worthington C. Ford (ed.), *Thomas Jefferson Correspondence, Printed from the Originals in the Collections of William K. Bixby* (Boston, 1916), 194.

32 Jefferson to Burwell, February 25, 1810, *ibid.;* Jefferson to Richard Peters, March 6, 1816, in Philadelphia Society for Promoting Agriculture . . . , *Memoirs,* IV (1818), 16–17; Jefferson to Tristram Dalton, May 2, 1817, in Paul L. Ford (ed.), *The Writings of Thomas Jefferson,* X, 79–80.

33 Taylor, *Arator,* 172.

34 Rodney H. True (ed.), "Minute Book of the Agricultural Society of Albemarle," in American Historical Association, *Annual Report,* 1919 (Washington, 1920), 236–37.

allowing trapped water to accumulate until a major break developed, led to the formation of the very sort of destructive gully which the system was designed to control. Finally, the hillside plow itself proved to be too expensive and was easily put out of commission.[35]

Yet, while farmers did not adopt all the features of the system, neither did they return to the old indiscriminate methods, which had prevailed earlier. Although extensive adaptations and alterations in his ideas were made, the general idea of plowing according to the land's contour was retained. Whatever his failures in other endeavors, Thomas Mann Randolph deserved the gratitude of his neighbors for "the *introduction* and adaptation" of the horizontal system to the "peculiar circumstances" of the Virginia Piedmont.[36]

Because Tom's lands yielded his livelihood, he felt the need to give himself largely to their best development. This devotion undoubtedly led him to develop horizontal plowing, just as it had led him to experiment with crop rotation. As far as the actual processes of cultivation were concerned, he seems to have been a careful, conscientious, and technically successful farmer. Not trusting everything to his overseers, he spent the long days of the planting and harvesting seasons in the fields, supervising very major operation. For rest, he would withdraw to the shade of the nearest tree and spend an hour "with a favorite Greek or Latin author,"[37] and sometimes he would give himself a day's vacation, exploring a field of wild flowers, for he still retained his old interest in botany.[38] Occasionally he gave way to impulsive eccentricity, at the expense of agricultural efficiency. Once, it is told, he rode his high-withered horse Dromedary at full gallop across the harvest field at Edgehill, scattering the shocks to right and left, because the hands had not set them up to his liking. After that escapade, he calmly informed the overseer that "the old bull" had gotten into the field and upset the shocks.[39]

35 Edmund Ruffin, "A Glance at the Farming of Albemarle," *Farmer's Register*, II (September, 1834), 237.
36 [N. F. Cabell], "Inquiry into the Origin of Horizontal Plowing," *ibid.* (April, 1835), 667–69.
37 [Thomas Jefferson Randolph] to Henry S. Randall, ca. 1855, in Randall, *The Life of Thomas Jefferson*, III, 327–28 *n.*
38 T. M. Randolph, Jr., to Francis Walker Gilmer, August 24, 1818, in Gilmer Papers, Alderman Library, University of Virginia.
39 Hamilton W. Pierson (ed.), *Jefferson at Monticello* (New York, 1862), 93. This volume is devoted to the reminiscences of Jefferson's overseer Edmund Bacon recorded forty years after the occurrence of the events.

In spite of such diversions, he usually succeeded in growing rich harvests, and he accomplished this "without in any way abusing or harassing his slaves." [40] He was generally considered by his contemporaries as a kind, humane master, and like Jefferson and many other Virginians, Thomas was keenly aware of the evil effects which slavery visited upon master and man alike. "What a hideous monster, among the various phenomena of the social state, is our Southern system!," he burst out sometime in 1818. "The greatest dastard might possibly have the feelings, moral and physical, as well as the comforts, of many a brave man entirely in his power, and dependent upon his caprice." He himself sought to "always scrupulously distinguish, and exempt, manly and moral character, when it shows itself with any steadiness of ray in the sooty atmosphere of our slave discipline," preferring to punish the disobedient by confinement in the county-jail rather than by use of "the man-whip." [41] Some, among them his eldest son, thought him too lenient,[42] but he felt his policy justified by the fact that he had "not in thirty years lost one month's work altogether" by runaways.[43]

Despite his efficiency as a cultivator and his real talent as an agricultural innovator which combined to bring him bountiful harvests, Tom failed to earn enough from his farms to make them pay, or to support himself or his large family in comfort, for he often failed to get those harvests to market "until the golden moment of disposing of them was over." [44] Such procrastination had almost caused him to lose Varina in 1800, and, despite his resolutions to be more alert, he continued to be dilatory. This trait naturally handicapped his effort to pay off the mortgages on his Henrico

---

Because of Bacon's mild bias against Randolph, the lapse of time between the incidents narrated and his relating of them to Pierson, this volume should be used with care.

40 Randall, *The Life of Thomas Jefferson*, III, 328.

41 T. M. Randolph, Jr., to Nicholas P. Trist, November –, 1818, in James Parton, *The Live of Thomas Jefferson* (Boston and New York, 1874), 694–96.

42 Thomas Jefferson Randolph, *The Last Days of Thomas Jefferson* (Charlottesville, 1873). A broadside account written late in life by Randolph's son to refute some of Bacon's anecdotes, as re-told by Pierson. The only known copies of this work of family piety are in the broadside collections of the Bostonian Society and of the Alderman Library, University of Virginia.

43 T. M. Randolph, Jr., to Trist, November –, 1818, in Parton, *Thomas Jefferson*, 694–96.

44 Randall, *The Life of Thomas Jefferson*, III, 328 *n*.

County plantation and the various other charges against his father's estate, the most serious of which remained the debt held by William Lidderdale, executor of John Lidderdale. Despite his efforts to clear himself, the burdens were increasing. His brother William became bankrupt in 1807,[45] and Tom was forced to assume both shares of the Lidderdale debt.[46] Late that same year he was forced to borrow $5600 from James Monroe's son-in-law, George Hay, and had to give a deed of trust on Edgehill as security.[47]

In this situation he found it necessary early in 1809 to consider the sale of Varina. Although he prized his Tidewater property as "the most valuable spot for a farm in the state," he had decided to sacrifice it in order to relieve himself from "insufferable torment." [48] He could have sold some of the sixty slaves at Edgehill to pay his debts, but he refused to consider such a course. His Albemarle land would be "worth nothing," without slaves to work it, and he had "raised" many of the Negroes himself and knew "them all well." [49] Thus he concentrated on disposing of Varina, but, failing to find a purchaser, finally abandoned the effort to sell it.

Jefferson, ever helpful, offered to sell two of his own tracts in Albemarle in order to relieve his son-in-law's "more valuable property from calls." It was unimportant, the older man insisted, whether the proceeds went to pay Tom's debts or his own, for he considered their respective estates as "a common stock for our joint family." [50] Tom must have been encouraged by this new demonstration of Jefferson's confidence, but he did not take advantage of the offer. Indeed, the old statesman had given abundant evidence of his trust. In 1808 he had instructed Edmund Bacon, the new overseer at Monticello, to take Tom's advice on all matters relating to that

45 Martha Randolph to Jefferson, January 2, 1808, in Edgehill–Randolph Papers.

46 T. M. Randolph, Jr., to William Randolph, July 8, 1809, in Creed Taylor Papers.

47 T. M. Randolph, Jr., to George Hay,—1807, in Albemarle County Deed Book No. 25, p. 471.

48 T. M. Randolph, Jr., to Jefferson, January 6, 1809, in Edgehill–Randolph Papers.

49 Albemarle County, Land Tax Book, 1809, in Archives Division, Virginia State Library; T. M. Randolph, Jr., to Jefferson, January 6, 1809, in Edgehill–Randolph Papers.

50 Jefferson to Randolph, Jr., January 31, 1809, in A. A. Lipscomb and A. E. Bergh (eds.), *The Writings of Thomas Jefferson*, (Washington, 1903) XVIII, 262.

property,[51] and the next year he authorized his son-in-law to act for him in the sale of part of his Bedford County property, explicitly avowing his confidence in the latter's "good sense and information" and in "the integrity and honor of his character." [52] However, when Jefferson returned to private life in 1810 he again resumed control of his own properties in Albemarle.[53]

In the same year Tom sold the 1000-acre plantation in Bedford County which had been Martha's dowry. He had shown little interest in this property, and was willing to sell it to John Watson for ten dollars an acre in his continuing efforts to obtain funds.[54] Jefferson still retained possession of Poplar Forest, of which the dowry had been a part, and by 1809 had already begun construction there of the octagonal house which was to be his favorite retreat from the noise and bustle of Monticello. Although that remote house in the fastnesses of Bedford was visited often by Randolph's children in the company of their grandfather,[55] Tom does not seem to have joined these family pilgrimages, preferring his own retreat at North Milton on the Rivanna.[56]

His family was still increasing, Meriwether Lewis having been born early in 1810.[57] Like his older brothers Benjamin Franklin and James Madison, he was named for his grandfather's friends and associates. Indeed, of all the Randolphs' twelve children, only Anne Cary, their first-born, carried a name from the Tuckahoe side.

Randolph apparently displayed little interest in his children's development, and the older ones, particularly, turned to their

51 Jefferson to Edmund Bacon, June 7, 1808, in Pierson (ed.), *Jefferson at Monticello*, 65–67; also in Betts (ed.), *Thomas Jefferson's Garden Book*, 371.

52 Jefferson to T. M. Randolph, Jr., December 15, 1809, in Jefferson Papers, Massachusetts Historical Society; Jefferson to James Steptoe, December 15, 1809, in W. C. Ford (ed.), *Thomas Jefferson Correspondence*, 191.

53 Jefferson to Mrs. Elizabeth Trist, February 10, 1810, in Betts (ed.), *Thomas Jefferson's Garden Book*, 433.

54 T. M. Randolph, Jr. and Martha Randolph to John Watson,—1810, in Jefferson Papers, Alderman Library, University of Virginia.

55 Randall, *The Life of Thomas Jefferson*, III, 341–45.

56 The town of North Milton, the site of which was about a mile from Edgehill, was established on part of Randolph's land by act of the General Assembly, January 8, 1801. See Samuel Shepherd (ed.), *The Statutes at Large of Virginia . . .* (New Series, Richmond, 1835–36), II, 270–71. Despite the hopes of its founders, North Milton never progressed beyond the village phase and soon disappeared altogether. Randolph owned lots there, on one of which was a store and a warehouse.

57 *Thomas Jefferson's Prayer Book.*

grandfather for stimulation and companionship. Jefferson was glad to supply it, particularly in the case of his oldest grandson and namesake. He was anxious that the boy acquire a firm foundation in "particular branches of science," and thus, in 1807, wrote his friend Caspar Wistar, professor of anatomy in the University of Pennsylvania, asking the latter's help in placing the youth in a school in Philadelphia.[58]

It is not surprising, then, to know that the youth omitted his father from his "earthly trinity," which included his grandfather, his mother, and his wife; or that he looked back on his boyhood at "Edgehill" as a period of privation.[59]

Late in life Jefferson Randolph recalled that he had often walked barefooted in snow and ice to school, that he had been accustomed to sleep in a "closet" with only a blanket for his bed, and that he had been reared on the plainest food. But these reminiscences of his childhood were probably colored by the unhappy relationship that developed between him and his father.

Jeff's older sister Anne Cary was also close to her grandfather, their mutual interest in flowers forging a strong bond between them. It was she who had looked after the gardens at Monticello in Jefferson's absence and who reported to him on their progress.[60] By 1808, however, the seventeen-year-old girl found other interests, and in September of that year she married Charles Lewis Bankhead of King George County.[61] Increases in the family circle at Edgehill were beginning to be offset by departures from it.

Thomas himself had few intimate friends in Albemarle or elsewhere, but he developed a warm regard for Francis Walker Gilmer, the young son of Dr. George Gilmer of nearby Pen Park. Both of the Randolphs had had an "old friendship" with the father, and Thomas began to correspond with Francis in 1809, when the eighteen-year-old youth was attending school in Georgetown. The latter's description of a Potomac flood had revealed an interest in natural phenomena which strongly appealed to the older man, who

58 Jefferson to Caspar Wistar, June 27, 1807, in Betts (ed.), *Thomas Jefferson's Garden Book*, 349.

59 Thomas Jefferson Randolph, "Reminiscences."

60 Jefferson to Anne Cary Randolph, June 7, 1807, in Betts (ed.), *Thomas Jefferson's Garden Book*, 349; Anne Randolph to Jefferson, November 9, 1807, *ibid.*, 352; Anne Randolph to Jefferson, March 18, 1808, *ibid.*, 367.

61 Jefferson to Eppes, September 20, 1808, in Jefferson Papers, Alderman Library, University of Virginia.

replied in complimentary terms.[62] With this beginning, the cordial relationship between the middle-aged Randolph and the youthful Gilmer flowered and expanded. Francis was grateful because the older man encouraged his love of abstract study, while Randolph apparently sensed that the introspective youngster was a kindred spirit.[63]

Although farms, family cares, and financial worries were important concerns during the years after he left Congress, Thomas retained his interest in public affairs, particularly those concerning the worsening course of Anglo-American relations. The strains and demands of Britain's long war with France had made her government increasingly reckless in its demeanor towards the United States and increasingly overbearing in its attitude towards American rights. The continuance of impressment, the paper blockade of the Continent promulgated by the Orders in Council and enforced by the royal navy, the insolence of diplomats like "Copenhagen" Jackson, and the meddling with the Northwest Indians by redcoat officials in Canada, all combined to magnify the Colonel's violent dislike of British policy and to inflame his warlike feelings.

By the early months of 1812 men like Wilson Cary Nicholas were proposing war "in a triangle" against both England and France, but Randolph cried out in March to Francis Gilmer's brother, Peachy, against this "damnable heresy." England was America's "natural enemy," he declared, and was alone to blame; the French, in his eyes, were merely acting in self-defense when they seized American ships in Continental ports, for most of those craft were sailing "on English account." Indeed, he believed that were the United States to declare immediate war upon Great Britain, Napoleon would come in upon the American side.[64] These observations convinced Gilmer that Randolph, while "brave, generous, and romantic," indeed "an eccentric man of genius," was "wild, visionary, and a victim to the delusions of a vivid imagination."[65]

Then, on June 18, 1812, the War Hawks in Washington finally

62 T. M. Randolph, Jr., to Francis Walker Gilmer, January 12, 1809, in Gilmer Papers, *ibid.*

63 Richard Beale Davis, *Francis Walker Gilmer, Life and Learning in Jefferson's Virginia* (Richmond, 1931), 14, 31–32.

64 T. M. Randolph, Jr., to Peachy R. Gilmer, March 30, 1812, in Randolph–Gilmer Letters.

65 Notation by Peachy Gilmer on back of Randolph's letter to him of March 30, 1812, *ibid.*

secured a declaration of hostilities, and the Colonel's opportunity to prove his prowess came. France did not rally to the side of America, for Napoleon was too busy on the Russian border and in Spain to send any of his fleet across the Atlantic. Thus the nation was forced to fight her old enemy without foreign assistance. Those patriots, like Randolph, who had long and ardently desired war, were now called on to back up their bellicose words with deeds.

CHAPTER VII

"Military Fever"

LIEUTENANT COLONEL RANDOLPH spent the first year of the war at home, and the experience must have aggravated such an impatient warrior. The fighting was confined to the Canadian frontier and to the high seas, while the Chesapeake area remained unmolested by the enemy. The American forces in the north were suffering reverses and defeats from Detroit to Queenston Heights, but the officers and men of the Virginia militia remained on their farms and in their shops and offices.

There was, of course, enough to occupy Thomas at home. His farms at Edgehill and Varina continued to demand close supervision, and the merchant mill on the Rivanna which he had leased from Jefferson the year before required his attention.[1] Also, he became involved that fall in the nation's first wartime presidential election. Most Republicans supported the incumbent Madison for a second term, and Randolph was named as an elector for the party's ticket in Virginia.[2] The President's supporters had no great difficulty in carrying the Old Dominion over the opposition party, led by De Witt Clinton of New York, and Thomas and the other twenty-four Madison electors in the state were chosen that fall by a comfortable margin. However, when those electors met in Richmond on December 6 to register the will of the voters, Colonel Randolph was absent,[3] an indication that he had not taken his responsibilities too

1 Jefferson to Charles J. Bankhead, June 10, 1811, in Betts (ed.), *Thomas Jefferson's Garden Book*, 458–59.
2 Richmond *Enquirer*, September 29, 1812.
3 *Ibid.*, December 8, 1812.

seriously. William Armistead of Amherst was chosen in his stead.

His absence, however, did not prevent his being nominated and accepted for a commission in the United States Army the following year. In February William A. Burwell, formerly one of Jefferson's secretaries and now a Congressman from Franklin County in Virginia, suggested to Madison that Thomas Mann Randolph would make "a most zealous and valuable officer" and recommended him for the command of a regiment in the national army.[4] Madison was impressed by the colonel's reputation for "superiority in the talents and military acquirements so much needed in our army." And although he must have realized the difficulties Randolph's family would face during his absence, he told Jefferson that he "could do no less than give the public a chance of having the benefit" of those talents.[5]

On March 3, 1813, therefore, Lieutenant Colonel Randolph of the Virginia militia was commissioned as a colonel in the Army of the United States and was given command of the 20th Regiment of Infantry.[6] This unit, which was to be raised in Virginia and Maryland, had been activated on July 6 of the previous year, but it had not been brought up to its designated strength of 1,094 men.[7] Thomas almost immediately began a recruiting campaign and by the middle of April he and his subordinates had enlisted four hundred men.[8]

While awaiting his marching orders, he busied himself in the settling of his affairs and in the completion of a speculative enterprise. Earlier in the war he had bought up 23,300 bushels of wheat and had it ground into flour, holding it off the market until he could sell it for a large profit in the northern ports. An unusually cold winter was followed by heavy onslaughts by the Hessian fly during the spring of 1813, and those calamities, by causing a near failure of the wheat crop, had heightened prospects for profit.[9] Circumstances, however, upset his calculations, for that same spring

4 William A. Burwell to Madison, February 19, 1813, in Madison Papers, Library of Congress.

5 Madison to Jefferson, March 10, 1813, *ibid.*

6 *American State Papers, Military Affairs* (Washington, 1832), I, 405.

7 *Ibid.*, I, 424.

8 Isaac Coles to T. M. Randolph, Jr., April 14, 1813, in Jefferson Papers, Massachusetts Historical Society.

9 T. M. Randolph, Jr., to Harry Heth, June 3, 1813, in Heth Papers, Alderman Library, University of Virginia.

a British naval squadron blockaded the mouth of Chesapeake Bay and thereby cut off the sea routes to New England. There were no buyers in Virginia for the 2,650 barrels of flour and Tom could not, except by exorbitantly expensive overland transit, deliver them to the ports of the northeast.[10]

In this situation his zeal for a continuance of the war flagged, and he began even to hope for a cessation of hostilities, but was careful not to express that hope too openly, since there were many, he discovered, who were "displeased at the mention of peace." Yet he was no defeatist, and resolved to do his duty as long as the war lasted. He assured a friend he had no "hope or wish for military renown," but he was fearful that hostilities might end before he and his regiment were called to active duty. If he were denied the opportunity of taking part in at least one great battle, he "would be unhappy for life." [11] To one who believed that "lead and even steel [made] very proper ingredients in serious quarrels," the prospect that the war might be fought without his presence on at least one bloody field must have been highly disturbing.

The colonel's eagerness to take the field was tempered by the realization that he might not survive the combat he so ardently desired. In May he copied out a war song by Tyrtaeus, the ancient Spartan poet, and sent the transcript to his young friend Francis Walker Gilmer. The verses which he chose, and which he then or later translated into English, indicated that death in battle, far from being dreaded, might be preferable to less noble ends.

> Where stood the foremost rank, how fair they lie,
> The brave and good who for their country die.
> How wretched he who leaves his native fields
> To beg the bread a foreign harvest yields!
>
> The land and those we love let *us* defend,
> Regardless when this anxious life may end.
> Young men! in firm array prepare to fight;
> Unfelt be fear, disdained be shameful flight;
> Let mighty hearts beat high in bosoms strong;
> Think not of life while in the hostile throng.[12]

10 *Ibid.*

11 Randolph, Jr., to Heth, June 12, 1813, *ibid.*

12 T. M. Randolph, Jr., to Francis Walker Gilmer, May 4, 1813, in Gilmer Papers, Alderman Library, University of Virginia, contains the Greek text. Randolph's translation, provided by Nicholas P. Trist, appears in Parton, *Thomas Jefferson*, 679. For a modern version, see John Maxwell Edmonds (ed. and tr.), *Elegy and Iambus, being the Remains of all the Greek*

Perhaps the precarious state of his financial affairs, culminating in the failure of his flour project, had led him to see a soldier's death as the easiest and most honorable way out of his difficulties. Even were he to return safely, he expected to become a victim of chronic rheumatism, and he gave himself, at best, only fifteen years more of life.[13] With such prospects he found it not too hard to face the probability that he might not return. He made arrangements, contingent upon his death in action, for a public trial of his horizontal plow, although he had hitherto repeatedly avoided such a demonstration.[14]

While Thomas awaited his orders with impatience, his family expressed little enthusiasm about the prospect of his impending departure. His son Benjamin's health was precarious that spring, and his father-in-law, then in his seventy-first year, could not walk no farther than his garden and was, in general, "weakening very sensibly." In such circumstances it was not unnatural that Jefferson should view Randolph's attack of "military fever" with misgivings. "He will be a great loss to his family," declared the ex-President sadly but helplessly, "and no man in the world a greater one to his affairs." [15] Yet neither Jefferson nor Martha apparently made any strenuous attempt to dissuade Thomas from his patriotic duty.

Thus beset by so many anxieties, he could not have been a comfortable or relaxed member of the Monticello circle during the spring and summer. The tensions at work within him must have been aggravated by the news of the British assault that June on Craney Island, one of the key points in the defenses of Norfolk.[16] The attack was beaten off, but only the continuing hope that he would see action in Canada could have compensated Randolph for the fact that he had taken no part in the first—and last—hostile action on Virginia soil.

Finally, in early August Secretary of War John Armstrong ordered the colonel to assemble all members of his regiment and

---

Elegiac and Iambic Poets from Callinus to Crates . . . (London and New York, 1931), I, 69.

13 T. M. Randolph, Jr., to Heth, June 3, 1813, in Heth Papers.

14 T. M. Randolph, Jr., to Joseph C. Cabell, July 20, 1820, in Randolph Papers, Duke University Library.

15 Jefferson to Mrs. Elizabeth Trist, May 10, 1813, in Jefferson Papers, Missouri Historical Society, St. Louis; text in Missouri Historical Society, III (April–June, 1936), 120.

Glimpses of the Past, "Correspondence of Thomas Jefferson, 1788–1826,"

16 Adams, *History of the United States*, VII, 271–77.

march to Sackett's Harbor on Lake Ontario, where they were to join General James Wilkinson's army for an attack down the St. Lawrence on Montreal.[17] Thomas immediately instructed his second in command, Lieutenant Colonel David Campbell of Washington County, to expedite preparations for the march north.[18] In spite of the colonel's zeal and energy, recruiting proceeded slowly.

In Annapolis the company which had been raised there was reduced by illness and desertion to seventy-five men, and a third of these were sickly. Nonetheless, Randolph ordered them north towards Lake Ontario. A company of volunteers at Richmond were sent to York, Pennsylvania, while Captain Richard Pollard's company was instructed to march to Upper Marlboro in Maryland; recruits enrolled in eastern Virginia were sent to the general rendezvous at Fredericksburg, there to await their commander's orders. While Colonel Randolph gathered his scattered columns east of the mountains, David Campbell was enlisting men west of the Blue Ridge. It was the commander's plan to have all of these detachments unite eventually at Harrisburg, Pennsylvania, from which point they were to move north into western New York and then to Sackett's Harbor.[19]

Pausing briefly in Albemarle late in August, Tom paused in his task of seeking recruits and collecting deserters to confer with Jefferson. He informed his father-in-law that he intended to abandon his lease of the latter's mill, and he may have discussed the matter of choosing a "principal assessor" for the county, a matter on which Jefferson had also consulted other neighbors.[20]

Hurrying north at last with all the troops he had been able to gather and collecting others along the way, he reached Carlisle, Pennsylvania, on September 12 with less than six hundred men, barely half of the authorized strength of his regiment.[21] From there

17 John Armstrong to T. M. Randolph, Jr., August 11, 1813, in Jefferson Papers, Massachusetts Historical Society.

18 T. M. Randolph, Jr., to David Campbell, August 14, 1813, in David Campbell Papers.

19 Randolph, Jr. to Campbell, August 20, 1813, *ibid.*

20 Jefferson to Yewen Garden, August 20, 1813, in Jefferson Papers, Massachusetts Historical Society, mentions the mill lease matter; Jefferson to Madison, August 23, 1813, in Madison Papers, Library of Congress, refers to the choice of an assessor.

21 Randolph's arrival at Carlisle and the strength of his regiment was reported by him to General James Wilkinson on September 12. This report is referred to in Wilkinson to T. M. Randolph, Jr., October 1, 1813, in Jefferson Papers, Massachusetts Historical Society.

the group resumed the march north. During the long and somewhat leisurely hike through Pennsylvania and western New York the colonel shared the privations of his men, sleeping on the ground with only a blanket and eating the common fare of a private. He made most of the march on foot, often letting some sick soldier ride his horse.[22] He probably paid conscientious heed to the appeals of anxious parents who asked him to look after their sons, particularly when those requests expressed confidence in his "benevolent temper." [23] When he discovered that a former employee at his mill was a private in Captain Peyton's company, the colonel made him his "bowman," or personal orderly, but when the miller took to drink, there was no compunction shown in returning him to the ranks.[24] By the time that the 20th Regiment reached the shores of Lake Ontario, nearly seven weeks after leaving Carlisle, the men undoubtedly knew something of the quality of their commander.

Randolph found that the main army had left Sackett's Harbor and was already encamped on Grenadier Island, near the entrance to the St. Lawrence. He received orders to hasten to the new rendezvous where, according to the optimistic Wilkinson, "scenes of the highest national import, of splendour, and . . . of glory" awaited him and his men.[25] But there were more delays before the march-weary men of the 20th were able to reach the army's base. The weather was "so boisterous," that Captain Isaac Chauncey, commanding the American squadron on the lake, was unwilling to risk his tiny transports on Lake Ontario's stormy surface until the tempests abated.[26] So it was not until the morning of November 3 that the colonel's command debarked on Grenadier Island. He reported with only 230 men, less than a quarter of his designated strength and less than half the number which had left Carlisle.[27]

It was not likely that he felt particularly honored by the prospect of serving under such a commander as Wilkinson. For this was the

22 T. J. Randolph, *The Last Days of Thomas Jefferson.*

23 George Evans to T. M. Randolph, Jr., September 22, 1813, in Jefferson Papers, Massachusetts Historical Society.

24 Virginia Jefferson Randolph to Nicholas P. Trist, March 21, 1824, in Trist Papers, Library of Congress.

25 James Wilkinson to T. M. Randolph, Jr., October 29, 1813, in Jefferson Papers, Massachusetts Historical Society.

26 Isaac Chauncey to T. M. Randolph, Jr., November 1, 1813, *ibid.*

27 James Wilkinson to John Armstrong, November 3, 1813, in James Wilkinson, *Memoirs of My Own Times* (Philadelphia, 1816), III, Appendix xxxviii.

same general whose chequered and often unsavory career had drawn on him the distrust of most of his brother officers and many of his civilian superiors. Congressman Randolph had been one of the general's severest critics, and early in 1807 he had privately argued that Wilkinson should be dismissed from the service because of his involvement with Aaron Burr.[28] When he had expressed those opinions, however, he had been a civilian; now, he was an officer subject to the orders of the pompous old intriguer. Furthermore he had reported for duty after long delay and with his command depleted well below the level of combat effectiveness. Former prejudices, therefore, must have been outweighed by a consciousness of present shortcomings. The course of wisdom for one in the colonel's position was to keep his mouth closed, to obey orders, and to make every effort to recoup his previous failure by distinguished service against the enemy.

At Grenadier Island, Tom must have seen that his prospects for achieving glory were far from encouraging. Despite Wilkinson's boasting to his subordinates, he was opposed to the campaign against Montreal and, in communications with his superiors, expressed his fears that the operation would fail.[29] Among his subordinates were able and experienced leaders like Brigadier General Jacob Brown and Colonel Winfield Scott, but there were also the aged and feeble Major General Morgan Lewis, and the Yankee adventurer and soldier of fortune Brigadier General John Parker Boyd, who, for all his experience as a commander of Sepoys in the wars in India, "never had the confidence of the army." [30] Furthermore, relations between Wilkinson and Major General Wade Hampton, with whom he was supposed to cooperate in the final assault on Montreal, were notoriously bad.[31] A large proportion of the seven thousand men under Wilkinson's command were "charged with deleterious matter, generated by poisonous provisions," and their commander himself was so gravely ill of dysentery, that he was, by his own admission, "incapable of the salutary exercise of military command." [32] Tom, inexperienced as he was in the ways of warriors, may not have

28 Plumer, *Memorandum*, 623, reports Randolph's remarks concerning Wilkinson on February 23, 1807.

29 Wilkinson, *Memoirs*, I, 587.

30 Adams, *History of the United States*, VII, 182–83.

31 *Ibid.*, VII, 188.

32 *Ibid.*, VII, 174–75; Wilkinson, *Memoirs*, III, Appendix vii; Wilkinson, *Memoirs*, I, 587.

understood all that he saw and heard during his first day in camp, or realized the disadvantages which the army faced.

After a false start on November 3, the expedition moved out two days later. Seven thousand men crowded into open barges on the shores of Grenadier Island and started down the wintry St. Lawrence toward Montreal.[33] Leading the way was the advance guard, which some were calling the "élite corps," commanded by Colonel Alexander Macomb and consisting of twelve hundred men. Randolph and the men of the 20th, travelling with the light artillery companies under Lieutenant Colonel Abraham Eustis, followed closely behind. Then came the four infantry brigades into which the rest of the army was formed, and finally the hospital, ordnance, and commissary barges.[34] Strung out along the river in this fashion, the flotilla was dangerously open to attack from the Canadian shore, along which the enemy had been hastily erecting fortifications; the elimination or neutralization of such obstructions was the responsibility of Macomb's advance guard. If a British blockhouse proved unduly obstinate, that responsibility might have to be shared by Randolph and his command, for their barges floated immediately behind those of the élite corps.

For the first two days the army moved downriver without opposition. On the morning of November 7, however, as the advance was nearing the "Long Sault," scouts reported that the British were concentrating at Fort Matilda, a log blockhouse near the entrance to that critical and narrow stretch of rapids, and were fortifying it with artillery. The ailing Wilkinson immediately sent an aide down the line of slow-moving boats with orders for Macomb to capture the fort. The commander of the advance then ordered Tom's men to join in the assault.

Macomb immediately pushed ahead downriver, but his boats moved sluggishly, and it was late in the afternoon when his troops reached Fort Matilda. In order to deploy his men properly the commander of the advance first landed them on the American side of the stream, almost directly opposite their objective. They were close enough to hear the Canadian militiamen and Indians across the

33 Wilkinson, *Memoirs,* III, 120; Adams, *History of the United States,* VII, 184.

34 *American State Papers, Military Affairs,* I, 477; Robert G. Hite, Asst. Adjt. Gen., to T. M. Randolph, Jr., November 6, 1813, in Jefferson Papers, Massachusetts Historical Society; Wilkinson's "flotilla plan," November –, 1813, *ibid.*

St. Lawrence "firing, whooping, and hallooing." The assault force was divided into two columns, with Colonel Winfield Scott in command on the right and Colonel Randolph assigned to lead the left wing. The rest of the corps was sent a short distance upstream to cut off the enemy's rear.[35]

It was dark before the Americans clambered into their barges again and began to cross the river. As they drew near the Canadian side, the enemy opened fire with rifles and muskets. Several shots struck the water near the boats, but Macomb's men went forward. Though delayed by eddies in the river, they landed without mishap, and the two columns marched against the fort. In the darkness, two American platoons fired on each other, but the commanders reasserted control before the confusion could spread.

Fort Matilda was lightly held, with only fifty or sixty militiamen in the garrison. As the attackers approached, the defenders fired five or six rounds apiece and then ran. The Americans immediately poured into the abandoned blockhouse, where they discovered that the reported cannon were not there. Then, under Macomb's orders, the victors set Fort Matilda afire.[36] The advance guard had carried out its first assignment, and the men of the 20th had borne their part of the assault without embarrassment to themselves or their commander. Colonel Randolph, his first combat experience behind him, was entitled to some fleeting moments of satisfaction as he watched the British blockhouse burning against the night sky.

The advance continued to move slowly down the river, while upstream the major action of the campaign was developing. A British force under Lieutenant Colonel J. W. Morrison had gathered along the Canadian shore, threatening the American rear, and Wilkinson sent his troops ashore to meet him. The badly led Americans, despite their numerical superiority, were beaten back at Chrystler's Farm and forced to withdraw to their boats. The next day Wilkinson and his army hastened downriver to rejoin the advance guard at the Sault, and there he subsequently announced his intention to abandon the campaign.[37]

35 Wilkinson to Alexander Macomb, November 7, 1813, in Wilkinson, *Memoirs,* II, 284; *American State Papers, Military Affairs,* I, 477; testimony of Macomb at Wilkinson's court martial, March 7, 1815, in Wilkinson, *Memoirs,* III, 168.

36 Testimony of Capt. Joseph Biddle, March 1, 1815, in Wilkinson, *Memoirs,* III, 303; Macomb's testimony, March 7, 1815, *ibid.,* III, 168.

37 Adams, *History of the United States,* VII, 187–89; Charles W. Elliott, *Winfield Scott, the Soldier and the Man* (New York, 1937), 130–31.

The colonel from Virginia must have felt considerable chagrin that he had missed the battle at Chrystler's Farm, and he undoubtedly experienced even greater disappointment when he learned that the army would go immediately into winter quarters. Even his promotion to the command of the élite corps, following Macomb's transfer to the 3rd Brigade of the army,[38] was not sufficient to reconcile him to inaction. He knew himself to be "naturally the most restless, unquiet, and impatient being in nature," and he found the thought of idleness unbearable. Already finding the continued absence from his family almost more than he could bear, it was natural that he should recall the unsettled state in which he had left his own affairs and that he should feel his time would be more profitably employed in Albemarle than in garrison duties on the St. Lawrence. Furthermore, his health was beginning to suffer from the wintry climate along the Canadian boundary. Duty remained "the first motive" with him, but he convinced himself that his obligations did not demand his presence once the campaign was over.[39]

Barely had his troops reached St. Regis on the New York side of the river and begun the construction of the log huts that were to house them during the northern winter, when Thomas applied to his commander for leave. Wilkinson granted the request, stipulating only that the colonel return in the spring and that he exert himself during his absence to fill up his regiment.[40] The general was not completely altruistic in making this gesture, for he was anxious to have Randolph, who had "been a Spectator of my conduct . . . in all the movements from Grenadier Island," give a favorable account to the Secretary of War.[41]

The homesick warrior therefore turned over his command to Lieutenant Colonel Campbell, gave a few parting instructions regarding the construction of quarters and the establishment of a sentry system, gravely reminded his successor of the importance of getting along with other officers, and departed for the south.[42] Passing through Malone and Albany, he reached New York City on

38 David Campbell, General Orders, November 15–16, 1813, in Jefferson Papers, Massachusetts Historical Society.

39 T. M. Randolph, Jr., to David Campbell, November 20, 1813, in David Campbell Papers; Joseph C. Cabell to John H. Cocke, December 15, 1813, in Cabell Papers, for Randolph's health.

40 James Wilkinson to T. M. Randolph, Jr., November 18, 1813, in Jefferson Papers, Massachusetts Historical Society.

41 James Wilkinson to John Armstrong, November 19, 1813 (copy), *ibid.*

42 T. M. Randolph, Jr., to David Campbell, November 20, 1813, in David Campbell Papers.

December 1, by which time Campbell was settling down to a winter of paperwork and courts-martial and the men of the 20th were making themselves as comfortable as they could in their log huts.[43]

Hurrying southward, the traveler reached Philadelphia, where he stayed long enough to be received into "the small circle of men of science" in that city. To some of these he may have been known for his development of the horizontal plow; to the rest, the name of Jefferson would have been sufficient introduction. Among those whom he encountered at this time was the Abbé José Francisco Corrêa da Serra, the learned Portuguese scholar then living in self-elected exile in the United States. Conversations revealed that the Abbé was deeply versed in history and political science, as well as in botany, the colonel's own favorite branch of learning. Furthermore, Corrêa knew Jefferson and had visited at Monticello the previous summer. Thus, mutual interests and associations drew together two men who were widely disparate in background and temperament, and the intellectual camaraderie that developed out of this meeting lasted as long as Corrêa was in the United States. At the time, however, the encounter meant little more to Randolph than a pleasant interval in his journey from one duty to another.[44]

He went on to Washington, arriving there by December 11, and learned that President Madison had appointed him federal collector of revenue for the congressional district which included Albemarle.[45] It was not, perhaps, the kind of post he would have requested for himself, but Martha had solicited it for him, and he had promised her the previous fall that he "would do anything rather than continue to live separate from her." Recalling his conjugal duties and taking into account his need for the annual salary of $4,000, he accepted, but without enthusiasm. "To assist in the conquest of Canada," he told the President, was still "a favorite object" with him, and he was loath to give up his opportunity of winning military distinction.[46]

Having thus committed himself, he resumed his homeward journey to be reunited with his family and friends. He was

43 Richmond *Enquirer*, December 7, 1813.

44 T. M. Randolph, Jr., to Francis Walker Gilmer, March 30, 1818, in Gilmer Papers, Alderman Library, University of Virginia.

45 Madison to T. M. Randolph, Jr., November 11, 1813, in Jefferson Papers, Massachusetts Historical Society.

46 T. M. Randolph, Jr., to Joseph C. Cabell, December 29, 1813, in Randolph Papers, Duke University Library; Randolph, Jr. to Madison, December 11, 1813, in Madison Papers, Library of Congress.

confronted with the usual quota of discouraging events—the mill was not flourishing, although it had been efficiently operated in his absence under the supervision of his oldest son Jefferson, and the harvest at Edgehill had fallen short of expectations.[47] Under the circumstances, the colonel may well have wondered why he had been so eager to leave the army. He told friends that he had determined to resign his commission because of the "unfitness of his constitution for the climate of Canada,"[48] but he had by no means abandoned his martial aspirations. So, when military opportunity beckoned again that December, he was more than willing to consider it.

This time it was the prospect of an important command in Virginia's own state forces which aroused his ambition. Brigadier General John Guerrant of the militia had just died, and the General Assembly was debating the choice of a successor to him. Late in December Thomas Mann Randolph was asked to become a candidate for the post. Supporting him within the legislature was Joseph Carrington Cabell, delegate from Nelson County, and backing him outside it was John Hartwell Cocke, the able young planter of Fluvanna who had already distinguished himself in the militia and who was also interested in the post. Both men were motivated as much by their fear that the Assembly might choose "some old woman" as by their conviction that the veteran of the St. Lawrence campaign deserved the assignment. Yet, Cabell recognized that the colonel's "late patriotic efforts" in Canada, as well as the rank he had already attained in the militia, were in his favor, and he began the maneuvers necessary to secure his election.[49]

Tom received the news of their efforts in a mood that was a mixture of interest and hesitation. His recent appointment as collector, he explained, would stand in his way of accepting the militia post: "The welfare of my family, indeed the preservation of what estate I enjoy, commands me to retain that place." Yet he was loath to reject the opportunity altogether, and a piece of military gossip then in circulation offered him a way out of his civilian commitment.

He had heard a report that Brigadier General Robert Barraud

47 Jefferson to T. M. Randolph, Jr., November 14, 1813, in Jefferson Papers, Massachusetts Historical Society.

48 Joseph C. Cabell to John H. Cocke, December 15, 1813, in Cabell Papers.

49 Flournoy (ed.), *Calendar of Virginia State Papers*, X, 295; Joseph C. Cabell to John H. Cocke, December 15, 1813 and Cocke to Cabell, December 15, 18, 28, 1813, in Cabell Papers.

Taylor, then commanding the defense of Norfolk, was also about to retire, and that Guerrant's successor would take over Taylor's duties. The prospect of replacing the hero of Craney Island was particularly appealing to the recent participant in the Battle of Fort Matilda, and he saw clearly that the Norfolk post would open a "field indeed worthy of ambition." Indeed, he declared that he was "impatient to risk honor, fortune, life, in such an undertaking as the defense of that place." Nor did he have any personal doubts as to his fitness for the assignment. The President and "many General Officers of the U.S. Army" would, he was sure, testify to his capability. His enthusiasm was tempered by a recollection of his responsibilities, and he left no doubt as to the conditions under which he would accept the brigadiership. "It is the command only I want. For nothing less could I give up my hopes of retrieving my affairs." [50]

By the time that he had made up his mind to allow his name to be used, it was too late. Cabell had waited two weeks for a reply, and on December 30 he abandoned the attempt to get him appointed and transferred his support to Cocke, who had been his first choice from the beginning. The latter was elected as Guerrant's successor on January 7, 1814, and Tom's name was not even submitted.[51]

The disappointed aspirant took his newest frustration in good face. He had realized from the start that his own financial predicament would have made his acceptance of a new military post a quixotic step, and the arrival on January 3 of a new daughter, christened Septimia,[52] had made his presence in Albemarle desirable for the immediate future. Accordingly he let it be known that he would "drop the subject" and turned to the problem of selling the large stock of flour which, because of the tightening blockade, still remained on his hands. A few weeks later, in his newly assumed role as federal collector of revenue, he was certifying that his father-in-law had paid the carriage tax, imposed by the federal government as a war revenue measure.[53]

Despite his earlier near-decision to resign his commission in the

50 T. M. Randolph, Jr., to Joseph C. Cabell, December 29, 1813, in Randolph Papers, Duke University Library.

51 Joseph C. Cabell to John H. Cocke, January 8, 1814, in Cabell Papers.

52 *Jefferson's Prayer Book.*

53 T. M. Randolph, Jr., to Joseph C. Cabell, January 8, 1814, in Randolph Papers, Duke University Library; Certificate, January 23, 1814, in Jefferson Papers, Massachusetts Historical Society.

national army, Tom had not done so, and he was still subject to recall to duty with the 20th. The prospect that his son-in-law might "try another campaign" in the spring was a source of anxiety to Jefferson, and friends felt that "one campaign was a great undertaking for a man with so large a family," [54] holding that the colonel had already done his duty. Nonetheless, Randolph did nothing until the middle of February when he received orders from Colonel John Walbach, Wilkinson's Adjutant General, to proceed to the regimental rendezvous at Leesburg, Virginia, and initiate recruiting for a new spring campaign.[55] Summons to such uncongenial duty led Tom, on February 23, to ask for a delay in departure until March, pleading duties "not of a private nature." [56]

He followed that with a request that he be allowed to "go on to the lines" instead, and he strongly intimated that he would rather resign his commission than become involved in recruitment procedures. This brought a swift and brusque retort from headquarters advising him that his "intimation" had been accepted as his resignation.[57] The 20th Regiment thus passed to the command of Lieutenant Colonel Gilbert Russell of Tennessee,[58] and Randolph's hopes of military renown in Canada came to an end.

Having thus written himself out of the 20th, Tom turned once more to the pursuits and problems of peace. Still striving to find a solution to his financial difficulties, he again considered the sale of Varina,[59] but he appears to have done no more than consider it. Instead, he gave a deed of trust on Edgehill (excepting a 250-acre tract he had already turned over to his oldest son) to a cousin, Thomas Eston Randolph, in order to secure needed cash.[60]

A more congenial subject which engaged his attention during the spring of 1814 was the attempt, fostered by his father-in-law, to establish an academy in Albemarle County. The trustees of this

54 Jefferson to Mrs. Elizabeth Trist, February 10, 1814, and Trist to Jefferson, March 5, 1814, in Jefferson Papers, Massachusetts Historical Society.

55 John Walbach to T. M. Randolph, Jr., February 10, 1814, *ibid.*

56 Randolph, Jr., to Walbach, February 23, 1814, *ibid.*

57 Walbach to Randolph, Jr., March 13, 1814, and note thereon by Randolph, *ibid.*

58 Francis B. Heitman (comp.), *Historical Register and Dictionary of the United States Army* . . . (Washington, 1903), I, 118, 853.

59 T. M. Randolph, Jr., to Harry Heth, April 17, 1814, in Heth Papers.

60 Deed, T. M. Randolph, Jr., to Thomas Eston Randolph, August 28, 1814, in Albemarle County Deed Book No. 25, p. 247, Albemarle County Clerk's Office.

embryo institution met on May 3, at which time Thomas Randolph, Thomas Jefferson, and Peter Carr were chosen to draft a petition to the General Assembly.[61] Long before the petition could be presented to the legislature, Randolph's stay at home was interrupted by a new threat of British invasion.

He had retained his commission as a lieutenant colonel in the Virginia militia even during the period of his service under Wilkinson, and he was still subject to a call to active duty with the state troops. Renewed enemy activity in the Chesapeake in the summer of 1814 led to such a summons. The principal British objective was the city of Washington, but Governor James Barbour and his military advisors, remembering 1781, feared that a blow might also be struck at Richmond. The militia was mustered to defend the state capital, and Lieutenant Colonel Randolph, this time wearing the uniform of the 2nd Regiment of Virginia Cavalry, returned to the wars.

Reporting for duty at Camp Fairfield outside of Richmond, he was again offered the opportunity to distinguish himself in the field. News had been received of the British attack on the national capital, of the flight of the American defenders, and of the burning of the city on August 24. To avoid a similar strike on the James, the Virginians decided to organize an élite corps and use it to guard the approaches to Richmond. Brigadier General John Cocke, who had been elected to the militia post which Tom had belatedly sought the previous winter, recommended his former opponent for the command of this mobile force, and he was appointed on September 1. A total of 629 men was drawn from other units and assigned to the corps, which was established as an independent command, reporting directly to Adjutant General Moses Green.[62]

The various components of this force were mustered at Camp Fairfield and on September 3 marched northward to the head of the York River, where they took up a defensive position at the ruins of Warrany Church near West Point. Their mission was to watch for hostile movements up the York, to resist any landing that the British

61 Albemarle Academy, Minutes, 1814, in University of Virginia, Board of Visitors, Minutes, 1816–1826 (bound ms. in Alderman Library, University of Virginia); Philip Alexander Bruce, *History of the University of Virginia* (New York, 1920–22), I, 115–31.

62 Peter Carr to T. M. Randolph, Jr., August 31, 1814, in Jefferson Papers, Massachusetts Historical Society; Claiborne Gooch, Asst. Adjt. Gen. Va., General Orders, September 1 and 2, 1814, in John H. Cocke Papers, Alderman Library, University of Virginia.

might attempt to the north of Richmond, and, if forced to withdraw, to fight a delaying action in the woods and swamps of New Kent County. On September 7, the corps arrived at its station around the abandoned church where they established a camp and sat down in "bush tents" to wait for the enemy.[63]

The command was a diversified one, but, in the words of one volunteer private soldier, it contained "the finest of the youth of Virginia." [64] Among the units attached to it were the organization later known as the Richmond Light Infantry Blues, commanded by Captain William Murphy; a rifle company from Chesterfield County; and a troop of cavalry led by Captain Samuel Carr of Albemarle. Supplementing these detachments was a company of flying artillery under the command of the literary lawyer William Wirt who, like the colonel, was an admirer of the Spartan poet Tyrtaeus. Thomas' principal subordinate was the gregarious Major David Watson of Louisa County, "a very genteel man" exuberantly addicted to snuff and Shakespeare. Not all of the gentlemen who served in the corps were officers. The colonel's eldest son Jefferson Randolph served as a private in the corps, as did his young friend Francis Walker Gilmer, then living in Richmond.[65] The veteran of Fort Matilda appears to have been particularly popular with these young gentlemen rankers, and at least one of them, William Fitzhugh Gordon, had refused a commission because he preferred "the situation of a private with Colonel Randolph." [66]

The commander of the élite corps, "with all his chivalry about him," prepared to beat off the anticipated British assault. The campsite was unhealthy, the weather was bad, provisions were few in the "poverty-stricken land," and there was little for the

63 William Fitzhugh Gordon to Mrs. Gordon, September [9], 1814, in Gordon, *William Fitzhugh Gordon*, 79; "Richmond Light Infantry Blues," *Tyler's Quarterly*, I (1919–20), 9–10; John S. Cutchins, *A Famous Command: The Richmond Light Infantry Blues* (Richmond, 1934), 20–21. For dates see Orderly Book of Capt. Benjamin Graves, July 2–December 7, 1814, manuscript in Virginia Historical Society, Richmond, Va.).

64 William Fitzhugh Gordon to Mrs. Gordon, September [9], 1814, in Gordon, *William Fitzhugh Gordon*, 79.

65 Claiborne Gooch, General Orders, September 1, 1814, in Cocke Papers; see Gordon to Mrs. Gordon, September [9], 1814, in Gordon, *William Fitzhugh Gordon*, 79, for comments on David Watson and Francis Walker Gilmer; Samuel Mordecai to Rachel Mordecai, September 11, 1814, *Virginia Magazine of History and Biography*, LIII (October, 1945), 285. For Wirt's opinion of Tyrtaeus, see William Wirt to Dabney Carr, Jr., August 23, 1813, in Wirt Papers, Archives Division, Virginia State Library.

66 William Fitzhugh Gordon to Mrs. Gordon, September [9] and 14, 1814, in Gordon, *William Fitzhugh Gordon*, 80.

men to do. To offset the effects of inactivity, training exercises were held twice a day for the first week, but these maneuvers soon began to wear out the horses. Enthusiasm remained high, however, as long as there was a chance that the enemy might try a landing, and morale was sustained both "by the occasion and by the devotion of every man . . . to our heroic commander." [67] There was an exhilarating flurry of martial excitement on September 13 when five strange sail were reported at the mouth of the York River, but the ships vanished up the bay and the mood quickly passed.[68] As September drew to a close, officers and men alike knew that the British had been repulsed in their attack on Baltimore and that the ships seen in Chesapeake Bay were no longer a grave danger.

Then the effects of monotony and sickness began to make themselves felt, and Tom once more discovered that there was more to warfare than combat. Many of the men were ill with fever, the result of drinking impure water, and their condition was made worse by living in their rude shelters during rainy weather. The rest were suffering from a lack of proper provisions, for when the corps first arrived at the encampment on the York, even potatoes were not to be had.[69] The inhabitants of the surrounding countryside were unwilling to provide any subsistence or equipment for their would-be defenders, and Randolph, armed with a military warrant, had to take supplies "by force after a painful search" and then had to pay for these articles at a price that was sometimes almost half again more than they were worth.[70] The farmers of New Kent and King William counties became more cooperative after the state succeeded in securing a loan of $150,000 from the Farmer's Bank of Virginia, and the supply situation had improved considerably by the last weeks of September.[71]

The belated increase in the flow of provisions did not offset the loss of enthusiasm that set in as soon as it was evident that there would be no British attack. The rank and file began to "murmur

67 Gordon to Mrs. Gordon, September [9] and 14, 1814, *ibid.*, 79, 81; William Wirt to Mrs. Wirt, September 9 and 12, 1814, in John P. Kennedy, *Memoirs of the Life of William Wirt* (Philadelphia, 1849), I, 377.

68 Wirt to Mrs. Wirt, September 13, 1814, in Kennedy, *Memoirs of William Wirt*, I, 377.

69 Wirt to Mrs. Wirt, September 9 and 12, 1814, *ibid.*, 377.

70 T. M. Randolph, Jr., to Jefferson, March 8, 1824, in Jefferson Papers, Library of Congress.

71 William Nekerves to James Barbour, September 8, 1814, in Flournoy (ed.), *Calendar of Virginia State Papers*, X, 386–87; William Wirt to Mrs. Wirt, September 26, 1814, in Kennedy, *Memoirs of William Wirt*, I, 378–79.

incessantly" and to grumble "about their wives,—their business, debts, sick children, &c, &c," and everyone wanted to go home. Intoxication, insubordination, and fights became frequent, and the officers were kept busy "listening to the everlasting and growing discontents of the men and trying their quarrels before courts-martial." [72] Officers of the corps were also being deluged with requests for furloughs, one member of Captain Graves's rifle company seeking leave "on account of his duties as sheriff." Some members of the command, disregarding the formalities, merely left camp and went home. Colonel Randolph proved to be an indulgent commander, bestowing furloughs with generosity and punishing deserters and other malefactors with mildness. Captain Wirt of the artillery protested that excessive leniency at the command level was encouraging the increasingly high rate of desertions, whereupon Randolph authorized his artilleryman to grant or refuse furloughs in his unit "at his own discretion." [73]

By the last week in September even the once enthusiastic gentleman rankers had become "tired of waiting for the British and gone home." Among those departing were Francis Gilmer and the colonel's own son, the conscientious Jeff Randolph. The commander himself remained, as did Captain Wirt and Major David Watson. The latter entertained his companions with lengthy quotations from Shakespeare and with spectacular demonstrations of his prowess as a snuff-taker, thrusting as much as two inches of the powder up "his bellows nostril," smiling all the while "at the luxury of the effort." For the delectation of the rank and file who were still present for duty, there was drilling and "firing national salutes for recent victories," but these pleasures did not end the grumbling, the quarrels, or the desertions. Many units were "unofficered," and sickness was so rampant in the ranks that Wirt became anxious about the health of the faithful few still on duty.[74]

But the ordeal of the élite corps was almost over, for it had become obvious that the danger of British invasion had passed and that the ailing troops were no longer needed on the York. The

72 Wirt to Mrs. Wirt, September 19 and 26, 1814, in Kennedy, *Memoirs of William Wirt*, 378–79.

73 Orderly Book of Capt. Benjamin Graves, in Virginia Historical Society; William Wirt to T. M. Randolph, Jr., September 19, 1814, in Jefferson Papers, Massachusetts Historical Society; Thomas Mann Randolph, General Orders, September 23, 1814, entered in the Graves Orderly Book under that date.

74 William Wirt to Mrs. Wirt, September 26 & 28, 1814, in Kennedy, *Memoirs of William Wirt*, I, 379–80.

detachment was ordered disbanded on September 30, tents and other equipment were turned back to the quartermasters, and the various components were assigned to other duties or discharged. The colonel had already made known his intention of "retiring from the service," but he departed for Albemarle with his superior's assurances that he would be recalled on the next approach of the enemy.[75] The occasion never arose, and Thomas Randolph, whose desire for martial glory had twice led him to seek service in the field, came to the end of his active military career.

That career had involved him in only one small skirmish, an encounter which proved little or nothing about his competence in combat. His effectiveness as a military man must be thus judged on the basis of his performance in other aspects of command, particularly in the routine fields of administration and discipline. While he did not deliberately shirk his duties as a military administrator, he did not take them seriously or consider them an important part of his responsibility as a commander. Nor did he have more than the most rudimentary notions of maintaining discipline.

He came nearer to possessing another quality of a good commander, for he was able to inspire the admiration and devotion of his men. Part of that devotion was no doubt inspired by his concern for their welfare and his willingness to share their privations, both of which qualities he had demonstrated on the march from Carlisle to Sackett's Harbor. Part of it was due to his ability to communicate, temporarily at least, his own martial spirit to his subordinates, as he had done at Warrany. However, part of it followed from his liberality with furloughs and his leniency with deserters. His failure as an administrator and as a disciplinarian diminished his effectiveness as a leader, even in a command whose members found him personally likeable and sympathetic.

In the years which followed he often looked back on his war experiences with mingled nostalgia and dissatisfaction. He continued to believe that he had "served with zeal and sought risks of all sorts," [76] but he must have realized, as he resumed the life of a farmer and a family man, that the risks had not materialized and that zeal alone had not been enough.

75 Orderly Book of Capt. Benjamin Graves, entry for October 1, 1814 in Virginia Historical Society; Claiborne Gooch, General Orders, September 30, 1814, in Cocke Papers, Alderman Library, University of Virginia.

76 T. M. Randolph, Jr., to Robert Brent, October 26, 1817, in Hench Collection.

CHAPTER VIII

"The Blunt School of Agriculture"

After the dissolution of the élite corps Thomas Mann Randolph returned to Albemarle County. He found everyone at Monticello and Edgehill in good health, but he also discovered that crops had been bad and learned from his father-in-law that taxes were "coming on . . . as an approaching wave in a storm." Jefferson, for his part, was sanguine about the future. The aging statesman did not doubt that he and his loved ones would "live as long, eat as much, and drink as much" as before and that "somehow or other these things find their way out as they came in." [1] There was little, however, to give the former soldier much hope that the particular wave rolling toward him would leave him afloat.

Many other Virginians faced the same storm wave in the years after 1814. Others struggled not only to pay their taxes but to discharge burdens of inherited debt. While not all planters were as unpunctual and careless in making their payments as Thomas often was, most of them were caught in the same hopeless spiral of mounting costs and falling prices.

Underlying their predicament was the continued decline of the Virginia tobacco economy, a decline which had its roots in the pre-Revolutionary past. The conditions under which colonial planters and British merchants had done business had produced a balance of payments in the former's disfavor, and independence had not

1 Jefferson to Mrs. Elizabeth Trist, December 26, 1814, in Randolph, *Domestic Life*, 360.

released Virginia planters from either their debts or the accrued interest on those debts. Furthermore, independence had ended the preferred position of Virginia tobacco in British markets.

Virginians of Randolph's day also suffered from the results of nearly two centuries of wasteful practices in cultivation. The soil in much of the Tidewater and the Piedmont had become exhausted by careless and improvident methods, with a consequent decline in agricultural productivity and in land values. The efforts of men like Randolph and Jefferson to adopt more scientific techniques were praiseworthy, as were their attempts to substitute grains and other crops for the Virginia weed, but relatively few of their neighbors followed their example.

The twenty-year-long European war which had just ended also contributed to the planters' difficulties. Not only had overseas markets been affected by the commercial restrictions imposed on neutral commerce by both sets of belligerents, but such American measures as the Embargo and the Non-Intercourse Act had served to keep American products from entering those markets. Then, with American entrance into the war in 1812, the British blockade had further denied Virginia wheat and tobacco access to the outside world.

This was the situation which faced Randolph on his return. From 1814 on, as the flood continued to rise, he was to be engaged in a struggle to surmount his enormous difficulties and to escape, if he could, complete financial inundation. Fortunately, he had lost none of his skill as a cultivator or his zeal for experiment. Jefferson continued to praise him as one of "our best farmers," to recommend his achievements as an agricultural innovator to others, and to adopt Randolph techniques himself.[2] The Randolph system of plowing, Jefferson reported enthusiastically in 1817, was "spreading rapidly" in Bedford, and he expressed his confidence that horizontal plowing would be "the salvation of that . . . part of the country," as it had been in Albemarle.[3]

Yet confidence in his son-in-law's capacities was not unlimited. In

2 Jefferson to Jean Baptiste Say, March 2, 1815, in Lipscomb and Bergh (eds.), *The Writings of Thomas Jefferson,* XIV, 260–63; also Jefferson to Tristram Dalton, May 2, 1817, in Paul L. Ford (ed.), *The Writings of Thomas Jefferson,* X, 79–80; Jefferson to Reuben Maury, February 21, 1819, in W. C. Ford (ed.), *Thomas Jefferson Correspondence,* 245.

3 Jefferson to George M. Jeffreys, March 3, 1817, in Betts (ed.), *Thomas Jefferson's Garden Book,* 567.

1815 Jefferson, then in his seventy-third year, realized that he was too feeble to continue personal supervision of his estates, and he turned, not to his son-in-law, but to his twenty-two-year-old grandson Thomas Jefferson Randolph.[4] That conscientious and devoted young man eagerly assumed the duties imposed upon him, partly because he had no immediate prospects of his own, and partly because he had a deep and genuine affection for his grandfather. Jefferson had seen to it that the youth had been educated at the University of Pennsylvania,[5] and had taken a much more paternal interest in him than his father had. Coupling ability with gratitude, Jeff Randolph quickly justified his senior's confidence. Within a year the patriarch was praising the "care and skill" of his youthful steward,[6] and by 1819 he was describing him as one of the "best farmers in the neighborhood." [7]

As the bonds between grandfather and grandson tightened, those between Jefferson and his son-in-law began to loosen. Perhaps the selection of Jefferson Randolph as farm manager at Monticello hurt Tom's pride. Perhaps he interpreted this family appointment as a reflection on his own abilities as a farmer, and he may have decided that his father-in-law was no longer well-disposed towards him.

Certainly, from 1815 on, Thomas Mann Randolph was forced to devote himself almost entirely to his desperate struggle against insolvency. He continued to feel that he could pay off most of his debts and lead "a more tranquil life," if he could only dispose of Varina, but he still could not find a purchaser.[8] By 1819 he was so wearied with his struggle to maintain his Henrico property that he was openly regretting that he had ever taken possession of it. The care of it, he confided to Francis Walker Gilmer, had ruined both his health and his fortune, and he recalled that Jefferson had advised against his acceptance of Varina in 1790. Indeed, he found a bitter satisfaction in blaming all his troubles on that fertile if unhealthy plantation.[9]

4 Jefferson to William P. Newby, June 21, 1815, *ibid.*, 546.

5 Jefferson to T. M. Randolph, Jr., November 22, 1808, in Lipscomb and Bergh (eds.), *The Writings of Thomas Jefferson*, XVIII, 522.

6 Jefferson to Eppes,—1816, in Randall, *The Life of Thomas Jefferson*, III, 433.

7 Jefferson to Reuben Maury, February 21, 1819, in W. C. Ford (ed.), *Thomas Jefferson Correspondence*, 245.

8 T. M. Randolph, Jr., to Harry Heth, September 17, 1815, in Heth Papers.

9 T. M. Randolph, Jr., to Francis Walker Gilmer, July 25, 1819, in Gilmer Papers, Alderman Library, University of Virginia.

Early in 1817 he was forced to borrow from the Richmond branch of the Bank of the United States, of which his friend Wilson Cary Nicholas was president.[10] His son Jefferson Randolph, and his neighbor Samuel Carr came forward as his securities, and he gave a deed of trust on Edgehill, the forty slaves there, and the twelve slaves at Varina, in order to provide a means of recompense if he defaulted.[11] This loan proved no more than a temporary solution, and Randolph had considerable difficulty in paying even the interest on it. In 1818, and again the following year, he had to sell a slave to Edmund Bacon, Jefferson's overseer at Monticello, to obtain ready cash.[12]

His constantly increasing family had always drawn heavily on his finances, and by 1818 there were five boys and six girls at Edgehill. His fifth son, born on March 10 and christened George Wythe Randolph after his maternal grandfather's law mentor, was the eleventh and last child,[13] but eleven must have been more than enough. By 1819 nine children were still living at Edgehill, and that small house probably seemed somewhat less than spacious when all of this brood were present. Randolph's situation was obvious to the older girls, and nineteen-year-old Ellen Wayles Randolph, visiting in Washington early in 1816, could barely enjoy her shopping tours for fear of distressing her "poor father" by her extravagances.[14]

Martha Randolph undertook most of the responsibility for rearing their children. Devoted and self-sacrificing, she maintained her calm and even-tempered disposition in the face of mounting difficulties.[15] Indeed it is not unlikely that her continued cheerfulness and her habit of humming and singing to herself as she went about her duties[16] were somewhat irritating to a man who was finding increasingly less reason to be cheerful about anything. Her greatest

10 T. M. Randolph, Jr., to W. C. Nicholas, April 13, 1817, in Wilson Cary Nicholas Papers, Alderman Library, University of Virginia. The amount of the loan was not specified.

11 Albemarle County Deed Book No. 21, p. 506.

12 Pierson, *Jefferson at Monticello*, 96–98, cites notes of Randolph to Bacon, October 9, 1818, and May 9, 1819, relating to these loans.

13 *Jefferson's Prayer Book*.

14 Ellen Wayles Randolph to Martha Randolph, January 3, 1816, in Jefferson–Coolidge Collection, Alderman Library, University of Virginia.

15 Pierson, *Jefferson at Monticello*, 86; Rayford H. Logan (ed.), *Memoirs of a Monticello Slave, as Dictated to Charles Campbell in the 1840's* (Charlottesville, 1951), 28.

16 Pierson, *Jefferson at Monticello*, 86.

happiness, she wrote in 1819, was that of her family's reflected.[17] Tom never deliberately sought to shirk any of his paternal obligations, but his lack of interest forced her to take a part in her children's affairs that should have been played by their father.

Persons outside of the family circle seem to have sensed her position. For example, in 1818 young Nicholas Trist, member of a family with whom Jefferson had long been intimate, fell in love with the colonel's seventeen-year-old daughter, Virginia, and approached the girl's mother, rather than her father, for permission to court her.[18] Randolph made no objection to the match, nor did he show any resentment that he had not been the first one to be consulted. Indeed, he had already become quite friendly with his prospective son-in-law, a cadet at the military academy at West Point, and wrote long letters to him on military affairs, slavery, and other subjects.[19]

Jefferson reveled in the role that propinquity as well as necessity, had imposed on him, and did much during these years for the well-being of his grandchildren. He genuinely enjoyed the company of his daughter's children, and had them brought singly and in groups to Monticello for long visits. There he took them for short walks around the grounds and gardens, which he often turned into miniature botanical field trips, participated in their games, made the little girls presents of clothes, books, trinkets, and other articles which their father was often unable to provide, and, in characteristic fashion, advised them on their reading.[20] Having already sent his eldest grandson to study at the University of Pennsylvania, the grandfather began to concern himself about the schooling of the younger boys. As James Madison and Benjamin Franklin Randolph reached their teens, Jefferson persuaded their father to let him assume responsibility for their further training.[21]

17 Martha Randolph to Virginia Randolph, April 23, 1819, in Trist Papers, University of North Carolina Library.

18 Nicholas P. Trist to Martha Randolph, September 10, 1818, *ibid.;* Martha Randolph to Trist, September 20, 1818, *ibid.;* Trist to Martha Randolph, September 9, 1821, *ibid.*

19 T. M. Randolph, Jr., to Nicholas P. Trist, November –, 1818, in Parton, *Life of Thomas Jefferson,* 694–96; Randolph, Jr. to Trist, August 15, 1819, Trist Papers, Library of Congress; Randolph, Jr. to Trist, June 5, 1820, Trist Papers, University of North Carolina Library; Randolph, Jr. to Trist, May 6, 1821, Trist Papers, University of North Carolina Library.

20 Randolph, *Domestic Life,* 340–48.

21 Jefferson to T. M. Randolph, Jr., October 8, 1820, in Jefferson Papers, Massachusetts Historical Society.

These children fondly reciprocated their grandfather's affection and devotion, and most of them obviously felt far closer to him than they did to their preoccupied and taciturn sire, for he apparently did little to win the love of his offspring. Since he was a sensitive man, he must have realized that he did not stand first in his children's affections, and that realization, coupled with the knowledge that he could not provide for them, must have added to his unhappiness. Also, his father-in-law's increasing dependence on Thomas Jefferson Randolph helped deepen his sense of alienation. While the colonel may not have felt any active resentment, he was no longer entirely comfortable in Jefferson's company. Sometime in 1815 he thought he began to detect a certain coolness in the old statesman's manner toward him,[22] and he had spent increasingly more of his time away from Monticello.

The unhappy situation of his daughter Anne Cary also contributed to his anguish in the years following the war. Her husband Charles L. Bankhead had fallen so deeply into debt by the spring of 1815 that he was faced with the loss of his farm. In April he and Anne Cary gave a deed of trust on Carlton, together with the slaves and other property there, naming Thomas Mann Randolph, Reuben Lindsay of Albemarle County, and John Bankhead of King George as trustees. Jefferson thereupon made over one of his tracts in Albemarle to his granddaughter and appointed Randolph, Lindsay, and Bankhead to administer this property for Anne, her husband, and their children.[23]

Perhaps under the strain of insolvency, Charles Bankhead had taken to drink, and by the fall of 1815 he had become an incorrigible and sometimes violent alcoholic. On one occasion Bankhead beat his wife in Martha's presence and then "ordered her out of the room, forbidding her to enter it again." Such abuses were for a while "very much unknown" to Tom, for Martha tried to conceal them from him. Instead, she "communicated such of them as happened under

22 Randolph, Jr., to Jefferson, July 8, 1825, in Edgehill-Randolph Papers. See also "Reminiscences of Ellen Coolidge," in Lipscomb and Bergh (eds.), *Writings of Thomas Jefferson,* XV, iii.

23 Deed of Trust, Charles L. Bankhead and Anne Cary Bankhead to Thomas Mann Randolph, Jr., etc., April 1, 1815, and Indenture, Thomas Jefferson to Anne Cary Bankhead, John Bankhead, Thomas Mann Randolph, and Reuben Lindsay, April 1, 1815, in Carlton Papers, Alderman Library, University of Virginia.

her eyes" only to Jefferson. He, in turn, informed the offender's father, Dr. John Bankhead, hoping that the latter would be able to restrain Charles.[24] The situation did not improve, however, and, despite family efforts at concealment, Tom eventually became aware of it.

A crisis was precipitated early in February, 1819, when Thomas Jefferson Randolph encountered the drunkard in the streets of Charlottesville. Young Randolph was apparently responsible for "commencing hostilities," and a heated quarrel developed. Bankhead attacked his brother-in-law with "a knife as long as a dirk" and stabbed him several times before bystanders stopped the fight. Randolph's wounds were not dangerous, but he was weakened by the loss of blood, and his grandfather was "dreadfully agitated" about his condition.[25]

Anne's father, who had been in Richmond, arrived on the scene on February 8. Everyone expected that he would "play the devil" with Bankhead, but he surprised them by behaving "quite cooly and dispassionately." [26] He did not take the matter lightly, however, and quickly took charge of farming operations at Carlton, ordered the overseer to disregard Bankhead's instructions, and made it clear that his son-in-law was "to have nothing to do with the plantation." [27] Charles, who had discreetly removed himself to his father's house in King George County, announced plans to move with his family to Kentucky. Randolph learned of the plan and announced that he "would oppose it strenuously," since "he could not suffer his daughter to go into a distant country with such a scoundrel." He warned that he would prosecute his son-in-law if he tried to leave the state, and there, for a while, the matter rested.[28]

But Tom Randolph was not one to conceal his resentment long. About this time he re-read the Book of Proverbs and copied out

24 Jefferson to Dr. John Bankhead, October 28, 1815, in Edgehill–Randolph Papers.

25 Hetty Carr to Dabney S. Carr, February 5 and 9, 1819, in Carr–Cary Papers; Mrs. Elizabeth Trist to Nicholas P. Trist, March 9, 1819, in Trist Papers, Library of Congress. See also Joseph Vance, "Knives, Whips, and Randolphs on the Court House Lawn," Albemarle County Historical Society, *Papers*, 1955–56, pp. 28–35.

26 Hore B. Trist to Nicholas P. Trist, March 22, 1819, in Trist Papers, Library of Congress.

27 Mrs. Elizabeth Trist to Nicholas P. Trist, March 9, 1819, *ibid.*

28 Hore B. Trist to Nicholas P. Trist, March 22, 1819, *ibid.*

from it the verse: "He that is slow to wrath is of great understanding, but he that is hasty of spirit exalteth folly." [29] He unfortunately found himself unable to follow this excellent maxim for long, and when he encountered Bankhead one day at Monticello, the latter's insolence provoked a collision. Charles, drunker than usual, had been refused brandy by Burwell, Jefferson's butler, and the slave had withdrawn just before Colonel Randolph entered the room. Hearing but not seeing Randolph, Bankhead took his father-in-law for Burwell and began cursing violently. Tom, who may have been somewhat intoxicated himself, let wrath have its way with him and charged his abuser.

In the resulting scuffle Tom, so overseer Bacon recalled many years later, struck at Bankhead with a poker, peeling the skin from his forehead and face and leaving him bleeding and almost insensible. Jeff Randolph, whose version was also prepared long after the event, insisted that the whole affair had been nothing more than "a row between two drunken men, in which neither skin was broken nor blood drawn." [30] Jefferson persuaded the combatants to go through the motions of a reconciliation, but there is no evidence that Tom regretted his hastiness or that he relented in his feeling toward Bankhead. Certainly his display of temper did nothing to improve a situation which already was probably past solution.

Always temperamental and excitable, Tom became even more eccentric in these troubled years. He apparently was somewhat "intemperate" at this time and was under the influence of drink the day he thrashed his son-in-law. Never too attentive to his dress, he grew increasingly careless of his appearance until he looked more like a poor tenant farmer than a Randolph of Virginia, and his

29 Commonplace Book of T. M. Randolph, Jr. The citation is to *Proverbs* 14: 29.

30 Pierson, *Jefferson at Monticello*, 99–100, contains Edmund Bacon's version of the affair. T. J. Randolph's *Last Days of Thomas Jefferson*, is a somewhat less sensational account. Both of these accounts were written many years after the affair took place, Pierson's transcript of Bacon's reminiscences appearing in 1862 and Randolph's in 1873. The principal difference in these accounts lies in their varying estimates of the battle damage. Joseph Vance, in "Knives, Whips, and Randolphs," places this incident *before* the clash in Charlottesville. While Bacon and Jefferson do not date the scuffle at Monticello, my own reading of the record leaves me convinced that this exchange of blows followed, rather than preceded, the one at the courthouse. The absence of any mention of a previous encounter between Randolph and Bankhead in the correspondence dealing with the knifing affray seems conclusive, if indirect, evidence on this point.

natural brusqueness of manner became more pronounced. When his displeasure was aroused, he was apt to let temper have its way with him, and "stormed . . . in his big grum voice, in his roughest manner." His feelings, so he said, had been "trained in the blunt school of agriculture," and he cared little for "forms, used for mere respect." [31]

His mood became increasingly more irritable in the years after the war, and he was prone to imagine slights where none were intended. He still kept his enthusiasm for scientific and political subjects, however, and he particularly enjoyed discussing these matters with young men like Francis Walker Gilmer. His young friend once told him of a "rich field" of wild flowers near Manchester, and he spent a day there late in the summer of 1818. He identified two "beautiful orchidae," an areal urchin, and an arethusa "like a head of clover," and returned to his harvest duties convinced that the place was everything Gilmer had said it was.[32] Both men were also ardent admirers of the Abbé Corrêa, and Randolph never wearied in his praise of that "inexhaustible machine of useful knowledge." Since their first meeting in 1813, Tom had looked up to the learned Abbé, and he once declared to Gilmer that, were he "single and without children," he would gladly follow Corrêa "with scrip and staff" for the rest of his life.[33]

As he could not play the part of a disciple, he had to content himself with corresponding with the master, praising him to his fellow disciple, securing his election to membership in the Albemarle Agricultural Society, and seeing him whenever he could. The Abbé made several trips to Virginia during the years after the war, and Tom looked forward to his visits with the eagerness of a schoolboy. Corrêa also thought highly of him and respected the latter's knowledge of botany. Late in 1818 the Abbé planned a trip to the Dismal Swamp and, through Gilmer, he invited Colonel Randolph to accompany him, but the distraction of the Bankhead affair, delayed his accepting the invitation. Corrêa, not willing to do without "such an addition" to the party, urged Gilmer to "employ every means in your power to engage him" for the exploration of

31 Pierson, *Jefferson at Monticello*, 93–94; T. M. Randolph, Jr., to John C. Calhoun, February 28, 1820, in War Department, Record Group 83, National Archives, Washington.

32 T. M. Randolph, Jr., to Francis Walker Gilmer, August 24, 1818, in Gilmer Papers, Alderman Library, University of Virginia.

33 Randolph, Jr. to Gilmer, March 30, 1818, *ibid.*

"this *avant poste* of . . . southern vegetation." Francis' pleas were made in vain, and the Abbé finally visited the place on his own in the summer of 1820.[34]

Later that year he left the United States for Brazil. He was not able to take personal leave of Jefferson and his kin, and he asked Gilmer to convey his respects to "the family I am most attached to in all America." [35] Though Corrêa never returned to the United States, the colonel ever cherished his memory. His children long took pride that their father had been the "sought and cherished companion of the Abbé," for they felt that "to be the selected associate of such a man was in itself an evidence of much culture." [36]

Randolph was also on cordial, although not intimate, terms with several planters in his own section of Virginia. While he did not have the same community of intellectual interest with them that he had enjoyed with Gilmer and Corrêa, he did share their desire to promote the prosperity and welfare of the Piedmont. There was, said Jefferson in 1815, "not a better country society in the United States" than the group of "plain, honest, and rational neighbors" living in Albemarle.[37] His son-in-law would have extended this description to include the whole Piedmont, an area which he considered the "best tempered, most famed region of our extensive country." [38]

Common concern for the agricultural condition of this section led in 1817 to the foundation of an organization "to promote the interests of Agriculture and Domestic Economy in general." On May 5 the first meeting of the Agricultural Society of Albemarle was held in Charlottesville, and Tom Randolph was one of the thirty gentlemen-farmers present. Most of the members were residents of Albemarle, but the counties of Fluvanna, Louisa, Nelson, and Orange were also represented, and the organization from the beginning had more of a regional character than its name implied.[39] Thomas Jefferson and Jefferson Randolph were in attendance, and so were Joseph Carrington Cabell of Nelson and John Hartwell

34 Corrêa to Gilmer, December 28, 1818, March 11, 1819, and August 31, 1820, *ibid.*

35 Corrêa to Gilmer, November 9, 1820, *ibid.*

36 Randolph, *Last Days of Thomas Jefferson.*

37 Jefferson to Jean Baptiste Say, March 2, 1815, in Lipscomb and Bergh (eds.), *Writings of Thomas Jefferson*, XIV, 260–63.

38 T. M. Randolph, Jr., to Francis Walker Gilmer, April 10, 1818, in Gilmer Papers, Alderman Library, University of Virginia.

39 True (ed.), "Minute Book of the Agricultural Society of Albemarle," 263.

Cocke of Fluvanna. At a subsequent meeting that autumn the venerable James Madison, then living in retirement at Montpelier in Orange County, was elected president of the society, and Thomas Randolph and Cocke were chosen first and second vice-presidents, respectively. Randolph, together with Cabell, Cocke, James Barbour of Orange, and David Watson of Louisa, was also named to the plans committee.[40]

From the beginning Thomas took an active and interested part in the work of the organization. Madison, as president, was not expected to be anything more than "an Honorary Head," and the two vice-presidents were responsible for shaping the policy and directing the activities of the society.[41] As chairman of the plans committee, Randolph helped to set the tone for the future development of the whole group. Similar organizations, he reported on November 4, 1817, had failed because of "the indefinite nature of the duties devolving upon the members." To remedy this he recommended that every affiliate report "on his own practices in Agriculture and Rural Economy, together with that which is pursued on the three or four farms nearest to his own Residence." [42] These suggestions were adopted, and the collection of information was begun.

Tom was not able, however, to devote as much attention to the affairs of the society as he would have liked. His farm business sometimes kept him busy "from the hour of breakfast until night" for days at a time, and "the time requisite for coming home in the dark and the effects of fatigue" prevented him from employing his evenings to good advantage. Yet he found opportunity to advocate that the society open a correspondence with "celebrated Agronomic Philosophers abroad," to serve on a committee which was endeavoring to import a Spanish stallion into Albemarle, to distribute seeds which the society had received from the Royal Gardens of Madrid, to establish a system of prizes for good crops,[43] and to prepare and deliver at least two lengthy papers to the organization.

The first of these, presented to the society on March 2, 1818, dealt

40 *Ibid.*, 270.

41 *Ibid.*, 272–73; T. M. Randolph, Jr., to Madison, October 14, 1817, in Madison Papers, Library of Congress.

42 True (ed.), "Minute Book of the Agricultural Society of Albemarle," 273.

43 T. M. Randolph, Jr., to Joseph C. Cabell, October 25, 1817, manuscript copy by Nathaniel Francis Cabell, in Cabell Papers; True (ed.), "Minute Book of the Agricultural Society of Albemarle," 277, 285, 286, 292.

with the Hessian fly. But if any of his hearers expected to be told how to rid their fields of this pest, they were disappointed. Nevertheless, his fellow-members expressed their appreciation of his effort, and the Society ordered that his address be printed in the newspapers.[44] A second paper, delivered more than a year later, also concerned an entomological subject. This time he lectured on the "Bott Fly of Horses." This paper, too, was respectfully received and, like its predecessor, subsequently appeared in print.[45]

In 1819, after twelve years of political inactivity, the fifty-one-year-old colonel made a new bid for public office. His participation in the work of a group as devoted to the common welfare as the Agricultural Society of Albemarle may have caused a renewal of his interest in public affairs. And he was deeply interested in the advancement of the University of Virginia, which had just been established by the General Assembly, and in the affairs of the James River Company. In March, 1819, he announced his candidacy for the House of Delegates,[46] and the following month he and William Fitzhugh Gordon of Edgeworth were chosen to fill Albemarle County's two seats in that body.[47] He spent the next few months in the usual hectic fashion, agonizing over his crops and his debts and bewailing his difficulties at Varina.[48] He took some consolation in the fact that he had escaped direct involvement when Wilson Cary Nicholas went bankrupt, but he had scant cause for comfort, since his father-in-law had suffered grievously from Nicholas' fall.[49]

One of the first tasks before the General Assembly was the election of a new governor, this power having been conferred on the legislature rather than on the people by the state constitution of 1776. On December 10, four days after the beginning of the

44 True (ed.), "Minute Book of the Agricultural Society of Albemarle," 277; *American Farmer*, VIII (August 5, 1825), 153–55.

45 True (ed.), "Minute Book of the Agricultural Society of Albemarle," 283; *American Farmer*, I (December 31, 1819), 315; article also appeared in Richmond *Enquirer*, February 1, 1820.

46 Hore B. Trist to Nicholas P. Trist, March 22, 1819, in Trist Papers, Library of Congress.

47 Richmond *Enquirer*, April 13, 1819.

48 T. M. Randolph, Jr., to Peachy R. Gilmer, June 9, 1819, in Randolph–Gilmer Papers; Randolph, Jr. to Francis Walker Gilmer, July 25, 1819, in Gilmer Papers, Alderman Library, University of Virginia.

49 T. M. Randolph, Jr., to Nicholas P. Trist, August 15, 1819, in Trist Papers, Library of Congress. See Randall, *Life of Thomas Jefferson*, III, 533–39, and Nathan Schachner, *Thomas Jefferson: A Biography* (New York, 1951), 968–69, for Jefferson's involvement.

legislative session, the two houses together met to choose a successor to James Patton Preston, who had just served the last of the three one-year terms allowed him by law. When nominations were opened, William Fitzhugh Gordon proposed Randolph's name, and he was seconded by Briscoe Baldwin of Augusta. The names of Burwell Bassett, Jr., delegate from James City County, and of Linn Banks, Speaker of the House of Delegates, were also put in nomination, and voting began.[50]

Bassett was supported by the colonel's old adversary, David Garland of Amherst, and also by William Cabell Rives from Nelson County, "a young man owing his reputation" to Jefferson. Rives had made caustic insinuations outside the hall about Randolph's financial difficulties, and he did his best "to sink him for ever in the public view." Cabell and the colonel's other friends, however, had succeeded in building such strong support among the western delegates that these defections were balanced, and Randolph was elected on the first ballot.[51]

His success gave great pleasure to his supporters in and outside of the General Assembly. William Fitzhugh Gordon reported that "the triumph" was "indeed pleasing," while Francis Walker Gilmer found the victory of his old friend a "doubly honorable" one in view of "the very means adopted to defeat him." [52] John Hartwell Cocke at Bremo hailed the Assembly's choice and predicted that Randolph would aid in "promoting the University and the various schemes of internal improvements," then before the legislature.[53]

Randolph himself, although confessing that he felt some "anxiety about the exact performance of the manifold duties" of his new office, promised his best efforts in the post to which his fellow citizens had called him.[54] At the age of fifty-one, Thomas Mann

50 *Journal of the House of Delegates . . . 1819* (Richmond, 1820), 17; Richmond *Enquirer*, December 11, 1819. See Swem and Williams (comps.), "Register of the General Assembly," 100–101, for names of legislators.

51 Joseph C. Cabell to John H. Cocke, December 12, 1819, in Cabell Papers; Richmond *Enquirer*, December 11, 1819. There is no record of the number of votes cast for the three candidates.

52 William Fitzhugh Gordon to Mrs. Gordon, December 23, 1819, in Gordon, *William Fitzhugh Gordon*, 69; Francis Walker Gilmer to P. Minor, December 19, 1819, in Gilmer Papers, Alderman Library, University of Virginia.

53 John H. Cocke to Joseph C. Cabell, December 20, 1819, in Cabell Papers.

54 T. M. Randolph, Jr., Message of Acceptance, December 11, 1819, in *Journal of the House of Delegates . . . 1819*, pp. 26–27.

Randolph had attained the greatest triumph of his political career. This tall, raw-boned man, swarthy as an Indian in complexion, indifferent in his dress and careless of his appearance,[55] had known years of unhappiness and frustration, years in which he had failed in nearly every capacity save that of a cultivator of the rich soil of Albemarle County. Ahead of him lay an opportunity, limited though it was by constitutional restrictions, to demonstrate that, as a Randolph and as a follower of Jeffersonian principles, he was fitted to preside over the affairs of a proud Commonwealth.

55 Pierson, *Jefferson at Monticello*, 93, gives Bacon's description of Randolph at a time approximately close to his election as governor.

CHAPTER IX

"No More Than A . . . Signing Clerk"

ON DECEMBER 13, 1819, the new governor appeared before John Adams, Mayor of Richmond, and took the prescribed oath of office.[1] The next day he met for the first time with the Council of State.[2] The eight members of this group, like Randolph, had been chosen by the General Assembly, and they likewise were subject to control by the legislative branch. The primary function of the council was to advise and assist the governor in his exercise of "the executive powers of Government, according to the laws of this Commonwealth" and the Constitution of Virginia.[3] Peter Vivian Daniel, the senior member, was also lieutenant governor and was authorized to preside over council meetings in the governor's absence. Other members were Jerman Baker, Joseph L. Fry, James Heath, John H. Martin, William Pendleton, William H. Roane, and Robert G. Scott.[4]

The Council of State had been created by the constitution makers of 1776 to act as a check on the governor, but Tom viewed the future with cheerful optimism. When he announced his acceptance on December 11, he had expressed confidence that relations would

1 John Adams, Certificate of Oath of Office of T. M. Randolph, Jr., December 13, 1819, in Executive Papers, Archives Division, Virginia State Library.

2 Journal of the Council of State of Virginia, 1819–20, manuscript volume in Archives Division, Virginia State Library.

3 "Virginia Constitution of 1776," in Boyd (ed.), *Papers of Thomas Jefferson*, I, 377–83.

4 Journal of the Council . . . 1819–1820, in Archives Division, Virginia State Library. Two members of the Council were dropped every three years by joint vote of the two houses of the General Assembly, and two new ones were chosen in their places.

be amicable. "The able support to the office of the Chief Magistrate, which a very judicious selection has provided in the council of state, gives me hope that all the duties of the Executive department will be performed to the general satisfaction." [5]

At least one of his advisors, however, was not in sympathy with him. Robert G. Scott had supported Bassett for the governorship, and he openly disagreed with the incumbent in the course of his first term. By the following May the governor was complaining about Scott's disrespectful attitude, a charge which the councillor hastily disclaimed.[6] No drastic break developed at this time, but the incident was a harbinger of future trouble.

The new governor soon found that a great deal of his time was taken up by routine matters which he did not consider important or, in some instances, even part of his job. "I am called on every hour," he protested in 1821, "to exercise . . . functions totally unconnected with my office, and the explanation of why I cannot take more time than would have been requisite to perform the acts." [7] It annoyed him when his meals were interrupted "by official business or callers," interruptions that occurred rather frequently during his terms of office. Even more aggravating was his discovery that his functions were not so exalted nor his office so dignifying as he had expected from his own interpretation of the Virginia constitution.[8]

It is somewhat surprising that a man who had studied the political history of the Commonwealth as thoroughly as he claimed to have done and who must have been familiar, through conversations on the subject, with Jefferson's experience in the gubernatorial chair expected to play a very important part in state affairs.[9] The powers of the governor of Virginia had been clearly and deliberately limited by the framers of the Constitution of 1776, and that document was still the organic act of the Commonwealth. It had been drafted by men who had an almost pathological fear of strong

5 T. M. Randolph, Jr., Message of Acceptance, December 11, 1819, in *Journal of the House of Delegates . . . 1819*, pp. 26–27.

6 Robert Scott to Joseph C. Cabell, May 14, 1820, in Cabell Papers.

7 T. M. Randolph, Jr., to Joseph C. Cabell, March 2, 1821, in Randolph Papers, Duke University Library.

8 T. M. Randolph, Jr., Message to the General Assembly, December 2, 1822, in Richmond *Enquirer*, December 3, 1822.

9 Malone, *Jefferson the Virginian*, 304–308 and 368–69, discusses Jefferson's ideas on the role of the executive during his own governorship, 1779–81.

VIRGINIA HISTORICAL SOCIETY

Thomas Mann Randolph of Tuckahoe (1740–1793), father of Randolph of Edgehill. Portrait by John Wollaston.

VIRGINIA STATE LIBRARY

Tuckahoe, the Randolph home in Goochland County, Virginia. A recent photograph showing the west court and entrance.

Edgehill, home of Thomas Mann Randolph and his wife Martha Jefferson in Albemarle County, Virginia. This photograph shows the house as it looks today after modernization.

VIRGINIA STATE LIBRARY

Thomas Jefferson, ca. 1804–1805, engraving by J. B. Forrest, after Gilbert Stuart.

COLLECTION OF ARTHUR ROTCH, MILTON, MASSACHUSETTS

Thomas Jefferson Randolph, oldest son of Thomas Mann Randolph. Portrait by Charles Willson Peale.

HOWARD C. RICE

Miniature of Martha Jefferson by Joseph Boze, painted in Paris, 1789, when she was seventeen. The original is in the American Embassy, Paris.

THOMAS JEFFERSON MEMORIAL FOUNDATION

Portrait of Martha Jefferson Randolph at age forty-nine, by Thomas Sully. The original is at Monticello.

VIRGINIA STATE LIBRARY

Virginia State Capitol at Richmond, ca. 1831. The building then looked much as it did when Thomas Mann Randolph sat in the House of Delegates 1823–25. Wings have since been added.

VALENTINE MUSEUM, RICHMOND

Governor's Mansion in Richmond, where Randolph lived during his years as governor, 1819–1822.

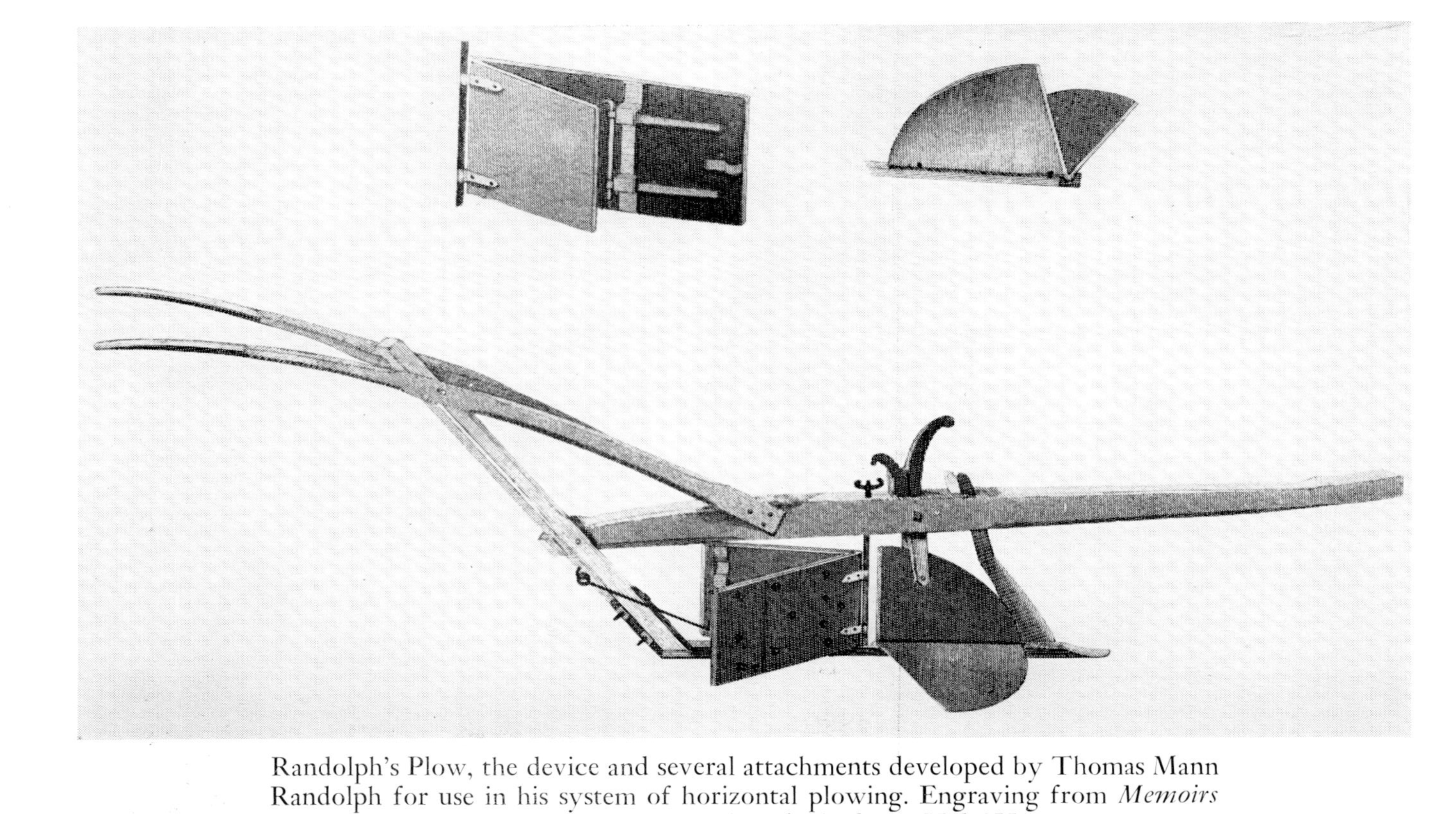

Randolph's Plow, the device and several attachments developed by Thomas Mann Randolph for use in his system of horizontal plowing. Engraving from *Memoirs of the Philadelphia Society for Promoting Agriculture*, Vol. IV, 1818.

THOMAS JEFFERSON MEMORIAL FOUNDATION

Recent photograph of the "office" at Monticello, a small building at the end of one of two walkways extending from the sides of the main house. Thomas Mann Randolph spent his last days here as a recluse.

executives, and in their zeal to forestall tyranny the constitution makers had created "a mere mongrel kind of Directory." [10] Ironically enough, one of those who had participated in the preparation of that document was Tom's father, who had attended the Convention of 1776 as a delegate from Goochland County.[11] The "Chief Magistrate" could neither prorogue nor dissolve the General Assembly, nor could he veto any bill which had been passed by that body. Furthermore, he was required to follow the advice of the Council of State, whose members were elected by the legislature, in the exercise of those few powers allowed him.[12]

The Governor-in-Council received all petitions and claims and referred them to the legislative branch for action, appointed justices of the peace and militia officers in the various counties, carried on correspondence with governors of other states, issued election writs, examined the accounts of the state treasurer and the state auditor, and supervised the state penitentiary. In such matters the governor acted only with the approval of his advisors, any four of whom constituted a quorum. Except when there was an evenly-divided vote, he could not cast a ballot.[13]

Randolph never expressed any objection to his domination by the legislature, but he gradually developed a bitter resentment of his subordination to the council. Eventually his defenders charged that over zealous councillors had taken advantage of the complacency of the governor's predecessors to usurp control of the executive branch,[14] but neither they nor he spoke out against the constitutional provisions that made both governor and councillors mere creatures of the General Assembly.

Nor did the new governor seem aware of the dominant role then being played in Virginia politics by the "Richmond Junto," a clique of bankers, editors, and state officers which had been exercising control over the Commonwealth's affairs for almost a decade. This body had maintained public support by its stands on behalf of states'

10 Jefferson to T. M. Randolph, Jr., July 30, 1821, in Jefferson Papers, Library of Congress.

11 Swem and Williams (comps.), "Register of the General Assembly," 242.

12 Irving Brant, *Madison, the Virginia Revolutionist, 1751–1780* (Indianapolis, 1941), 263–65.

13 Journal of the Council . . . 1819–20, 1820–21, 1821–22, *passim.*, in Archives Division, Virginia State Library.

14 Martha Randolph to Nicholas P. Trist, January 8, 1822, in Trist Papers, University of North Carolina Library.

rights, internal improvements, and other popular causes, but its real power rested largely on its ability to fill the key posts in the state with its own men. Among its leaders were Spencer Roane, Senior Judge of the Court of Appeals; Thomas Ritchie, editor of the Richmond *Enquirer* and almost perpetual public printer; Dr. John Brockenbrough, president of the Bank of Virginia; Wilson Cary Nicholas, president of the branch Bank of the United States at Richmond; Philip Norborne Nicholas, president of the Farmer's Bank; and John Preston, treasurer of Virginia. The Junto had also penetrated the council, where its interests were represented by Peter V. Daniel, William H. Roane, and the dissident Robert G. Scott.[15]

One of the few privileges vouchsafed the governor was that of submitting messages to the legislature, and he availed himself of this right several times during the early months of his first term. The members of the Assembly, of course, were in no way obligated to follow his suggestions, but the practice did give the Chief Magistrate an opportunity to instruct public opinion and, thus, indirectly to influence legislation. Furthermore, on many topics the governor and the legislature were in agreement.

For example, both governor and Assembly were disturbed by the Supreme Court's decision in the case of *McCulloch* v. *Maryland* and by the debates in Congress on the admission of Missouri to the Union. On these issues the governor took a firm and unequivocal states' rights stand. Like his father-in-law and many other prominent Virginians, Randolph was opposed to the McCulloch decision, which upheld the constitutionality of the law creating the Second Bank of the United States and which was based on the old Federalist doctrine that the national government possessed implied powers. Much of the opposition to this decision in Virginia had been inspired by agrarian antagonism to the Bank itself and by the suffering in that state as a result of the panic of 1819, but a great deal of the resistance stemmed from fears of federal encroachment. The governor was similarly disturbed by the attempt of James Tallmadge, Jr., of New York, and other northern Congressmen to bring Missouri into the Union as a free state.

Governor Randolph referred to both of these matters by implication in his message of acceptance on December 11, 1819, at which time he called on the Assembly to make "some endeavors to check

15 Harry Ammon, "The Republican Party in Virginia, 1789 to 1824" (Ph.D. dissertation, University of Virginia, 1948), 396–97.

the progress of a decline so fatal in its aspect." [16] The House of Delegates, most of whose members were inclined to the same opinion, heeded this suggestion by adopting two resolutions, one of them protesting the Bank decision,[17] and the other condemning any congressional interference with slavery in Missouri or elsewhere.[18] The more conservative senate rejected the attack on the Bank, but approved the resolution concerning the Tallmadge amendment.

Randolph was also on safe ground when he recommended state support of a program of internal improvements. He had declared his interest in such a program when he accepted the governorship,[19] and he forwarded a special message on the subject to the House of Delegates on January 25, 1820. On this occasion he submitted a recommendation of the state's Board of Public Works that a canal be built along the James River from Richmond to Covington and a road from that point to the Kanawha.[20] The governor gave his warmest endorsement to this project for joining the Chesapeake to the Ohio Valley. He predicted that the proposed improvements, when completed, would enable Virginia to compete successfully with New York—then engaged in the construction of the Erie Canal —for the trade of the trans-Allegheny region. Let this link with the rich lands of the Great Valley be forged, he proclaimed, and Virginia would have "a great and flourishing commerce, populous and wealthy cities, re-occupied plains on the east, and peopled mountains on the west." Thus would be forged, he continued, "a connexion founded on mutual interests with the great population of the western states," and, finally, "the preservation of order, free principles, and union in the Confederacy." [21]

The instrument chosen for the achievement of these goals was the James River Company, which had been incorporated by the General Assembly in 1785. That privately owned and privately financed organization had been created for the purpose of "clearing and improving the navigation of James River . . . from tidewater upwards to the highest parts practicable on the main branch

16 T. M. Randolph, Jr., Message to the General Assembly, December 11, 1819, in *Journal of the House of Delegates . . . 1819*, p. 27.

17 *Ibid.*, 57–65.

18 *Ibid.*, 76–77.

19 *Ibid.*, 27.

20 Wayland F. Dunaway, *History of the James River and Kanawha Company* (New York, 1922), 64–65.

21 *Journal of the House of Delegates . . . 1819*, p. 144. See also Richmond *Enquirer*, January 27, 1820.

thereof," so as "to make the river well capable of being navigated in dry seasons by vessels drawing one foot water at least." The company was authorized to sell stock in the enterprise and to charge "reasonable tolls." [22]

During the thirty-five years of its existence the company had completed a 7-mile canal around the falls of the James at Richmond, and had improved the upper part of the river as far west as Botetourt County by the construction of sluices. Farmers living along the James between the Blue Ridge and the fall line benefited from the company's improvements, but the long-range aim of providing better transportation for the western sections of the state had not been attained.

On February 17, 1820, the supporters of the project in the Assembly secured passage of an act "for clearing and improving James River." The old company was designated as the state's agent to carry out the plan. Work on the canal proceeded quite slowly, however, and only thirty-four miles of it had been completed four years later.[23]

The new governor was also a staunch friend of the University of Virginia, the cherished project of his father-in-law's old age, and his enthusiasm was shared by several influential members of the legislature. This institution had been conceived first as Albemarle Academy in 1814 and had received its charter as a university from the legislature early in 1819, but it was still far from completion. Only five of the ten pavilions, as the buildings designed for use of the professors were called, had been finished, and work on the remaining buildings was languishing for lack of funds. On January 4, 1820, therefore, Randolph called on the Assembly to appropriate additional funds for the university. As if he anticipated arguments by economy-minded legislators, he declared that "the annual diffusion of knowledge" by the institution would more than justify the cost of construction. Like Jefferson, he was appalled by "the vast waste now made of the efforts of native genius," and he was convinced that such waste, if left unchecked, was far more of a drain on the resources of the Commonwealth than the expense incurred in developing latent talents. He took this occasion to pay tribute to the

22 William W. Hening, *The Statutes at Large . . .* (Richmond, 1809–23), XI, 450–62; Dunaway, *History of the James River and Kanawha Company*, 21–49.

23 Dunaway, *History of the James River and Kanawha Company*, 66–73.

beauty of the university's buildings, the plans for which he had undoubtedly seen on Jefferson's drawing board, and to predict that these buildings, based "on the pure models of ancient times," would inspire a general improvement of architectural taste.[24]

The legislators, prodded by such men as Joseph Cabell and Chapman Johnson in the Senate and by William Fitzhugh Gordon and James Breckinridge in the House, responded favorably to this appeal. On February 24, 1820, a bill was passed authorizing the university to borrow $60,000 from the Literary Fund.[25] This fund has been created in 1810, when the Assembly set aside all fines, forfeitures, and similar revenues of the state for educational purposes. Disbursements were handled by the Literary Board, composed of the president and directors of the Literary Fund, of which Randolph was ex-officio chairman.[26]

The governor succeeded in getting many of his policies adopted, but his triumphs were possible because his views coincided with those held by most members of the legislature. Whenever he took an independent stand, the lawmakers demonstrated their power by ignoring his wishes.

Thus when the Dismal Swamp Canal Company sought permission to convert its stock from real to personal property, Randolph opposed the petition in vain. That company, which was chartered in both North Carolina and Virginia, had in 1805 completed a canal through the great morass south of Norfolk. North Carolina had given her approval to the proposed change in 1819 but had made that approval contingent upon similar action by Virginia. Sentiment in the Assembly at Richmond favored the change, but Governor Randolph felt that the invitation to imitate North Carolina should be rejected. When he submitted the pertinent documents in the matter to the House of Delegates on January 17, he expressed his opposition in firm and forthright terms.

The shares of the Dismal Swamp Canal were, in his opinion, more valuable as real estate than as personal property. Once the company's stocks were converted into personal property, they were likely to become pawns in "the fascinating game of stockjobbing." He drew an alarming picture of shares being passed from hand to hand with every rise in value, until most of the stock would be owned by

24 *Journal of the House of Delegates . . . 1819,* pp. 99–100.
25 Bruce, *History of the University of Virginia,* I, 290–93.
26 *Ibid.,* 199.

persons who had paid too much "to allow any deduction for further improvements." [27] In spite of this lecture on economics, a bill authorizing the desired conversion was passed by the House of Delegates without debate on January 25 and was then approved by the Senate.[28] Since the governor had no power of veto, the measure then became law.

The Assembly adjourned on February 25, and the members scattered to their homes throughout the Commonwealth, not to gather again until the following December. Thomas, however, remained in Richmond, attending meetings of the council and of the Literary Board and carrying on the routine duties of his office. He lived alone, except for a few servants, in the square and massively built Governor's House, for his wife and family remained in Albemarle during most of his governorship. He felt the separation very keenly and since they, preoccupied with domestic affairs, seemed unable to come to him, he went to them at every opportunity. He formed the habit of going home on weekend visits, leaving Richmond after supper on Saturday, riding all night on his gaunt steed Dromedary, and arriving in Albemarle in time for Sunday breakfast. After spending the day with his family and visiting his aging and increasingly feeble father-in-law, he made the return trip to the capital on Monday.[29]

He also left Richmond occasionally to look after his plantation at Varina, but he was generally attentive to his official duties and spent most of his time in the capital. The financial needs of the university continued to demand his attention, and that March he pressed the Literary Board to release the $60,000 loan authorized by the General Assembly at its previous session. The board agreed to pay two-thirds of that sum immediately.[30] At this time the governor, eager to "keep the remainder of the Loan constantly in view," persuaded his colleagues to agree to pay the remaining $20,000 in October, but no record of this decision was made.[31] Thus, when the board met again on July 30, Randolph was surprised and chagrined to discover that

27 *Journal of the House of Delegates . . . 1819*, pp. 124–25.
28 *Ibid.*, 138, 150, 169.
29 Pierson, *Jefferson at Monticello*, 95; Randall, *Life of Thomas Jefferson*, II, 225 *n.*
30 Literary Board, Minutes, March 23 & 25, 1820, extract in Jefferson Papers, Alderman Library, University of Virginia.
31 T. M. Randolph, Jr., to Jefferson, October 12, 1820, *ibid.;* Literary Board, Minutes, March 23, 1820, *ibid.*

the other members had "no recollection of the occurrence" and that there was no mention of it in the minutes of the previous meeting.[32] Spurred on by Jefferson,[33] he kept the matter alive and was able to forward a bond for the balance of the loan on October 12.[34] The "old sachem" was gratified by his son-in-law's "zeal for the institution" but, realizing much still had to be done, he called on Thomas to make additional efforts to place the institution on more secure ground.[35]

Governor Randolph's first term was now drawing to a close. The legislators reassembled on December 4, 1820, and on that date he submitted his annual message to the body.[36] Therein he recommended that the state penitentiary, in use since 1800 and already overcrowded, be rebuilt so as to provide a separate cell for each convict. He further proposed that the inmates, hitherto employed in the institution's workshops, be assigned useful tasks that they could perform in their own cells.

Another of his recommendations concerned education. He was keenly interested in efforts to give poor children an opportunity for schooling, but he was aware that many parents were too proud to apply for public assistance. He therefore suggested that the magistrates in each county certify all cases of need known to them and that all those who taught poor children be paid directly from the Literary Fund on the basis of such certifications. He also proposed that schools should offer training in the mechanical arts as well as instruction in the more formal branches of learning, and he argued that such an extension of the curriculum would prove of incalculable benefit to those pupils not suited for a collegiate or classical education.

The governor also recommended the popular election of juries, called for a more intensive program of training for the militia, deplored the increasing popularity of paper money, proposed that state taxes be collected in specie, declared his continuing devotion to the cause of internal improvements, and alluded briefly to the case of

32 Randolph, Jr., to Jefferson, October 12, 1820, *ibid.*

33 Jefferson to Randolph, Jr., September 16, 1820, *ibid.;* Jefferson to Randolph, Jr., October 8, 1820, in Jefferson Papers, Massachusetts Historical Society.

34 Randolph, Jr., to Jefferson, October 12, 1820, in Jefferson Papers, Alderman Library, University of Virginia.

35 Jefferson to Randolph, Jr., November 20, 1820, in Jefferson Papers, Massachusetts Historical Society.

36 *Journal of the House of Delegates . . . 1820* (Richmond, 1821), 7–12.

Cohens v. *Virginia*, then pending before the United States Supreme Court. Philip J. and Menendez Cohen, both of them "venders of Lottery tickets" from the District of Columbia, had been arrested in Norfolk the preceding summer for plying their trade and had been convicted by the court of that borough. Although a Virginia statute of 1820 clearly prohibited the promotion of such enterprises within the Commonwealth, the Cohen brothers pleaded that their activities were authorized by an act of Congress. When the Virginia Court of Appeals refused to review the decision of the Hustings Court of Norfolk, the Cohens took their case to the Supreme Court on a writ of error.[37] The Governor-in-Council had already appointed Philip Pendleton Barbour and Alexander Smyth to represent the Commonwealth before that tribunal,[38] but no further action had been taken on this matter when Randolph addressed the legislature. Now he contented himself with a few pungent remarks concerning the evils of gambling and the perils of lotteries and with a prediction that the federal tribunal might render a "strange opinion."[39]

Although Randolph's statements on these matters attracted little notice, other portions of his message, particularly those dealing with slavery and religion, did. Indeed, they aroused opposition against him within the Assembly itself.[40] To be sure, his proposal for a gradual reduction of Virginia's Negro population was mild enough, especially in comparison with those then being advanced in other quarters. Nor were his ideas on this subject particularly novel. St. George Tucker, while serving as a judge of Virginia's General Court, had recommended a plan for "gradual abolition" in 1796, and others had proposed that the emancipated slaves be removed to Africa, to the wilds of Louisiana, and to other places not then inhabited by white Americans.[41]

Randolph's views on slavery apparently were shaped by recent events in Virginia, as well as by his own experience as a master. In

37 Albert Jeremiah Beveridge, *The Life of John Marshall* (Boston, 1916–19), IV, 342–45.

38 T. M. Randolph, Jr., to James Barbour, October 27, 1820, in Executive Letter Book (1816–22), manuscript volume in Archives Division, Virginia State Library.

39 *Journal of the House of Delegates . . . 1820*, pp. 7–12.

40 Joseph C. Cabell to Jefferson, December 22, 1820, in Cabell Papers.

41 St. George Tucker, *A Dissertation on Slavery, with a Proposal for the Gradual Abolition of It in the State of Virginia* (Philadelphia, 1796); Ludwell L. Montague, *Haiti and the United States, 1714–1938* (Durham, 1940), 68; Early Lee Fox, *The American Colonization Society, 1817–1840* (Baltimore, 1919), 45–75; Charles S. Sydnor, *The Development of Southern Sectionalism* (Baton Rouge, 1948), 96–97.

February, 1820, there had been rumors of an intended slave insurrection in Petersburg,[42] and he probably had not forgotten the excitement generated by those reports. Even before he submitted these thoughts to the Assembly, Thomas had come to the conclusion that it was "impossible that the slave system should continue," unless some effort was made to check the rapid increase of the slave population, and he feared that a bloody racial war would be the eventual result of inaction.[43] He did not propose "general emancipation, however gradual" and he greatly doubted the possibility of "lessening the evil in a sensible degree" in his own lifetime. He was, nonetheless, convinced that a "just responsibility to posterity" made some action mandatory, and he suggested that "a fair proportion" of slave youths in the different parts of Virginia be manumitted every year. To accelerate the process, he recommended further that "a double proportion of females" over males be released annually. While he did not make a definite proposal concerning compensation of the owners, he suggested that the project could be financed out of the proceeds of the state's tax on slaves.[44]

Men like St. George Tucker had proposed that freedmen be denied the enjoyment of civil and political rights as long as they remained in Virginia, but the governor recommended that transportation be made a condition of emancipation. In setting this condition, however, he was only recognizing a statute in force since 1806, which provided that if "any slave hereafter emancipated shall remain within this commonwealth more than twelve months after his or her right to freedom shall have accrued, he or she shall forfeit all such right." [45] He further suggested that those manumitted under his program be sent to the island of Santo Domingo, which was "sufficiently near to admit of emigration at little cost," and where a self-governing community of liberated Negroes was already in existence.[46] Jefferson praised Tom's courage in making this proposal, but his

42 Journal of the Council . . . February 29, 1820, in Archives Division, Virginia State Library.

43 T. M. Randolph, Jr., to Nicholas P. Trist, June 5, 1820, in Trist Papers, University of North Carolina Library.

44 For Randolph's views on slavery, see his Message, December 4, 1820, in *Journal of the House of Delegates . . . 1820*, pp. 10–11; for Tucker's scheme, see his *Dissertation on Slavery*, 54–58. See also Sydnor, *Development of Southern Sectionalism*, 96, for a critical estimate of Randolph's plan.

45 Shepherd (ed.), *Statutes at Large of Virginia*, III, 251.

46 Jefferson to D. B. Warden, December 26, 1820, in Paul L. Ford (ed.), *The Writings of Thomas Jefferson*, X, 178.

plan, particularly the suggestion that slave owners themselves be called on to finance the dissolution of their own laboring force, could hardly have attracted very widespread support.

However, it was the comments on religion which he included in his message that provoked the most vociferous and immediate opposition at the time. In the course of a routine tribute to the spirit of toleration, Randolph spoke enthusiastically of "that unassuming and silent system of religious doctrine, which manifests itself in an enthusiastic and persevering study of the attributes of the author and sovereign of nature, as they are unfolded in visible works and revealed further by the power of the human mind." He openly admitted that he preferred to "substitute patient resignation for prayer, and silent admiration for labored praise or ceremonious worship." [47] A skeptic and a deist since his student days in Scotland, the governor had never made a secret of his beliefs. His friends were familiar with his conviction that the study of "the wonders of creation" was a "a sublime Religion in itself" and that prayer had "an inevitable tendency to render Religion purely Scenic." [48] But it was one thing to discuss such ideas with men like Joseph C. Cabell, and quite another to give voice to them in a public statement, in a day when more and more Virginians were turning again to sectarian conformity.[49]

Such words aroused resentments that were not forgotten when the two houses of the Assembly met together ten days later to select a governor for the ensuing year. The governor, whose term had expired on December 11, was nominated to succeed himself, and the name of Hugh Nelson, member of the House of Delegates from Albemarle County, was also proposed. Nelson's principal supporters, were David Garland of Amherst and Walter Fontaine of Buckingham. They did not hesitate to use Randolph's recent words against him, and the charge of impiety was used freely.[50] These opponents may also have sought to capitalize on Thomas' unorthodox views on slavery.

His friends in the Assembly closed ranks around him, even though

47 T. M. Randolph, Jr., Message, December 4, 1820, in *Journal of the House of Delegates . . . 1820*, pp. 7–8.

48 T. M. Randolph, Jr., to Joseph C. Cabell, August 5, 1820; Randolph, Jr., to Cabell, August 11, 1820, in Randolph Papers, Duke University Library.

49 Sydnor, *Development of Southern Sectionalism*, 56; Clement Eaton, *Freedom of Thought in the Old South*, (New York, 1951), 280–85.

50 Charlottesville *Central Gazette*, January 5, 1821.

some of them privately regretted his indiscretion.[51] Cabell did what he could in conferences with individual members to counteract "the scandalous attack" on Randolph's character,[52] while General Samuel Blackburn, delegate from Bath County, made an eloquent speech on his colleague's behalf on the floor of the Assembly. "The business of this day," declared Blackburn, "is not to elect a Bishop, a confessor, or a dervish but a Governor." The proper questions to ask concerning any aspirant for that office, he said, should be: Was he a Virginian? A supporter of the Union? A friend to states' rights? A kind husband, a tender parent, and good neighbor? Arguing that his principal was satisfactory on all these counts, the delegate from Bath besought his hearers to remember "the Act . . . establishing Religious Freedom" and to reelect Colonel Randolph.[53] Blackburn was only one of those who took part in the fight, and the lively debate, carried on before a crowd of spectators, ended in a sweeping victory for the incumbent who received 164 votes to Nelson's 38.[54] Two days later Thomas Mann Randolph took the oath of office for the second time.[55]

Emboldened by victory, he made a move which may have been contemplated for some time and launched his first public attack on the council in his message of acceptance, delivered on December 19. He spoke of the relations between "the acting and the deliberating branches of the Executive authority," and his remarks indicated that he found that relationship far from satisfactory. The governor, he complained, had no real power and was merely "a passive instrument" whose only function was to sign commissions.[56] He felt that he should have the power to act "in any civil matter" without the council, to determine the order of business and even to have a casting vote, while the council should hold no sessions unless "the Constitutional President thereof" was present. His remarks were comparatively restrained, but the tone of his complaint indicated an impatience that would not long be held within reasonable bounds. Undoubtedly he had interpreted his reelection as an unqualified

51 Joseph C. Cabell to Jefferson, December 22, 1820, in Cabell Papers.
52 Cabell to Jefferson, December 20, 1820, *ibid.*
53 Charlottesville *Central Gazette*, January 5, 1821.
54 Richmond *Enquirer*, December 19, 1820.
55 John Adams, Certificate of Oath of Office of T. M. Randolph Jr., December 17, 1820, in Executive Papers, Archives Division, Virginia State Library.
56 *Journal of the House of Delegates . . . 1820*, pp. 53–54.

endorsement of his policies, and he apparently believed that the legislators who had voted to continue him in office would back him up in future disputes with the council.

He soon was reminded, however, that the members of the Assembly had no intention of issuing such a blank check. None of the legislation proposed in the message of December 4 was adopted, and most of his suggestions were merely referred to committees and then forgotten.[57] While his plan for gradual emancipation did reach the floor of the House of Delegates on February 19, 1821, the members immediately voted to table it.[58]

Though the early months of the second term were disappointing in matters of legislative achievement, there were personal compensations for him during that period. Martha came down from Albemarle to spend a few weeks with him in Richmond, and she apparently encouraged him to entertain more than he had done during her absence. David Campbell, who had been Tom's second-in-command during the luckless St. Lawrence campaign in 1813, was a member of the Virginia Senate that session, and he paid a call at the executive mansion soon after his arrival at the state capital. Randolph greeted his guest in "very friendly" fashion, introduced him to Martha, "and, like a great man, retired." But Campbell, who must have heard a great deal about the lady in earlier days, was not so impressed with her as were most of his contemporaries. She was, in the senator's opinion, vain and sarcastic.[59] Even though Campbell did not like her, he seemed almost alone in his unflattering opinion. Perhaps her notably even disposition had begun to turn sour after thirty years of marriage to the high-tempered Randolph. Perhaps she merely did not approve of her husband's old army friends.

Soon enough, however, Martha returned to her aged father's side, and her husband quickly reverted to his old solitary habits.[60] He shortly discovered new sources of aggravation in the attitude toward the university displayed by some of his fellow directors of the Literary Fund. The board was showing an irritating indifference to the needs of the institution at Charlottesville, and Thomas was finding it increasingly difficult to secure even their attendance at

57 *Ibid., passim; Acts Passed at a General Assembly . . .* (Richmond, 1821), *passim*, does not include any legislation covering any of these proposals.

58 *Ibid.*, 203.

59 David Campbell to John Campbell, January 22, 1821, in David Campbell Papers.

60 John Campbell to David Campbell, June 20, 1821, *ibid.*

meetings. In the spring he spent three weeks, he complained, "trying & failing every day to have a council," and he had almost as much trouble in July assembling a quorum of the board.[61]

Even then he encountered resistance. The preceding session of the Assembly had appropriated $60,000 for the university, but the directors refused to release more than $29,100 of that sum at their July meeting, pleading that the common schools throughout the state were constantly drawing on the Literary Fund and that no more money was available. Governor Randolph argued that the fund was constantly being replenished by fines and forfeitures, but he could not overcome the opposition of his colleagues. Their intransigence convinced him that "hostility" to the university lay at the bottom of the whole matter, and he was confirmed in this opinion when the directors agreed to use part of the fund to purchase shares in the James River Company. Since James Heath, state auditor and member of the board, had proposed this diversion of money, the governor concluded that Heath had "gone over to the enemy." [62]

Not discouraged by this setback, the friends of the institution were exploring a new source of financial aid. In the spring of 1821 Tom opened negotiations with the treasurer of the United States for settlement of the claims arising from Virginia's defense expenditures during the War of 1812.[63] The principal of this obligation, assumed by the national government, had been paid, but not the interest which, according to the governor's calculations, amounted to $30,-000. He hoped that this sum could be obtained for the university [64] and had Cary Selden appointed to act as Virginia's agent in the negotiations.[65] There, for a while, the matter rested.

Even more annoying and exasperating was the situation in the Council of State. From the beginning of the second term Thomas'

61 T. M. Randolph, Jr., to Jefferson, July 30, 1821, in Edgehill-Randolph Papers.

62 Randolph, Jr. to Jefferson, July 31, 1821, in Jefferson Papers, Massachusetts Historical Society.

63 T. M. Randolph, Jr., to Thomas Tucker, May 8, 1821, in Executive Letter Book (1816–22), manuscript volume in Archives Division, Virginia State Library.

64 Bruce, *History of the University of Virginia*, I, 300–301.

65 T. M. Randolph, Jr., to Thomas Tucker, May 8, 1821, in Executive Letter Book (1816–22), manuscript volume in Archives Division, Virginia State Library; Randolph, Jr., to Jefferson, July 31, 1821, in Jefferson Papers, Massachusetts Historical Society.

relations with that body grew steadily worse. Peter V. Daniel, the lieutenant governor, was still a member, and the others in 1821 were William H. Roane, Robert G. Scott, William Robertson, William Selden, John Campbell, William Pendleton, and A. L. Botts. Scott had been an opponent of the governor from the beginning,[66] and the willingness of the others to cooperate vanished after the incumbent's remarks on "the acting and deliberating branches" in his message of acceptance. From that point on the council began to show its independence of the Chief Magistrate at every opportunity. By March he was convinced that his advisors were endeavoring "to render totally insignificant an office already reduced far below what was ever contemplated by the Constitution Framers." [67]

One fundamental point of disagreement concerned appointments. During 1821 the councillors often decided that the governor's recommendations be deferred, and they frequently advised that applications for the formation of new militia units be rejected, although such requests usually were supported by Randolph.[68] He was particularly offended when his colleagues refused to allow certain volunteer companies from Norfolk and Richmond to parade on the public square in front of the Capitol as part of the celebration of the Fourth of July. The council opposed the demonstration because they feared it would damage the grounds which had been recently graded and seeded. When he argued that he was the commander of the militia, the councillors replied that civic groups assembled on ceremonial occasions were not part of the militia and therefore were not under his direction or protection.[69]

Even more galling was the fact that the council met more and more often in his absence. While Randolph sought to attend sessions as often as possible, he found it necessary to leave the capital several times during 1821 to inspect his property at Varina, but he seldom was gone for more than a day or so at a time.[70] The councillors'

66 Journal of the Council . . . 1821–22 contains names of the councillors; for Scott's opposition to Randolph see Robert G. Scott to Joseph C. Cabell, May 14, 1820, in Campbell Papers.

67 T. M. Randolph, Jr., to Joseph C. Cabell, March 2, 1821, in Randolph Papers, Duke University Library.

68 Journal of the Council . . . 1821–22, *passim,* in Archives Division, Virginia State Library.

69 Memorial of the Council, December 19, 1821, in Richmond *Enquirer,* December 20, 1821; T. M. Randolph, Jr., to Thomas Ritchie, December 21, 1821, *ibid.,* December 22, 1821.

70 Richmond *Enquirer,* December 20, 1821.

claims that the matters dealt with in these sessions were too urgent to allow of delay did not impress him, and he grew increasingly suspicious and resentful. When he was present, his colleagues sometimes instructed their clerk "to serve their advices" without first securing the governor's assent.[71]

Long before these differences exploded into open warfare, Thomas seems to have brooded over his troubles, becoming gloomier and more withdrawn in his manner. Not only were his dress and appearance "as bad as they well could be," but he took no pleasure in himself or in anyone else. He was a guest at a bachelor party given in June by Philip Norborne Nicholas, but he was unable to share in the festivities, not even smiling at the sallies of James Barbour, who reputedly could make "the dead laugh." While everyone else became completely hilarious, the governor sat abstracted and in deep thought, unmoved either by Barbour's jokes or Nicholas' liquor.[72]

His quarrels with the council and with the Literary Board were not the only reasons for his state of mind that summer. Family worries and financial troubles were also distracting him, and his numerous creditors were pressing him hard. "I am harassed until life is a torment," he cried to his son Jeff,[73] and he had reached the point where he had almost given up hope of ever freeing himself from his burdens. But it was the tribulations of office which were most irksome, and he looked forward, with increasing impatience, to the day when he could retire "to Botany, Poetry, and the fields with their delightful silence." [74] His dissatisfaction with his office became well known in Richmond, and rumors multiplied that he would not seek a third term.[75]

Nevertheless, there was no hint of any intention to retire in his address to the opening session of the next legislature. He spoke approvingly of "the two great common objects of public instruction and territorial improvement" and declared that a "grand approach

71 T. M. Randolph, Jr., to Thomas Ritchie, December 20, 1821, in Richmond *Compiler,* December 21, 1821.

72 John Campbell to David Campbell, June 20, 1821, in David Campbell Papers.

73 T. M. Randolph, Jr., to T. J. Randolph, June 11, 1821, in Edgehill-Randolph Papers.

74 T. M. Randolph, Jr., to James Monroe, June 1, 1821, in Monroe Papers, New York Public Library.

75 John Campbell to David Campbell, June 20, 1821, in David Campbell Papers.

towards perfection" would be attained if all state revenues were devoted to these purposes. He dwelt at length on the implications of the Cohen decision, in which Chief Justice Marshall had rejected Virginia's contention that suits against a state could not be appealed to the national courts. The Constitution was "not a mystic writing given in charge to the federal judiciary as to a priesthood," and he proposed that Virginia sponsor a constitutional amendment "confining both the powers claimed and the jurisdiction asserted, within such well-defined limits as may make the state governments secure" against all efforts to reverse their decisions "upon matters of their own policy." [76] His suggestion, similar to one advanced by Spencer Roane,[77] undoubtedly enhanced his popularity in the legislature, for Marshall's assertion of Federal jurisdiction in the Cohen decision was highly unpopular.

By this time Randolph had decided to become a candidate for reelection. Unfavorably disposed delegates like William Mason Rives of Campbell County hinted that the governor sought the office again only because he needed the salary of $3,333.34 a year, but Rives nonetheless supported him. Burwell Bassett of James City, who had been the incumbent's opponent two years before, was the only alternative, and Rives had an even less favorable opinion of him. The incumbent, after all, could serve only one more term, while Bassett might become entrenched in office for the full three years allowed him. Other members, according to Rives, shared this feeling.[78] If so, Randolph's victory over Bassett on December 8 was hardly a sweeping endorsement of his program. Nonetheless, his triumph was statistically impressive, for he received 146 out of the 189 votes cast.[79] Whatever the intentions of his supporters, he interpreted his reelection as an expression of legislative confidence, and once again he let the wine of victory go to his head.

On December 14 he notified the House of his acceptance, and he made use of the occasion to deliver a violent frontal attack on the council. In angry and bitter language he reviewed the disputes over appointments, over the control of the militia, and over the practice of meeting without him, and he explicitly charged the councillors

76 T. M. Randolph, Jr., Message, December 3, 1821, in Richmond *Enquirer,* December 4, 1821.

77 "Spencer Roane," *Dictionary of American Biography,* XV, 642–43.

78 William M. Rives to William C. Rives, December 31, 1821, in William C. Rives Papers, Library of Congress.

79 Richmond *Enquirer,* December 11, 1821.

with unconstitutional encroachment on his office.[80] No steps to check this usurpation were revealed. Probably he had formed no definite plan of action beyond an attempt to turn the legislature against the "plural branch of the executive."

If such was Randolph's purpose, the tactic did not succeed. Far from winning him support, his outburst merely stiffened the opposition against him. Colonel David Campbell's brother John, a member of the council, attributed the attack to a "love of posterity," and he thought that he had provoked hostility where none had existed before. Characterizing the governor as a "curious eccentric" with much book learning but with "no useful sense at all," Campbell, who had hitherto been friendly to him, tartly observed: "He does not suit the world and he had better quit and *go home*." [81] As if to hasten that abdication, Campbell joined his colleagues of the council in a counterattack. On December 19 all the members of that body issued a memorial which they published in Thomas Ritchie's *Enquirer*. They denied the charges of usurpation and encroachment and defended their occasional meetings without the governor on the ground that he had been "inaccessible" on his estate. As for his view of the executive power, they declared that such theories were "never known anterior to the induction into office of the present incumbent." [82]

When this rebuttal came to the governor's attention, he was unable to contain his rage. Accustomed to keeping himself in his official residence and seeing no one,[83] he now went forth into the streets "like a mad bull, cursing and denouncing" the council to everyone who would listen. He was particularly abusive, so it was reported, in his comments on Lieutenant Governor Daniel and on councillors Scott, Roane, and Selden.[84] Not content with this display, he gave further release to his feelings in scathingly hostile letters to the press. In the first, published on December 21 in the *Compiler*, he reiterated all of his previous complaints. "The Governor of Virginia for the last five years," he raged, "has been no more than a reading and signing clerk to the Council" and was allowed no

80 *Journal of the House of Delegates . . . 1821* (Richmond, 1822), 40.

81 John Campbell to James Campbell, December 19, 1821, in David Campbell Papers.

82 Richmond *Enquirer*, December 20, 1820.

83 John Campbell to James Campbell, December 19, 1821, in David Campbell Papers.

84 John Campbell to Maria Campbell, January 1, 1822, *ibid.*

more part in their decisions "than the Foreman of a Petty Jury has with the verdict." [85] A second missile, launched the next day in the *Enquirer*, sputtered with charges of folly and bigotry, but this angry communication was mainly concerned with a review of the quarrel of the previous summer over the proposed militia parade on the Capitol grounds and the council's summary prohibition of that Fourth of July demonstration.[86]

Governor Randolph publicly retracted some of his more violent expressions three days later,[87] but considerable damage to his popularity had already been done. Friends were distressed by his intemperate behavior, and some of them, like David Campbell, turned against him. "We view the state as degraded in his conduct," wrote the colonel's former second-in-command, who also hinted that the governor was often intoxicated.[88] Men like Joseph Cabell were not yet ready to abandon the man they had three times helped to put in the governor's chair, but Cabell lamented the style of Randolph's rebuttals and felt that his acrimonious language had obscured the real issues at stake. Fearing that a continuance of hostilities would harm the university, he urged Jefferson to try to restrain his son-in-law's zeal in the future, although he himself had already dissuaded Tom from sending any more letters on the subject to the newspapers.[89]

Martha put the best interpretation she could on her husband's actions. She wholeheartedly endorsed his motives, but she admitted that he had shown a regrettable amount of "warmth" in the dispute.[90] Jefferson made no direct allusion to the affair at the time, but less than three weeks after the quarrel reached its height, he pointedly assured his son-in-law of his continued "affection and respect." [91] Swayed by these moderating influences, Tom abandoned his open warfare against the council, but he apparently made no effort to compromise his private differences with that body.

85 Richmond *Compiler*, December 21, 1821.
86 Richmond *Enquirer*, December 22, 1821.
87 Wilson J. Cary to Virginia Cary, December 25, 1821, in Carr–Cary Papers.
88 David Campbell to Maria Campbell, January 1, 1822, in David Campbell Papers.
89 Joseph C. Cabell to Jefferson, January 3, 1822, in Jefferson Papers, Alderman Library, University of Virginia.
90 Martha Randolph to Nicholas P. Trist, January 8, 1822, in Trist Papers, University of North Carolina Library.
91 Jefferson to T. M. Randolph, Jr., January 6, 1822, in Jefferson Papers, Alderman Library, University of Virginia.

Meanwhile he was making a belated but determined effort to enlist the support of individual members of the legislature. Conscious of the need for allies in his dispute with the council, he seems also to have become aware of a growing opposition to the university in the General Assembly.[92] So the reticent governor, who previously had lived almost as a recluse, now began to entertain delegates and senators in weekly parties at the executive mansion.

Every Saturday night during the session of 1821–22, a young kinsman reported, he invited "a score of savages from the west" to dine with him. His niece Harriet was spending the winter with him, as were his daughters Virginia and Cornelia, and they began protesting against "these rowdies" from the mountain counties. "Uncle Tom" gracefully yielded to their petition "that the company be varied a little" and let the girls draw up "a list of fourteen." The governor approved, and they "had a very genteel party" at which only "the cream of the legislature" were present. The respite, however, was a brief one, and the next Saturday the company was made up of "savages" from the Dismal Swamp counties.[93] After that the young hostesses resigned themselves to the situation and made no more efforts to influence his choice of guests.

If the newly generated hospitality was designed to win him support in the Assembly, Tom's experiment was a failure so far as the interests of the university were concerned. The opposition against that studentless institution, far from being checked, continued to grow, and the Assembly made unmistakably clear its reluctance to appropriate further public funds for Jefferson's "academical village." The opposition of the clergy was one factor in this hostility,[94] but the slow rate of progress being made at Charlottesville must have provoked the more impatient members of the legislature. By the end of 1821 only six of the proposed ten pavilions had been completed, and work on the remaining buildings was behind schedule. Not a professor had been engaged; not a student had been matriculated.[95] With so little to show after almost three years of public support, the "county interest" had become "much stronger than the academy,"

92 Randolph, Jr., to Jefferson, January 3, 1822, in Jefferson Papers, Library of Congress.

93 Harriet Randolph to Jane Hollins Randolph, February 1, 1822, in Edgehill-Randolph Papers.

94 Joseph C. Cabell to Jefferson, January 21, 1822, in Campbell Deposit, Alderman Library, University of Virginia.

95 Bruce, *History of the University of Virginia*, I, 251.

and many delegates had come to the conclusion that the proceeds from the Literary Fund could be used for other purposes.[96]

A prime reason for failure during the session, however, was the disappointment of the governor's hopes concerning the interest due Virginia from the federal government. He had counted heavily on a large sum from that source and had relied on using this sum, which he had estimated at $30,000, to liquidate the university's debt.[97] Late in January he impatiently urged Cary Selden, the Commonwealth's agent in Washington, to secure an early settlement of the claim,[98] and he seems to have expected prompt and favorable action. More than a month passed before Selden reported, and the news he brought was discouraging, for it revealed that the general government was unwilling to pay more than $6,000 in interest on Virginia's war claims.[99] When a final adjustment was made and when Selden's commission had been deducted, the Commonwealth received only $5,692.93.[100] The governor had to content himself with that pittance and with an additional loan from the Literary Board.[101] Construction was thus enabled to go forward, but the institution's future was still clouded by uncertainty.

Once the Assembly had adjourned, the governor apparently lost most of his interest in public affairs. He found time that spring to consider other things, among them the most efficient way of harnessing a horse to a threshing machine. This result could be achieved, he decided, "by leaving the body unconfined from the shoulders hindward & allowing him to move in perpetually shifting tangents to the circle," and he prepared a model to demonstrate his ideas.[102] He obviously was looking forward to the day when he could devote all of his attention to such matters. He still managed to pay fairly frequent visits to Albemarle, and made no secret of the

96 T. M. Randolph, Jr., to Jefferson, January 3, 1822, in Jefferson Papers, Library of Congress.

97 Bruce, *History of the University of Virginia*, I, 300–301. See also T. M. Randolph, Jr., to Joseph C. Cabell, January 31, 1822, in Randolph Papers, Duke University Library.

98 T. M. Randolph, Jr., to Cary Selden, January 20, 1822, in Executive Letter Book (1816–22), Archives Division, Virginia State Library.

99 T. M. Randolph, Jr., to Speaker of the House of Delegates, February 28, 1822, *ibid.*

100 T. M. Randolph, Jr., to Cary Selden, April 21, 1822, *ibid.*

101 Jefferson to T. M. Randolph, Jr., January 31, 1822, in Jefferson Papers, Library of Congress.

102 T. M. Randolph, Jr., to J. H. Cocke, April 22, 1822, manuscript copy by N. F. Cabell, in Cabell Papers.

fact that Richmond was an increasingly irksome place. He spent several days with his family in September and then made his usual departure "even more unwillingly than usual." [103] Additional incentive to resume his rural activities must have come the next month, when he learned that the Albemarle Agricultural Society, meeting on October 7, had paid tribute to him for the introduction of horizontal plowing into the county and voted him a silver plate.[104]

Then, with less than a month of his term remaining, he again became embroiled with the council. This time Jefferson had innocently furnished ammunition to his opponents. Councillor John Campbell had written to the patriarch of Monticello, seeking documented information on certain events that had taken place during the latter's own governorship. In his reply Jefferson had stated that he had retained no papers on this subject, since he had considered that the pertinent documents "belonged to the records of the Council." [105] Campbell was quick to show this communication to his fellow councillors and then to the governor. The latter, feeling his own reputation was at stake "at this most critical juncture of circumstances," asked his father-in-law somewhat testily for an explanation, complaining that Jefferson's letter to Campbell had furnished the council with "a great triumph," as it had recognized that group "as a Body distinct from and independent of the Governor." He felt that all of his efforts to maintain the opposite point of view had been undermined, and he was frankly bewildered and upset by Jefferson's attitude. But he was even more resentful of the use to which the council had put his father-in-law's letter. All of the aggravations of the past three years were still vividly fresh in his mind, and his protest to Jefferson ended on a note of anguish. "For my part," he cried, "I could flee to the grave . . . to escape such hatefull sophistry & such unprincipled conduct and opinions as I have been compelled so long to witness and hear." [106]

The tired old man at Monticello, ever ready to mollify his angry son-in-law, chose to disregard the more extreme statements, and he addressed himself to the original point in dispute. As governor, said

103 Virginia Randolph to Nicholas P. Trist, September 17, 1822, in Trist Papers, Library of Congress.

104 True (ed.), "Minute Book of the Agricultural Society of Albemarle," 299.

105 John Campbell to Jefferson, November 10, 1822, in Jefferson Papers, Library of Congress; Jefferson to Campbell, November –, 1822, *ibid.*

106 T. M. Randolph, Jr., to Jefferson, November 21, 1822, *ibid.*

Jefferson, he had always exercised his own judgment as to whether a letter to himself was official or personal, and he had always retained communications in the latter category as part of his own papers. However, he did not neglect to strike a soothing note of sympathy. Perhaps remembering the relief with which he had laid down his own public burdens, the retired veteran expressed delight that Tom would soon exchange "official troubles and jealousies for family love, peace, and comfort."[107] The older man was undoubtedly sincere in wanting his son-in-law home again, but he must also have been relieved that the pugnacious governor's term was drawing to a close.

And indeed there were signs that Randolph meant to leave office in an atmosphere of geniality and good will. When the legislature convened on December 2, Senator David Campbell decided to pay a last call on his old commander. Stopping at the Governor's House that morning, he found Thomas in an unusually cheerful mood.[108] Two hours later Campbell and his fellow legislators gathered to hear a reading of the governor's message, and the reasons for his good humor soon became apparent. Prolix and rambling, much of the address was above reproach. There was an appeal for more research into the causes of "autumnal disease;" there were cautiously optimistic reports on the progress of the James River Canal and of the University; there was a warm tribute to the militia, "an old companion and devoted friend." Once these topics were disposed of, he proceeded to repeat most of his previous complaints against the council and to mention some new onces. Its obstructionist members had refused, for example, to pay for sixty dollars worth of powder discharged by an artillery company the previous Fourth of July. He referred to the charge that he wished to change the executive department, declaring that the charge was unjust. "Outcry against innovation is an old way of disguising and perpetuating encroachments," he proclaimed, and then proceeded to catalogue other encroachments. Having thus exhausted the subject, he closed with a vindication of his own conduct:

My enthusiasm may have been excessive, my zeal perhaps indiscreet, but it is manifest from my age and the narrow views to which I am necessarily confined by the circumstance of my situation in private

107 Jefferson to Randolph, Jr., November 24, 1822, *ibid.*

108 David Campbell to Maria Campbell, December 3, 1822, in David Campbell Papers.

life, that I could not have been influenced by any selfish motive whatever. . . . My efforts have been the best that my powers could afford and I trust the ends of those who sent me forth have been sufficiently answered.[109]

It seems, however, that neither Thomas Mann Randolph nor those who sent him forth could have been satisfied with the record he had made. Certainly defects of temperament had impaired his usefulness and had indeed reduced his capacity for accomplishment. Although he had worked loyally and diligently for the university and for other useful projects, his effectiveness had been curtailed by quarrels with the council and the Literary Board and by the tactics he had employed in waging war against them. While his attempt to increase the power of the governor was laudable, the intemperate violence with which he had sought that end destroyed any chances that might have existed for strenghtening the executive in his own time.

Although he may have been influenced to some degree by "love of posterity," as John Campbell suggested, it is more likely that he was swayed by pride and by resentment of the inferior status of his position. Virginians of his day expected their governors to be figureheads, and Randolph was not temperamentally fitted for that role. It is by no means certain that he would have functioned more effectively and with less friction if he had been able to perform his executive duties in a different constitutional atmosphere, or that he would not have quarreled just as vociferously with the General Assembly, had there been no council to question his activities and so attract his animosity. Even though the very nature of the governorship in his day would have vexed and angered any man of pride and independence, other such men understood the situation and did not expose themselves to humiliation. Colonel Randolph did so, not once but three times, and his refusal to accept the consequences led him into the campaign of recriminations that continued until his last week in office.

Nine days after the last volley in this campaign, his final term as governor expired. On December 12 James Pleasants, Jr., of Goochland County, succeeded him, and the Albemarlian was free at last to escape "to Botany, Poetry, and the fields." Once his official connection with the government had ended, however, he showed no inclination to leave Richmond, and he lingered there for almost two

109 Richmond *Enquirer*, December 3, 1822.

weeks longer; not until December 23 did he go home.[110] Martha, sensing his need for "Peace and Quietness," prepared one of the "skylight rooms" at Monticello for him,[111] and there he attempted to settle down again to the routines of country life.

For a brief while, at least, the change appeared to stimulate him, and he began the new year in a mood of unusual optimism. He was full of hopes for the future, spoke of making "great profits at Varina," and generally seemed to be in "very good spirits." [112] For the next few months he spent most of his time at Monticello, looking after his property at nearby Edgehill and leaving there only for occasional trips to Varina. Except for occasional rheumatism, his health was good,[113] and his burden of debt, although no lighter, seemed to rest less heavily on his shoulders. However, he was not, completely content with the life of a private citizen and, for all of his earlier disillusionment, had not abandoned interest in public affairs nor lost his taste for public office. That spring he offered himself as a candidate for one of the county's two seats in the House of Delegates, and he and his old friend William Fitzhugh Gordon were easily elected.[114]

Perhaps he sought an opportunity to redeem his failure in the governorship; perhaps he was inspired by a desire to further the cause of the university, for that cause then needed every supporter it could get. All ten pavilions and most of the dormitories had been completed,[115] but work had not yet begun on the Rotunda, which was to house the library and serve as the intellectual heart of the academic community. Furthermore, the institution's debt still acted as a brake on all development. Indeed, friends of the university had begun to fear that the "orient beam which was to enlighten our state & bring back her departed glories" would prove "an *ignis fatuas* only." [116]

At any rate, his election to the General Assembly, so soon after

110 David Campbell to Maria Campbell, December 22, 1822, in David Campbell Papers.

111 Mrs. Elizabeth Trist to Nicholas P. Trist, December 23, 1822, in Trist Papers, Library of Congress.

112 Wilson J. Cary to Virginia Cary, January 2, 1823, in Carr–Cary Papers.

113 Virgnia Randolph to Nicholas P. Trist, May 13, 1823, in Trist Papers, Library of Congress.

114 Richmond *Enquirer*, April 11, 1823.

115 Bruce, *History of the University of Virginia*, I, 251.

116 Dabney Carr to Peter Minor, February 1, 1823, in Watson Papers, Alderman Library, University of Virginia.

his noisy and unseemly exit from the governorship, must have given Thomas both encouragement and incentive. In choosing him to represent them in the legislature, the freeholders of Albemarle County gave him another chance to show that he had political ability, another chance to work for cherished measures, another chance to prove himself worthy of his heritage and his connections.

CHAPTER X

"*My Ruin Is Inevitable*"

WHILE AWAITING THE reassembling of the legislature, the new delegate from Albemarle busied himself with his own affairs. The care of his farms and the demands of his creditors engaged most of his time and attention throughout the summer and fall of 1823, as he attempted to recover the ground lost during the three years of his governorship. Debt continued to be his most pressing problem, and late in October he made a trip to New York in an effort to find financial aid. With him he took a letter of introduction from his father-in-law to Henry Remsen, a merchant of that city who had been chief clerk of the State Department during Jefferson's tenure there.[1] Thomas remained in New York for more than a month seeking to borrow money on Varina, but he succeeded in obtaining only temporary relief. Nonetheless, he was duly appreciative of Remsen's sympathetic interest, and left New York with renewed confidence and determinations. Still "quite a robust man and a very experienced farmer," he had hopes that he might yet succeed through renewed toil and the careful application of the best agricultural techniques.[2]

It was in this mood that he returned to Virginia late in November. Travelling by ship from New York, he went at once from Norfolk to Richmond,[3] for the session of the General Assembly was beginning. Taking lodgings at Mrs. Higginbotham's boardinghouse

1 Jefferson to Henry Remsen, October 26, 1823, in Jefferson Papers, Alderman Library, University of Virginia.

2 T. M. Randolph, Jr., to Henry Remsen, December 3, 1823, in Hench Collection.

3 Virginia Randolph to Nicholas P. Trist, December 6, 1823, in Trist Papers, Library of Congress.

on Main Street, he was soon engaged in conferences with Joseph C. Cabell and William Fitzhugh Gordon at the nearby Eagle Tavern.[4]

On December 2 he took his seat and was appointed to three committees, all of dealing with subjects within his field of interest and concerning which he had considerable knowledge. As a member of the Committee on Schools and Colleges, he would be in a strategic position to advance the welfare of the still unfinished "academical village" at Charlottesville; as a member of the Committee on Roads and Internal Navigation, he would have an opportunity to promote the interests of the James River Canal; and as chairman of the Committee to Examine the Penitentiary, he would be able to apply some of his ideas on penal reform.[5]

He had lost none of his enthusiasm for the university, and he faced his assignment with enthusiasm and confidence. Joseph Cabell, remembering Randolph's previous efforts and enthusiasm, may have had some reservations about the latter's tact, but he was also aware that he came as close as any member of the Assembly to being the founder's representative. From the beginning, therefore, he resolved to keep his friend informed on all developments and to "consult with him on everything."[6]

Randolph made a good beginning, and by the end of the first week of the session, so the loyal William Fitzhugh Gordon reported, he was "making the true impression which his science, intelligence, and patriotism should always command."[7] Thomas was particularly active that session in the campaign to secure additional funds for the university. Although a loan of $60,000 had been obtained the previous session for the completion of the Rotunda, no money had yet been provided to purchase books and scientific apparatus. The Assembly had already approved a bill liquidating the institution's debt to the Commonwealth, and Cabell hesitated to request further appropriations. He and his followers, therefore, decided to ask for the bonus of $50,000 which the Farmer's Bank of Virginia had agreed to pay into the state treasury for a new

4 Joseph C. Cabell to Jefferson, December 3, 1823, in Jefferson Papers, Alderman Library, University of Virginia.

5 *Journal of the House of Delegates . . . 1823* (Richmond, 1823), 13.

6 Joseph C. Cabell to Jefferson, December 3, 1823, in Jefferson Papers, Alderman Library, University of Virginia.

7 William Fitzhugh Gordon to Mrs. Gordon, December 7, 1823, in Gordon, *William Fitzhugh Gordon*, 70.

charter. While the senator from Nelson County led the fight in the upper house, Randolph and Gordon were "breasting the storm below." This proposal passed the House of Delegates but was defeated in the Senate, where it was decided to allot the bonus to the Improvement Fund instead.[8]

The bill rechartering the Farmer's Bank was then returned to the House of Delegates for its approval of the Senate's amendment, and, in the ensuing debate, delegate Randolph made a spirited but unsuccessful attempt to regain the bonus for the university. He reminded his fellow legislators that the university would need a superior library and the best scientific apparatus available if it were to fulfill its purpose, and he appealed to them to provide the requisite funds at once. Both Jefferson and Madison, he pointed out, were admirably qualified to select books and equipment, but they could not be expected to live much longer. Despite his efforts, the House adopted the Senate amendment,[9] and except for Randolph and Gordon, even the Piedmont delegates voted for internal improvements. The two men from Albemarle, however, had done everything that Cabell had "expected of them." [10]

Randolph also proved himself still a friend of the James River Canal, when its interests did not conflict with those of the university. The canal was still far from completion, and critics like Joseph S. Watkins of Goochland County had protested against further state aid. But Randolph argued for a continuance of public support of the project, and on February 21 he spoke in favor of a proposed $40,000-loan. A majority of the delegates agreed, and the loan was approved.[11]

Meanwhile he had played an even more active role in the deliberations of the penitentiary committee. This group was principally engaged in the preparation of concrete proposals for the construction and government of a new state prison to replace the one that had burned the previous summer. When the committee submitted its report to the House on February 3, 1824, many of the changes it recommended were similar to those that former Gover-

8 Joseph C. Cabell to Jefferson, February 19, 1823, in Jefferson Papers, Alderman Library, University of Virginia; Bruce, *History of the University of Virginia,* I, 303–307; Carol Tanner, "Joseph C. Cabell, 1778–1856" (Ph.D. dissertation, University of Virginia, 1948), 160–62.

9 *Journal of the House of Delegates . . . 1823,* pp. 194–97; Richmond *Enquirer,* March 2, 1824.

10 Joseph C. Cabell to Jefferson, March 7, 1824, in Jefferson Papers, Alderman Library, University of Virginia.

11 Richmond *Enquirer,* February 24 and March 9, 1824.

nor Randolph had previously suggested. Separate cells for each convict were requested, and the segregation of the younger prisoners from the older ones was advised to protect the former from "instruction in the craft of roguery." The committee also recommended that four workshops be provided, so that the inmates could engage in useful crafts and, at the same time, defray the cost of their upkeep. It was further suggested that corporal punishment be abolished and that refractory prisoners be thereafter assigned to heavy physical labor instead of being disciplined by the lash. A bill incorporating most of these proposals was subsequently passed by both houses.[12]

Besides exerting himself in committee work, Tom took the floor to renew his vendetta with the council. The Constitution provided that two members of that group be removed by the Assembly every three years and that two new men be elected. On January 8, therefore, the names of William Fitzhugh Pendleton, William Robertson, and William Selden were nominated for elimination. Each of them had been on the council during Randolph's last term as governor, and two of them, Robertson and Selden, had signed the manifesto of December 19, 1821, against him. Pendleton had been the only member who had failed to endorse that hostile petition, and Tom was as grateful to him as he was vindictive toward the other two. He accordingly recommended Pendleton's retention in warm and friendly tones, criticizing Robertson and Selden with vigor and passion.[13] In spite of the intemperate nature of his remarks, he won enough support in the House to secure the removal of his enemies and to condemn his friend to another year of service on the despised "plural branch."[14]

Not only councillors but also presidential candidates were scrutinized during the course of the legislative session, for 1824 was an election year. Delegate Randolph, like most of his fellow lawmakers, was a Republican, and he accordingly belonged to the party's caucus in the Assembly. The principal activity of that unofficial and extralegal group, of which there were counterparts in other states, was the nomination of presidential and congressional candidates.

By 1824 this system was coming under increasingly heavy attack.

12 *Journal of the House of Delegates . . . 1823*, pp. 153–57; *Acts of the Assembly . . .* (Richmond, 1824), 15–21.

13 Richmond *Enquirer*, January 10, 1824. Reports of debates which are given in this newspaper are much more detailed than those given in the official *Journals*, which are often confined to a mere calendar of the proceedings.

14 *Journal of the House of Delegates . . . 1823*, p. 111.

Early in the session the Assembly had received a copy of the "Tennessee Resolutions," which proposed that the caucuses be abandoned and that presidential candidates be nominated by national conventions. Thomas Randolph was appointed to a committee, headed by John Tyler of Charles City County, to consider this proposal, which was palpably designed to further the aspirations of Tennessee's favorite son General Andrew Jackson.[15] The committee recommended that the "Tennessee Resolutions" be rejected,[16] with Tyler offering a resolution on the floor that the caucus system be positively endorsed, but this was defeated by a narrow margin. Although Tom did not take part in the debate on Tyler's proposal, he was one of those voting against it.[17]

He was still a member of the Republican caucus, however, and met with that group on February 21, 1824, when it chose a ticket for the coming election. He was one of the 139 members who voted to support William Harris Crawford of Georgia, then Secretary of the Treasury in President Monroe's cabinet. The fact that Crawford had recently had a paralytic stroke which left him incapacitated did not deter his supporters in Virginia or elsewhere. The remaining 24 votes were divided among John Quincy Adams, Nathaniel Macon, Andrew Jackson, and Henry Clay. Four days later Randolph was selected as the presidential elector for his Congressional district on the Georgian's ticket, defeating his former enemy "Old Davy" Garland for the position.[18]

Conscious that he must otherwise "sink to the earth," he began seeking more remunerative employment than that afforded him as a gentleman farmer. Ambition and wishful thinking revealed themselves in his hope that he might be chosen as a successor to John Taylor, when and if that statesman-author resigned from the United States Senate, and in his fleeting notion to seek an appointment to the faculty of the university.[19]

Alluring as those prospects were, he did not press either, and finally set his sights on nothing less than the postmastership of

15 *Ibid.*, 55.
16 *Ibid.*, 74–76.
17 Richmond *Enquirer*, January 1, 1824.
18 *Ibid.*, February 24, 1824, February 26, 1824; Joseph C. Cabell to Jefferson, March 17, 1824, in Jefferson Papers, Alderman Library, University of Virginia.
19 T. M. Randolph, Jr., to Henry Remsen, February 16, 1824, in Miscellaneous Manuscripts, Alderman Library, University of Virginia.

Richmond, with its salary of $2,000 per year. The venerable William Foushee, then the postmaster, was "very near his end" by February, 1824, and Tom saw no reason why he could not be appointed to succeed him. He sought recommendations not only from Virginia's representatives in Congress but also from President Monroe himself. As if to make assurance even more certain, he also asked Henry Remsen to use his not inconsiderable influence with the Chief Executive and to persuade other New York merchants to do the same.[20]

The lobbying was unsuccessful, however, and although the coveted postal appointment went to an ex-governor of Virginia, it was Randolph's predecessor, James Patton Preston of Montgomery County and Richmond, who was so honored.[21] There was nothing for the colonel to do but return to Albemarle and run for reelection. William Fitzhugh Gordon was also a candidate, as was Dr. Charles Cocke, a strong supporter of Henry Clay for the presidency. Gordon led the field easily with 369 votes, while Randolph barely edged out Cocke for the county's second seat in the House, gaining 246 to the other's 227.[22] Only "the exertions of his friends in canvassing" had saved him from defeat, and Francis Gilmer's brother, Thomas, predicted that Randolph "could not be elected again if there was the slightest opposition." [23]

Tom's near defeat was a clear demonstration that he had become unpopular in his adopted county. Undoubtedly his irascible temper and irresponsible behavior had contributed to this decline, but he soon proceeded to alienate his constituents further by espousing a cause that was anathema to many of them. By the late spring of 1824 he had joined the movement for a constitutional convention. Virginia's western counties, most of them larger and containing more white inhabitants than the ones in the Tidewater, had long resented the domination of the state by the eastern planters, and they wanted the distribution of Assembly seats to be based on the free white population rather than on a total that included slaves. The westerners, together with a few easterners, also wished the freehold qualification for voting abolished, but the Tidewater jealously

20 Randolph, Jr. to Remsen, February 16, 1824, *ibid.*

21 "James Patton Preston," in Louise Catterall (ed.), *Richmond Portraits* (Richmond, 1949), 162.

22 Richmond *Enquirer*, April 13, 1824.

23 Thomas Walker Gilmer to Francis Walker Gilmer, April 6, 1824, in Watson Papers, Alderman Library, University of Virginia.

guarded the power it retained by virtue of this and other inequalities. As recently as 1821 Colonel Randolph himself had declared that there was no serious need for an extension of the suffrage,[24] but, by the end of his first term in the House of Delegates, he had recognized that need, and accordingly, began to work actively for its satisfaction.

A group of his friends and neighbors met at Charlottesville on April 30, 1824, to discuss the issue of constitutional reform, and he appeared and spoke warmly in favor of a convention.[25] It was decided to hold a poll at the courthouse, so that all citizens of the county could express their sentiments. Adult white males who lacked the property qualifications for participation in regular elections were allowed to vote in this poll, but their ballots were counted separately. As might have been expected, the latter group supported the convention, but they favored it by a majority of barely more than 3 to 2, while the freeholders rejected it by a far wider margin. The convention proposal was defeated by a vote of 222 to 182.[26] The subject was then temporarily dropped, but Randolph did not cease to agitate for reform.

Meanwhile he had found a temporary solution to his financial problems by transferring them to his oldest son Jefferson Randolph. The latter, now managing Jefferson's property, agreed to assume his father's various debts, which amounted to more than $23,000. In return the senior Randolph gave a deed of trust for both Varina and Edgehill, together with the forty-nine slaves on those estates. Francis Walker Gilmer and Valentine W. Southall, both of Charlottesville, were named trustees and were authorized to sell any part of the property necessary to discharge the obligation to Jefferson Randolph.[27]

Not anticipating the tragic contretemps of this agreement, Thomas relaxed that spring by preparing two papers for presentation to the Albemarle Agricultural Society. One was devoted to the ubiquitous horse nettle, a plant of which the author had both botanical knowledge and practical experience. His paper recounted that a flock of sheep turned loose in his fields when the flowers of

24 *Journal of the House of Delegates . . . 1821*, p. 6.

25 Richmond *Enquirer*, May 14, 1824.

26 Ira Garrett to Joseph C. Cabell, March 7, 1825, in Cabell Papers. See also Richmond *Enquirer*, May 14, 1824.

27 Deed of Trust, T. M. Randolph, Jr., to V. W. Southall & F. W. Gilmer, April 1, 1824, in Albemarle County Deed Book No. 24, pp. 268–70.

that hardy pest first showed themselves had done their work so thoroughly that "not a trace of the mischief" remained.[28] His other contribution concerned vetch, a bean-like, highly nutritious plant, which he believed might become "a valuable acquisition to the husbandry of an elevated, uneven, and stony country." His researches, he said, demonstrated that botanical studies might be practically applied and render "the present race of men in Virginia healthier and longer-lived than the last." [29] Both of these papers were found so interesting and instructive that the Society ordered them to be printed.[30]

Thomas Mann Randolph continued to live at Monticello, but he was coming to feel increasingly ill at ease there. He showed little inclination to join in company conversation, and there were times when he became so irritable that he refused to speak to Jefferson or to contribute even a word to family discussions.[31]

Meanwhile he continued to enjoy the qualified esteem of many of his fellow citizens. When a meeting was held in Charlottesville on September 20, 1824, to discuss the forthcoming visit of the Marquis de Lafayette, Tom was chosen to act as chairman. He was also named to the standing committee which was appointed at the time to arrange a proper reception for the distinguished Frenchman. As one who admired and respected Lafayette for "the eventful philanthropy" of his life,[32] Tom was undoubtedly eager and willing to serve, but he was also pleased at the chance to participate in the work of a group which included the most distinguished citizens of the county. He needed every token of public esteem he could get, for he had come to believe that "life itself" was "lengthened by the physical effects of praise." [33]

As an elector for William Harris Crawford, the colonel was also involved in the presidential campaign which raged through the summer and fall of 1824. The election ended in an impasse. Andrew

28 For text of Randolph's "paper," see *American Farmer*, VI (July 8, 1826), 96.
29 *Ibid.*, 97.
30 True (ed.), "Minute Book of the Agricultural Society of Albemarle," 303–304.
31 Horace Holley to Orville L. Holley, September 6, 1824, typed copy in University of Virginia Collection, Alderman Library, University of Virginia.
32 Richmond *Enquirer*, September 28, 1824.
33 T. M. Randolph, Jr., to Francis Walker Gilmer, December 1, 1824, in Gilmer Papers, Alderman Library, University of Virginia.

Jackson of Tennessee led the field, but John Quincy Adams was close behind. Crawford ran a poor third, winning the electoral votes of only Virginia and Georgia. Since neither Jackson nor Adams had a majority, the choice of a successor to James Monroe therefore devolved upon the House of Representatives. One contender who could not be ruled entirely out of the race was Henry Clay, and Randolph seized a convenient opportunity late that fall to meet with the Kentuckian, who had been a fellow lodger at Frost's Congressional boardinghouse seventeen years before. Clay passed through Virginia late in November on his way to Washington and, as a matter of course, stopped at Monticello to pay his respects to Jefferson. Tom Randolph had already gone down to Richmond to attend the opening of the General Assembly, but he made a hurried ride back to Albemarle on the 27th, travelling "a great part of the night to hear the conversation of Henry Clay."

Whatever his reasons for exposing himself to the Kentuckian's noted charm, Thomas was not conquered. He admitted that Clay had "fine dramatic talents," but he found him surprisingly uninformed "in the statesman's science," a man of "weak judgment and principles really dangerous." Randolph disapproved equally of Clay "the advocate of commercial restriction;" of Clay "the supporter of slavery as a permanent establishment;" of Clay "the encourager of profusion in government." Indeed, when the discourse was ended, Tom professed himself unable to understand why anyone would prefer "the encourager of profusion" to Crawford or even to John Quincy Adams. As for the hero of New Orleans, Randolph hoped only that the other candidates would "certainly keep out Jackson." [34]

If the hasty trip to Albemarle had been motivated in any way by the thought that Clay might prove an acceptable substitute for Crawford, his interview was disillusioning. Tom returned to Richmond on November 28, resolved to carry out his duty to the ailing Georgian. Like his fellow electors, he rejected all suggestions that they turn to John C. Calhoun. On November 30 Virginia's twenty-four electors met at the capitol and faithfully discharged their political obligations to Crawford.[35]

The new session of the Assembly was beginning, and Randolph took part in the organization of the House. He also listened with some impatience to the message of Governor James Pleasants, which

34 *Ibid.*
35 Richmond *Enquirer,* November 30 and December 2, 1824.

he described afterwards as a mere "effusion of piety." [36] On November 30 he was chosen chairman of the penitentiary committee, and was also named to the Committee on Schools and Colleges and the Committee to Examine the Militia.[37] Before those groups settled down to their respective affairs, however, there was a matter of more pressing importance to be decided.

John Taylor of Caroline County, the senator whom Randolph had once had fleeting thoughts of replacing, was dead, and both houses of the Assembly met in joint session to choose a successor. The names of John Tyler of Charles City County and of Littleton Waller Tazewell of Norfolk Borough were placed in nomination, and Randolph threw his influence behind the latter. Tyler was backed by equally eloquent supporters, and a warm debate developed on the floor of the Assembly. John Armistead of Charles City, David Garland of Amherst, and Scervant Jones of York spoke for Tyler; Randolph, Abel P. Upshur of Accomac, and George Loyall of Norfolk Borough replied for Tazewell.

Randolph charged in his address that Senator James Barbour had come down from Washington to get Tyler elected, an accusation that Armistead vehemently denied. The "gentleman from Albemarle" then repeated the charge in even more heated tones. Near the close of the debate, David Garland struck at Tazewell directly, decrying the latter's support of Federalist measures in 1798 and 1799. Tom, returning to the attack, cried that he "would rather be like a bird in the air leaving no trace behind it than leave a trace that is only marked by its corruption." Whatever was the effect of his oratory on this occasion, he was on the winning side. Tazewell won easily, defeating Tyler by 139 to 80 votes,[38] and proceeded to Washington where he soon was opposing the policies of John Quincy Adams, who had been elected President by the House of Representatives on February 9, 1825.

Randolph's displeasure with this outcome led him to abandon his customary position as an advocate of a strong national defense. On February 12 Jones of York County had proposed that Virginia's representatives in Congress be instructed to seek federal aid for the construction of a fort on the York River. The veteran of "Camp Warranigh," who might have been expected to support such a

36 T. M. Randolph, Jr., to Francis Walker Gilmer, December 1, 1824, in Gilmer Papers, Alderman Library, University of Virginia.

37 *Journal of the House of Delegates . . . 1824* (Richmond, 1824), 9–10.

38 Richmond *Enquirer,* December 9, 1824.

proposal, balked at the idea "of going begging so soon to a New England President," even in a good cause. In a speech designed both for the economy-minded and for the enemies of John Quincy Adams, he spoke of the great expense of the proposed fortification. Jones' proposal was defeated by a wide margin, and the vulnerable York remained undefended.[39]

Randolph, in his capacity as chairman of the penitentiary committee, meanwhile recommended legislation to restore the governor's pardoning power, which had been drastically restricted at the preceding session. This effort succeeded, and the bill passed.[40] But, as in the previous session, he was most active in his endeavors on behalf of the University of Virginia, ready at last to receive students. Supporters of the College of William and Mary were proposing that the older school be moved from moribund Williamsburg to the more stimulating atmosphere of Richmond, and friends of the university feared the consequences of this relocation. Jefferson was well aware that the college might thereby become a serious competitor to his "academical villege," and he urged his cohorts to oppose the move with all the powers at their disposal.[41] Cabell, leading the fight in the Senate, showed "the old sachem's" letters on the subject to Randolph, to Gordon, and to a few other close subordinates. He also authorized Randolph to exhibit the documents to other members at his discretion.[42]

The removal bill was by then before the Committee for Schools and Colleges, and John Tyler moved that group be discharged from all further consideration of the measure. Randolph supported the motion, and during the debate which followed he declared that the funds of the college would not be sufficient to support "an institution worthy of the metropolis of this great state." [43] Despite his plea, the motion was lost, and the schools committee continued deliberations on it. On January 30 they reported it favorably to the floor of the House, where it was defeated by a vote of 112 to 88. Thomas Randolph was one of those arrayed against it.[44]

39 *Ibid.*, February 12, 1824.
40 *Ibid.*, December 31, 1824 and January 4, 11, 1825.
41 Bruce, *History of the University of Virginia*, I, 308–14; Tanner, "Joseph C. Cabell," 162–66.
42 Joseph C. Cabell to Jefferson, December 31, 1824, in Jefferson Papers, Alderman Library, University of Virginia.
43 Richmond *Enquirer*, January 18, 1825.
44 *Journal of the House of Delegates . . . 1824*, pp. 113, 142, 147.

Before the session ended, he was privileged to perform a far more congenial service for the university. The ship *Competitor* arrived in Hampton Roads the second week in February, bringing several of the British professors who had been appointed to the faculty at Charlottesville. Jefferson's son-in-law was one of those who went to City Point to welcome them to Virginia [45] and see them safely started on the road to Albemarle County.

During the same session Tom took a vigorous and enthusiastic part in the debates on the convention question. A bill authorizing the meeting of such a group was brought before the House of Delegates, and Randolph supported it with all the ability and eloquence at his command. He voted against a proposal that consideration of the bill be postponed indefinitely, as did a majority of his fellow delegates.[46] He also strenuously opposed the effort of Thomas Jefferson Stuart of Augusta County to restrict the convention's powers, arguing that the members of that body should have a free hand to amend the constitution of the Commonwealth in any way they wished. His point of view was shared by others, and the House decided to submit the convention question to the freeholders of Virginia. If a majority approved, a convention of unlimited powers would be held.[47]

He was less successful in his suggestion that all free white males over twenty-one be permitted to vote in this referendum.[48] That effort failed, and Thomas, who avowed himself the representative of all the people in his constituency,[49] made another proposal. On February 5 he recommended that separate poll books be opened in each county for freeholders and for non-freeholders—the same device that had been used in Albemarle County the previous summer—but that both groups of votes be counted toward the result. During the debate which ensued, his listeners were warned of riots at the polls if the interests of the disenfranchised were disregarded, but his proposal was beaten by the narrow margin of seven votes.[50]

The convention bill, containing the orthodox suffrage restrictions,

45 T. M. Randolph, Jr., to Nicholas P. Trist, February 13, 1825, in Trist Papers, Library of Congress.
46 *Journal of the House of Delegates . . . 1824*, p. 140.
47 Richmond *Enquirer*, February 1, 1825.
48 *Ibid.*, January 18, 1825.
49 *Ibid.*, February 1, 1825.
50 *Ibid.*, February 8, 1825.

went to the Senate, where it encountered the opposition of the conservative Joseph C. Cabell, a man as hostile to constitutional change as he was friendly to educational improvement. Due largely to his efforts, it was defeated and, with it, the hopes of those desiring a convention. Tom thereupon turned against Cabell, and the two former allies soon became badly estranged as a result of their disagreement on this crucial question.[51]

Randolph had taken a stand on the convention issue that was unpopular with many of his constituents, and he further damaged his local popularity by the position he took on internal improvements. A bill was before the House which authorized a loan of $200,000 to the James River Company, to which a "ryder" had been added increasing the tolls on tobacco. He was aware that the added charge was contrary to the interests of his tobacco-growing constituents, and voted against it. The "ryder" passed, however, and Tom, as a staunch friend of the canal project, voted for the bill in its amended form,[52] which then went to the Senate, where on Feburary 16 it was passed without change.

Meanwhile he had second thoughts on the subject, and the following day he offered a resolution that the tobacco tolls be decreased and that the loan to the company be reduced proportionately. This "extraordinary" proposal found no favor in a House that had already approved the measure, and George C. Dromgoole of Brunswick snorted that his fellow delegate was seeking to repeal a law passed only one day before. The latter replied that he had voted for the bill only because he had expected the Senate to reduce the tolls, but this explanation did him no good, and his resolution was defeated by a majority of more than two to one.[53] He felt, so he said, that he had acted as his constituents would have wanted him to, and could not understand why he was "charged with inconsistency." Subsequently, he protested that it was always his principle to support the sectional interest "until a fair compromise of all interests" was reached, and he declared that he had followed such a course in his vote on the James River bill.[54] Yet Tom's maneuvers in

51 Tanner, "Joseph C. Cabell," 225; William H. Cabell to Joseph C. Cabell, March 17, 1825, in Cabell Papers.

52 *Journal of the House of Delegates . . . 1824*, p. 175; Richmond *Enquirer*, February 17, 1825.

53 Richmond *Enquirer*, February 19, 1825.

54 T. M. Randolph, Jr., to Nicholas P. Trist, March 30, 1825, in Trist Papers, Library of Congress.

that instance indicated neither clarity of thought nor devotion to his principle, and his effort to repeal the tolls did him more harm than good in Albemarle.

The session ended on February 1, its record being, in the opinion of many, "a history of abortions." [55] Randolph returned home to face his constituents and to renew his struggle against insolvency. He was, he said, "heartily tired of everything" in Richmond,[56] but he was shortly engaged in an effort to return there. Opposition to him, already strong, had increased because of his course on the James River bill, and he was soon trying to justify his vote for higher tobacco tolls.[57] William Gordon, who was also running for reelection, constituted no threat to Randolph, but Rice W. Woods, a Charlottesville attorney who was the third candidate in the field, was in a position to challenge the unpopular incumbent.

As if his own campaign were not task enough, Tom took on the added burden of securing the defeat of Senator Joseph C. Cabell. He had become "really hostile" to his onetime ally, largely because of Cabell's opposition to a constitutional convention, and he sought to convert others to his opinion.[58] This effort to purge one of the most influential members of the legislature not only failed, but it probably ruined whatever chance Tom himself had for victory. Cabell was easily returned to the Senate, and Gordon maintained his seat in the House of Delegates. But Randolph suffered a humiliating defeat, receiving only 79 votes to the 215 cast for attorney Woods.[59] His legislative career thus came to an end, and he was not again elected to public office.

After this blow, Tom turned to fight one last battle with his creditors. His debts, now amounting to $33,500, had been assumed by Jefferson Randolph, who had been made the beneficiary of a deed of trust on Varina and Edgehill.[60] Early in 1825 Jeff decided that he must sacrifice those estates to save his own property. By

55 Richmond *Enquirer*, February 19, 1825.
56 T. M. Randolph, Jr., to Nicholas P. Trist, February 13, 1825, in Trist Papers, Library of Congress.
57 Randolph, Jr. to Trist, March 30, 1825, *ibid.*
58 William H. Cabell to Joseph C. Cabell, March 17, 1825, in Cabell Papers.
59 Richmond *Enquirer*, April 8, 1825.
60 Account of Thomas Jefferson Randolph with T. M. Randolph, Jr., July 4, 1826, in Trist Papers, Library of Congress; Albemarle County Deed Book No. 24, pp. 268–70. This deed of trust was supplementary to that given by Randolph to Jefferson Randolph for Edgehill alone in 1817, *ibid.*, No. 21, p. 506.

July, therefore, Varina had been sold to Pleasant Aitken of Petersburg,[61] and the trustees were making preparations for a similar disposition of Edgehill.

Randolph surrendered the Henrico plantation with little protest, but he was so embittered by the imminent loss of his Albemarle property that he turned against the son who was about to take possession of it from him. When the proposals for the sale became known, he convinced himself that he was being treated unfairly, protesting vehemently to the trustees that Jefferson Randolph was motivated only by "coldblooded avarice." All he sought or desired, he fumed, was to retain a few hillside acres where he could make a vineyard and from which he could take timbers for a sawmill, but his son would not agree to this proposal. He also objected to Jeff's plan to raise tobacco and breed slaves in order to pay off the family's debts.[62]

Jefferson, grieved by the quarrel that was disturbing the peace of his old age, tried to recall Tom to his responsibilities. The weary patriarch was so debt-ridden himself that he could give no material aid, but he could still offer both sympathy and good advice, and he dispensed those commodities in abundance. Recommending "a ready submission to the law" as the only course left open, he advised his son-in-law to surrender "the afflicting concerns" which had become such "sources of pain and labor" and to forget them in more congenial activity. He pleaded with him to restore himself to the society of his family, pointing out that he would need "the soothing balm of their affections" more than ever. Nor need Tom, even in retirement, "want employment for the mind," for there were always the fruits of his "varied education and the resources of books" to stimulate study and to inspire thought. If he sought "some excitement to bodily exercise," that could be found, so Jefferson advised, in agricultural experiments or, perhaps, in "some call into public service." The most important thing, he insisted, was to accept the inevitable and to become a member of the family again.[63]

But Tom, although grateful for his father-in-law's sympathy,[64] was in no mood to accept his counsel. He had declared open war

61 T. M. Randolph, Jr., to Francis Walker Gilmer, July 12, 1825, in Gilmer Papers, Alderman Library, University of Virginia.

62 Randolph, Jr. to Gilmer, June 21, 1825, *ibid.*

63 Jefferson to T. M. Randolph, Jr., July 5, 1825, in Edgehill–Randolph Papers.

64 Randolph, Jr., to Jefferson, July 8, 1825, *ibid.*

against his eldest son, and he was unwilling to consider any move that would bring him into the latter's company. Thus, he spent his days at North Milton, going to Monticello only after dark, and seeing no one there but his wife.[65] He was "broke to atoms, in mind, body, and estate," observed his young friend Francis Gilmer in June, and, after an interview with the colonel, he expressed the fear that once "turned out to roam the world, houseless and pennyless," Randolph would "rave as wildly as Lear." [66] John Randolph, himself no stranger to fits of despondency, commented from afar: "Poor TMR—I heartily pity him. . . . He has no more self-command than a child." [67]

Tom was not yet ready to quarrel with everyone around him or to press all of the earlier quarrels in which he had involved himself. Indeed, in July he even made his peace with Joseph C. Cabell, through their mutual friend, Craven Peyton. Cabell waited a few days after receiving the overture, then expressed his willingness "to give to the wind the occurrences of the winter and spring." Thus "a breach which never ought to have been open" was closed.[68] Tom, however, refused all suggestions that he become similarly reconciled with his son and creditor.

Even Jeff Randolph's support of constitutional reform did not lead to a healing of the breach between them. Indeed, this common interest led to an incident which widened the distance between them. In June, 1825, a call for a "constitutional convention" to meet in Staunton the following month had been made by a group of citizens in Loudoun County. In response to this summons, a number of Albemarlians, including Colonel Randolph and his estranged son, met on July 4 at the courthouse in Charlottesville.[69] Some of those present expressed opposition to any participation in the Staunton meeting, and the elder Randolph found himself compelled to "make

65 See note by Randolph concerning Jefferson's letter to him of July 9, 1825, published (with the letter) in the Richmond *Enquirer*, September 14, 1827. Randolph had these and other papers published in order to refute charges that he and Jefferson were estranged during the last year of the latter's life.

66 Francis Walker Gilmer to Peachy R. Gilmer, June 19, 1825, in Gilmer Papers, Virginia Historical Society; Francis W. Gilmer to John Randolph of Roanoke, June 23, 1825, in Gilmer Papers, Alderman Library, University of Virginia.

67 John Randolph to Francis Walker Gilmer, July 2, 1825, in John Randolph Papers, Library of Congress.

68 Craven Peyton to Joseph C. Cabell, July 7, 1825, in Randolph Papers, Duke University Library; Joseph C. Cabell to Peyton, July 29, 1824, *ibid.*

69 Richmond *Enquirer,* July 22, 1825.

a warm, unpremeditated, & wholly unexpected effort to save the question." In the course of his remarks, he recalled—and repeated—a political conversation he had had with Jefferson in 1798, nearly thirty years earlier. Jefferson, so the Colonel told the men sitting in the courthouse at Charlottesville, had told him, that if Federalist rule continued indefinitely, "we should then carry Virginia westward & settle down with it somewhere in the Wilderness where we could . . . perfectionnate our political system."[70] He probably meant to suggest that the west was, by Jeffersonian definition, the true seat of Republican principles and that the voice of that section should be given more attention, but he did not state the point too precisely. Nonetheless, his speech was not without effect. His audience chose to accept the invitation to the Staunton convention, and Tom Randolph was one of the four delegates chosen to represent Albemarle County. The others were Thomas Walker Gilmer, Valentine Southall, and Jefferson Randolph.[71]

Word that the elder Randolph had quoted Jefferson in his "unexpected effort" was quickly carried to Monticello, and Tom, assuming that Jeff had done the telling and fearing that the latter had misrepresented his remarks, did not even wait for Jefferson's reaction but scrawled off a long explanation of his remarks. He was never, he protested, "much in the habit" of discussing his father-in-law's opinions, "even when it was most necessary to propagate them, for the good of the Republican cause," but sometimes he was compelled to repeat "strong sayings" that had made a particularly vivid impression on his mind.

But he was most concerned with a need "to counteract the misrepresentations" which, he was convinced, had been made concerning his Charlottesville speech. Randolph felt that the truth about himself had "but seldom reached" his father-in-law "since 1815," at which time "the close alliance" between them had begun to loosen. From that point on, he fretted, they had become "more and more estranged, until at last for some considerable time there has scarcely been any intercourse at all," much less "any interchange of thought or social feeling." The distraught writer named no names, but he obviously blamed his son, whom he had come to regard as the

70 T. M. Randolph, Jr., to Jefferson, July 8, 1825, in Edgehill-Randolph Papers.

71 Richmond *Enquirer*, July 22, 1825.

author of all his misfortunes. "I am too well convinced that my ruin is inevitable," he raged, "but I am the victim of the avarice of one, encouraged . . . by the vengeance of many." [72]

Jefferson did all he could to convince Tom that those obsessions were ill-founded and to assure his son-in-law of his own continued regard. Admitting that he might have given an impression of reserve, the statesman attributed such behavior to increasing deafness. Jefferson also denied that any individual had expressed hostile opinions in his presence. Again he urged Tom to "return & become a member of the family" in spirit as well as in body; again he pleaded with him not "to continue in solitude brooding over . . . misfortunes and encouraging their ravages "on mind and body." [73] But, unwilling to be consoled or cajoled, Randolph held to the course he had set for himself. He was still convinced that he was being treated "with great rancor as well as the utmost rigor" by his son, and found it impossible, he replied, to "suppress feelings & restrain resentment." [74]

Self-discipline became even more difficult after he learned the proposed terms of the sale of Edgehill, which had been set for August 8. He objected to the provision that the slaves be sold apart from the land, charging that such a procedure would result in the loss of his crop. For the same reason, he protested the provision wherein the purchaser was promised immediate possession. Above all he was angered by the decision of the trustees to sell the farm by parcels rather than as a unit. The lines which they had drawn ignored topography and, cutting through his "tillage beds of 32 years standing," ran "transversely, diagonally, and with every degree of obliquity, so as to disfigure the estate and diminish its value." He was positive that this had been done deliberately so that his son could acquire the land for "almost nothing." He tried, therefore, to persuade the trustees to allow the prospective buyer of Edgehill to give notes payable at the end of 1825, at which time, he argued, the property could be disposed of without loss.[75] When this

72 T. M. Randolph, Jr., to Jefferson, July 8, 1825, in Edgehill–Randolph Papers.

73 Jefferson to Randolph, Jr., July 9, 1825, *ibid.*

74 T. M. Randolph, Jr., to Francis Walker Gilmer, July 9 and 12, 1825, in Gilmer Papers, Alderman Library, University of Virginia.

75 Randolph, Jr. to Gilmer, July 9, 1825, *ibid.;* Randolph, Jr. to Creed Taylor, October 29, 1825, in Creed Taylor Papers.

failed, he obtained an injunction from Virginia's Superior Court of Chancery, and the sale was delayed until the fall.[76]

Meanwhile he found other activities to occupy him. The "constitutional convention" met in Staunton on July 25, and Randolph was present as a delegate from Albemarle. Lynchburg, Richmond, and a few Tidewater and Piedmont localities were represented at Staunton, but most of those present came from the west of the Blue Ridge. A committee on resolutions was organized the first day, and Thomas Mann Randolph was chosen as Albemarle's representative on that group.[77] The committee submitted its report on July 27 and recommended changes which had been suggested many times before by proponents of reform. Representation in the General Assembly should be reapportioned; the Council of State should be abolished; the suffrage should be extended; and provision for easier amendment of the Virginia Constitution should be made. These recommendations, and various other resolutions made from the floor, were then referred to a subcommittee of seven, one of whom was the elder Randolph.[78]

The debate that followed demonstrated that "no 2 friends of change" could "agree about the supposed defects" of Virginia's organic law.[79] In that discussion, Randolph took issue with the proposal, contained in the report of the resolutions committee, that the right to vote be extended only to those "furnishing sufficient evidence of permanent common interest" in their communities. Perhaps conscious that he was soon likely to be propertyless and therefore voteless, he appealed to the convention to endorse the principle of free white male suffrage, but his argument was not successful.[80] He also failed to persuade his colleagues that their demand for a convention should be made in an address to the people rather than in a memorial to the legislature. Nonetheless, he was appointed to the committee named to draw up the memorial.[81] That document was completed by July 30, and the Staunton meeting, its business done, adjourned. Despite the hopes and efforts of its

76 John Forbes to Jefferson, July 22, 1825, in Jefferson Papers, Massachusetts Historical Society; Hetty Carr to Dabney S. Carr, Jr., August 7, 1825, in Carr–Cary Papers.
77 Richmond *Enquirer*, August 2, 1825.
78 *Ibid.*, August 2 and 5, 1825.
79 *Ibid.*, August 9, 1825.
80 *Ibid.*, August 11, 1825.
81 *Ibid.*, August 5, 1825.

members, the long-desired changes had not been brought substantially closer to reality, and the convention they sought did not meet for another four years.

Randolph had done all that he could at this time to advance the cause of reform, and he returned to Albemarle to resume the hopeless struggle for Edgehill. By delaying the sale of that farm until fall, he had not rendered the final outcome any less inevitable, and, in winning a respite for himself, he had only worsened the predicament of Jefferson Randolph. That harried young man, who was still obligated to pay off the colonel's debts, was forced to advertise his own property to satisfy his father's creditors.[82] The senior Randolph had practically ceased going to Monticello, and he was significantly absent when the Marquis de Lafayette was entertained there on August 20.[83] He seldom saw Jefferson, although on one occasion late in 1825 he and his father-in-law conversed at some length on presidential politics and the relative merits of John Quincy Adams and Andrew Jackson, both of whom were expected to be candidates in 1828. As Randolph recalled this discussion two years later, the old statesman expressed misgivings concerning Adams' policies and indicated that Jackson would be his choice in the next election.[84]

Arrangements for the sale of Edgehill had gone forward, and Tom, who previously had regarded the trustees as impartial "arbiters and umpires," became convinced that they, and particularly Gilmer, were leagued against him.[85] He made a personal attempt to sell the property, but the farm was finally put up for public sale on January 6, 1826, with George Eskridge, marshal of the Superior Court of Chancery, in charge of the proceedings.

First, the Edgehill Negroes, including some of "the best trained farm servants anywhere to be found" and "many valuable tradesmen" were sold for cash in Charlottesville. Then the farm itself, containing 1,952.5 acres and located "in the healthiest climate of the whole earth, sheltered by the mountains from the westerly winds of winter, and enjoying the cool breezes invariably descending from wooded crests in summer nights," was put on the block. The

82 Hetty Carr to Dabney S. Carr, Jr., August 7, 1825, in Carr–Cary Papers.
83 Richmond *Enquirer,* September 6, 1825.
84 Note by T. M. Randolph, Jr., in Richmond *Enquirer,* August 24, 1827.
85 T. M. Randolph, Jr., to Francis Walker Gilmer, July 9, 1825, in Gilmer Papers, Alderman Library, University of Virginia; Randolph, Jr. to Creed Taylor, October 29, 1825, in Creed Taylor Papers.

property had been divided into five nearly equal parts, a device that Jeff had recommended the previous July, and each parcel was disposed of separately.[86] As the elder Randolph had long foreseen, his son succeeded in obtaining the whole estate. The personal property brought $5,000, and the farm was disposed of for $23,000. The new owner, according to terms previously agreed upon, was given three years to pay.[87]

Thus Thomas Mann Randolph lost the farm which had inspired him to stimulating activity. Although it had caused him such anguish and tribulation, of all his estates, it had been the one he cherished most deeply, and no man every surrendered a favorite mistress more unwillingly. When he had assumed its care, it had been "in a ruinous state," but he had "not only reclaimed it but made it the most beautiful in the state." [88] He yielded it, even as he had acquired it, in an atmosphere of family dissension and strife. If deeper animosities had been aroused by the transfer of 1826 than by that of 1792, so the plight of the yielder was far graver when Edgehill passed, for the second time, from a reluctant father to an importunate son. The master of Tuckahoe had still been a man of considerable possessions when he surrendered his Albemarle farm to Jefferson's son-in-law, but the bankrupt colonel had nothing left but his library and his five-room house at North Milton, which his creditors had allowed him to retain. In losing his real property, he had also lost the right to vote or to hold office in Virginia. It is little wonder that he sank even deeper into despondency and withdrew even further from a world that had once promised so much and now offered so little.

86 Richmond *Enquirer*, November 21, December 17, 20, 1825.

87 Account of T. J. Randolph, July 4, 1826, in Trist Papers, Library of Congress.

88 T. M. Randolph, Jr., note, Jefferson to Randolph, January 8, 1826, in Richmond *Enquirer*, July 14, 1827; Paul L. Ford (ed.), *The Writings of Thomas Jefferson*, X, 361 n.

CHAPTER XI

The Last Years

RANDOLPH'S SITUATION, harsh though it was, could have been worse. Although he had become a bankrupt, he was not yet homeless, and he had not been "turned out to roam the world" as Francis Gilmer had once feared.[1] There still remained to him the solace of domestic affection and sympathy if he could bring himself to accept Jefferson's repeated invitations to return to Monticello; there were still the consolations of study and experiment if he chose to grasp them.[2] But he was temperamentally unable to make any effort toward reconciliation, and, playing the role of Timon rather than that of Lear, he burrowed more deeply than ever into his hermitage at North Milton.

On February 11, 1826, Anne Cary Bankhead, Tom's firstborn, died, her passing undoubtedly hastened by her tribulations and suffering as the wife of the "scoundrel" who survived her.[3] Two weeks later Francis Walker Gilmer, friend of the family and Tom's onetime protege, succumbed to tuberculosis.[4] Jefferson's health and strength were failing rapidly. The venerable statesman, then approaching his eighty-third birthday, could no longer hide from

1 Francis Walker Gilmer to John Randolph of Roanoke, June 23, 1825, in Gilmer Papers, Alderman Library, University of Virginia.

2 Jefferson to T. M. Randolph, Jr., January 8, 1828, in Jefferson Papers, Library of Congress.

3 Notes by Jefferson in *Jefferson's Prayer Book;* Sidney Nicholas to T. J. Randolph, February 3, 1826, in Edgehill-Randolph Papers; Nicholas to Mary Randolph, February 11, 1826, for Ann's last illness, in Edgehill-Randolph Papers.

4 Davis, *Francis Walker Gilmer,* 252–53.

himself or from others the fact that he had "one foot in the grave and the other uplifted to follow it." [5]

Jefferson composed his will on March 16, and, when he did so, he took a compassionate but utterly realistic view of "the insolvent state of the affairs" of his "friend and son-in-law." He realized that his own property, or that part which would still be left after all debts were paid, would be "the only resource against the want" in which Tom's family "would otherwise be left." He felt that the younger man should also understand that situation: "It must be his wish, as it is my duty, to guard that resource against all liability for his debts, engagements, and purposes whatsoever, and to preclude the rights, powers, and authorities over it which might, . . . independently of his will, bring it within the power of his creditors." He thereupon appointed Jefferson Randolph, Alexander Garrett, and Nicholas Trist as trustees during Tom's lifetime and empowered them to administer the property "for the sole and separate use" of Martha Randolph. Jefferson Randolph was made sole executor,[6] an appointment that outraged his father.

When he had done what he could to guard his family's future, Jefferson applied himself once again to the cause of his beloved university. He spent the last spring of his life overseeing the unpacking of the books for the institution's library, speeding the completion of the Rotunda, helping to select a professor of law, and worrying about student discipline.[7] His son-in-law was meanwhile spending his solitary days at North Milton, and he may have at this time first conceived the idea of translating foreign works on agriculture into English.[8] So far as it can be determined, he saw nothing of Jefferson during the last few months of his father-in-law's life, and made no gesture toward the reconciliation that would have cheered the patriarch's final days.

5 Jefferson to Frances Wright, August 7, 1825, in Lipscomb and Bergh (eds.), *The Writings of Thomas Jefferson,* XVI, 119–20. See also Jefferson to W. F. Gilmer, January 12, 1826, in Paul L. Ford (ed.), *The Writings of Thomas Jefferson,* X, 358–59; Jefferson to Thomas Walker Maury, March 3, 1826, contemporary copy in Jefferson Papers, Alderman Library, University of Virginia.

6 Will of Thomas Jefferson, March 16–17, 1826, in Albemarle County Clerk's Office.

7 Jefferson Papers, Alderman Library, University of Virginia, March–June, 1826, *passim.*

8 T. M. Randolph, Jr., to William Cabell Rives, June 15, 1827, in Rives Papers, refers to this activity.

Indeed, Randolph did not show himself at Monticello even during the hot days of early summer when the old man laying dying in his room there. Friends and members of the family were in constant attendance; Martha kept a vigil at her father's bedside; Jefferson Randolph, young Trist, and others stood within call; but Thomas Mann Randolph did not come for a last word with the man who had been his patron, philosopher, and party chief. Early on the afternoon of July 4, 1826, Jefferson died without having had an opportunity to bid farewell to his son-in-law.[9]

It is barely possible that Tom did not know of his father-in-law's critical condition until it was too late. Jefferson's imminent death was not a matter of such common knowledge in the nearby community as to prevent a group of students at the university from celebrating the Fourth of July on the very morning that their rector was drawing his last labored breaths.[10] Immured in his refuge at North Milton, he may not have been aware of the situation, and his neighbors, with good reason, may have neglected to tell him. But his deep rancor against Jefferson Randolph was probably even stronger than his affection and respect for the dying man, and he may have chosen to wait out the news in sullen isolation rather than to share his sorrow with his son, and now enemy. Whatever the reasons, his absence at the moment of loss alienated him further from his family.

To be sure, Randolph seemed "to mourn exceedingly," but some of his neighbors alleged that his show of grief was feigned.[11] Certainly his conduct during the weeks following Jefferson's passing seems to have been inspired more by rancor for the living than by sorrow for the dead, and he was undoubtedly angered by the terms of his father-in-law's will. The situation must have been uncomfortably reminiscent of the death of his own father almost thirty-three years before and of "the suspicion of inability" which he had then read into the provisions of his parent's will. Then he had been

9 All accounts are based on family reminiscences. Parton, *Thomas Jefferson*, 732–34; Randall, *Life of Thomas Jefferson*, III, 541–52; and Randolph, *Domestic Life*, 421–29, fail to mention Randolph's presence at Jefferson's deathbed, and his absence must therefore be presumed. See, however, the communication signed by him to Philip Hone, July 23, 1826, and appearing in the Richmond *Enquirer*, August 11, 1826, which indicates a personal acquaintance with the circumstances of Jefferson's death.

10 Bruce, *History of the University of Virginia*, II, 332.

11 Mrs. Louise McIntire, to Jane Margaret Carr, July 6, 1826, in Carr–Cary Papers.

denied the guardianship of his younger brothers and sisters; this time he was deprived of any role whatsoever. Stung by an even more sweeping "suspicion of inability," he declared that he no longer considered himself "a member of the family at all," and he denied that he felt "bound to consult with any member of it" on his own actions. He withdrew completely from Monticello, where he long had maintained no more than a token residence, and from then on spent both his days and his nights at North Milton.[12]

From his refuge he continued to fling out charges of injustice and demands to be recognized as the titular head of the family. These accusations were not warranted, but by 1826 Randolph was no longer rational and was unable to look at the situation except in terms of his own prejudices and injured pride. Friends of the family were shocked and outraged to see the effect of these outbursts, and one of them wondered how even "an angel" like Martha could have so long endured his "cruel, barbarous, and fiendlike behavior." [13]

Unable to bear the tension any longer, she at last fled Monticello for a less stormy atmosphere. By August she was in Washington,[14] and that fall, at the strong urging of Jeff and his family, she departed for a long visit with Ellen and Joseph Coolidge in Boston,[15] taking with her the two youngest children eight-year-old George Wythe, and twelve-year-old Septimia. Her oldest son had been seeking to persuade her "to open a boarding school in Charlottesville in the spring," but this was a project that did not attract her.[16]

Her husband, badly in need of employment, had meanwhile applied to William Wirt, Attorney General of the United States, for a position with the federal government. Wirt had nothing in his own department to offer his onetime commander, and so he referred him to another Virginian in the Adams cabinet, Secretary of War James Barbour.[17] That official, who may have chosen to forget Colonel Randolph's charges against him in the House of Delegates two winters earlier, was in a position to be more helpful. The

12 T. M. Randolph, Jr., to Nicholas Trist, July 6, 1826, in Trist Papers, Library of Congress.

13 Ellen Carr to Jane Hollins Randolph, July 22, 1826, in Edgehill–Randolph Papers.

14 Martha Randolph to T. J. Randolph, August 24, 1826, *ibid.*

15 Sarah Elizabeth Nicholas to Jane Hollins Randolph, September 26, 1826, *ibid.*

16 Peggy Nicholas to Jane Hollins Randolph, December 22, 1826, *ibid.*

17 William Wirt to T. M. Randolph, Jr., November 6, 1826, in Jefferson Papers, Massachusetts Historical Society.

previous Congress had authorized a survey of the disputed boundary between the state of Georgia and the territory of Florida, and on November 7 Barbour offered to appoint Randolph as the federal member of the boundary commission.[18]

Thomas asked for further information as to "the plan of the technical and scientific processes" which would be employed,[19] but President Adams, to whom his "sundry questions" were referred, merely ordered that he be issued general instructions and authorized to coordinate the details with the Commissioner of the State of Georgia "at his discretion." [20] Randolph was still not satisfied, and he was disturbed because he did not know the name of the surveyor with whom he would have to work. Yet he probably realized that he was in no position to be a chooser, and on November 22 he informed Secretary Barbour of his acceptance.

Although his superiors expected him to leave for the south immediately, he tarried in Virginia for nearly eight weeks, much to the irritation of his son's family.[21] Severely cold weather and an attack of the gout accounted for much of the delay,[22] but he was not idle during the long interval before his departure. He spent part of that time in efforts to recruit helpers in Albemarle and the surrounding counties, since Barbour had authorized him to select his assistants wherever he could find them.[23] He received several applications for employment as "pioneers" and chainmen from students at the university and from other young men in the vicinity, and older citizens like Craven Peyton and Alexander Garret recommended their sons and youthful neighbors.[24] He even considered taking along his own son Meriwether Lewis Randolph, but the mere

18 James Barbour to T. M. Randolph, Jr., November 7, 1826, in *Documents Accompanying the President's Message at the First Session of the Twentieth Congress,* Senate Document 1 (Washington, 1828), 106. This work is hereinafter designated as *Documents . . . 20th Congress.*

19 T. M. Randolph, Jr., to James Barbour, November 12, 1826, in *Documents . . . 20th Congress,* 108–109.

20 John Quincy Adams, *Memoirs . . .* , ed. Charles Francis Adams (Philadelphia, 1874–77), VII, 179.

21 Peggy Nicholas to Jane Hollins Randolph, December 12, 1826, in Edgehill-Randolph Papers; Sarah Nicholas to Jane Hollins Randolph, February 12, 1827, *ibid.*

22 T. M. Randolph, Jr., to James Barbour, February 2, 1827, in *Documents . . . 20th Congress,* 111–113.

23 Barbour to T. M. Randolph, Jr., November 23, 1826, *ibid.*, 110.

24 Sydney R. Pettit to T. M. Randolph, Jr., December 7, 1826, and eight other applications, in Alderman Library, University of Virginia.

suggestion of carrying that sixteen-year-old "upon such a business" aroused such a storm of family protest[25] that Tom abandoned the idea. Indeed, he failed to employ any of his neighbors for the survey.

In addition to his search for assistants, Randolph also made a study of the complicated history of the disputed boundary. Georgia based her claim on the Treaty of Paris of 1763, by which Spain had ceded Florida to Great Britain. That document had described the boundary as a line running westward from the "most southern stream" of St. Marys River to the junction of the Flint and Chattahoochee rivers. However, when Florida was restored to Spain at the close of the Revolutionary War, the "head of the St. Mary's River" had been substituted for the "most southern stream" in the terms describing the boundary, and this definition was repeated in the Treaty of San Lorenzo of 1795, by which the disputed boundary between the United States and Spanish Florida was settled. The boundary commission appointed to survey the line of demarcation included Andrew Ellicott, acting for the United States, and Don Estéban Minor for His Most Catholic Majesty. Their party had worked eastward in 1800 from the Mississippi to the Flint and Chattahoochee and thence to the upper waters of the St. Marys. There they began a search for the source of that little-traveled stream, but the thick vegetation and the swampy soil made a thorough exploration extremely difficult, while the unfriendliness of the local Indians made a prolonged stay in the area something less than advisable. They failed therefore to find the head of the St. Marys, and they contented themselves with the erection of a mound in the general vicinity of where they thought it was. Ellicott, on the basis of the observations he was able to make from the top of the mound, decided that the source of the river was one mile to the north, but he and Minor did not survey the line back to the Chattahoochee.

Georgia, for understandable reasons, had never accepted this vague effort at location, and never abandoned its insistence that the correct point of departure was "the most southern stream," as specified by the 1763 treaty. When East Florida was ceded to the United States in 1819, the Georgia authorities, led by the excitable Governor George Michael Troup, began to press the issue anew,

25 Peggy Nicholas to Jane Hollins Randolph, December 12, 1826, in Edgehill–Randolph Papers.

and in 1825 they instructed the state's representatives in Congress to secure federal cooperation in a definitive survey of the dividing line. A law was passed on May 4, 1826, which authorized President Adams to name a commissioner for this purpose and which specified that the spot marked by Ellicott be accepted as the head of the St. Marys.[26]

From the beginning, however, the Adams administration showed little interest in implementing the law which had been forced upon it. The President let five months pass without selecting a federal commissioner, and the appointment was finally made almost on the spur of the moment by the Secretary of War. In choosing a known states' rights firebrand like Randolph to represent the United States and in the casual attitude he displayed toward the latter's repeated requests for detailed instructions, Barbour showed an indifference to the whole matter that is only partially explained by the long and debilitating illness which troubled him through the last months of 1826.[27] Personal pique may have motivated the Secretary to send Randolph on what proved to be a fool's errand, but the attitude of the whole administration was negative.[28] Already involved in a delicate dispute with Georgia over the Creek Indians living in that state,[29] the administration may have hesitated to push its legitimate interests in the Florida boundary too strenuously or otherwise to provoke controversy with a Georgia governor whom Barbour had described as a madman.[30]

Even before he left Virginia, Randolph may have been aware of some of these inconsistencies. From the first he tried to secure copies of the San Lorenzo Treaty and of Ellicott's report.[31] Barbour promised to procure the necessary papers from Secretary of State Henry Clay,[32] but Tom had still not received this material when he left Richmond on January 14 for Georgia. He did locate and purchase

26 E. Merton Coulter, *Thomas Spalding of Sapelo* (Baton Rouge, La., 1940), 195–99.
27 Adams, *Memoirs*, VII, 179.
28 John Quincy Adams barely mentions this matter. Adams' admirer Samuel Flagg Bemis in his *John Quincy Adams and the Union* (New York, 1956) makes no mention of it.
29 Bemis, *John Quincy Adams*, II, 79–87.
30 Adams, *Memoirs*, VII, 3.
31 T. M. Randolph, Jr., to James Barbour, December 16, 1826, in *Documents . . . 20th Congress*, 110–11.
32 Barbour to Randolph, Jr., December 23, 1826, *ibid.*, 111.

a copy of Major Ellicott's personal *Journal*, published in 1803, and on his way south he apparently studied those parts of it dealing with the Florida boundary.

On February 1 he reached Milledgeville, capital of Georgia, and conferred with Governor George Michael Troup and other state officials. Learning that they considered the personal *Journal* authentic and reliable, he decided to follow it and to be "very exact in the applications of the information it contains." [33] He had previously expressed a determination to be "expeditious, accurate, economical, accomodating to the other party," and he bore himself so well in his discussions with the fiery Troup that the latter soon accepted him as a man of "high and honorable character." [34] But Randolph was by no means ready to concede everything to the Georgians. He was well aware that they wanted the boundary located as south as possible, and he thought it likely that "some of the most fertile lands of all the South" might lie in the area in dispute.[35]

From Milledgeville he rode across the state to Darien on the coast, where on February 8 he joined Thomas Spalding, Georgia's representative on the commission. Spalding was a native Georgian, six years younger than Randolph, who had had an active and successful career as a legislator, banker, and planter and who had been an active promoter of turnpikes in his state. Being of a somewhat experimental bent, Spalding had introduced the cultivation of sugar cane into Georgia and had been the first to grow Sea Island cotton successfully on the mainland.[36] This mutual interest in agricultural innovations gave the two men a common bond and may have helped to foster the generally harmonious relations which prevailed between them during their association together on the boundary line.[37]

The two commissioners spent several days at Darien in preparations for their expedition. Chainmen, cooks, axmen, and porters were hired; provisions and equipment were procured and assembled. Since the federal government had not appointed a surveyor, Randolph agreed to the employment of a Georgian, John McBride.[38]

33 Randolph, Jr., to Barbour, February 2, 1827, *ibid.*, 111–13.
34 George M. Troup to Thomas Spalding, March 15, 1827, *ibid.*, 130–33.
35 T. M. Randolph, Jr., to James Barbour, February 2, 1827, *ibid.*, 111–13.
36 Coulter, *Thomas Spalding, passim.*
37 *Ibid.*, 202.
38 T. M. Randolph, Jr., to James Barbour, February 14, 1827, in *Documents . . . 20th Congress*, 113–14; Proceedings of Commissioners, February 12, 1827, *ibid.*, 115–16.

On February 28, 1827, "fully equipped and provided," the party left Darien and proceeded down the coast to the mouth of the St. Marys, sixty miles to the south. There they turned to follow the river upstream and by March 8 were in the swamps, searching for the mound which Ellicott had erected twenty-seven years before. Spalding preferred to ignore that marker and to look for the real source of the river, but Randolph, remembering his instructions, insisted on beginning at the point designated in 1800. The Georgian finally agreed, and the party marched due north of the mound for a mile and then began to run the line.[39]

They proceeded westward through the Okefenokee Swamp. The denseness of the underbrush and the marshy condition of the soil, made progress slow and difficult at first, but when they reached drier ground beyond the Suwanee River they were able to move more swiftly. As they passed through the thick, luxuriant southern forest, filled with a variety of subtropical plants, the botanist in Randolph must have exulted—here was an unequalled opportunity for the study of his favorite subject. Other factors combined to make this stage of the expedition a pleasant one. The weather remained fine, and Spalding proved to be an interesting and congenial companion.[40]

The Virginian, however, did not find everything to his satisfaction. Although robust for his age, the fifty-eight-year-old man found the primitive conditions of life in the open increasingly uncomfortable.[41] Furthermore, the "rudeness" of some of the chainmen and camp-servants was "truly painful" to him.[42] He was not alone in this resentment, for his fellow commissioner also objected to the "boisterous hilarity" of the men.[43]

Other and more serious difficulties arose to plague them. Surveyor John McBride had made miscalculations from the start, and the "experiment line" began diverging too far to the north. By early April it became obvious that this error would cause the line to strike

39 T. M. Randolph, Jr., to James Barbour, March 24, 1827, in *Documents . . . 20th Congress*, 121–22; Thomas Spalding to Randolph, April 9, 1827, *ibid.*, 136. Early in the expedition, Randolph and Spalding agreed to exchange written communications on all important points in order to make them a matter of record.

40 T. M. Randolph, Jr., to James Barbour, March 24, 1827, *ibid.*, 121–22.

41 T. M. Randolph, Jr., to Thomas Spalding, April 4, 1827, *ibid.*, 135–36; Randolph, Jr. to Barbour, April 7, 1827, *ibid.*, 123–24.

42 Randolph, Jr., to Spalding, April 26, 1827, *ibid.*, 143.

43 Spalding to Randolph, Jr., April 27, 1827, *ibid.*, 143–44.

the Chattahoochee several miles above its junction with the Flint.[44] Spalding suggested that the party proceed at once to the confluence of those two rivers and there begin anew.[45] Randolph, however, argued against abandoning a line of which 115 miles had already been run and proposed that they complete the survey and correct the error on the return to the St. Mary's.[46] The federal commissioner's will prevailed, and they continued until they reached Ellicott's western extremity.

Events soon revealed a fundamental difference between the points of view of the two men. Spalding, as a loyal servant of Georgia, was determined to protect her interests and to secure as much of the disputed territory for her as possible. Colonel Randolph, although not without a "predilection" for that state, was also motivated by "an enthusuastic republican honesty" and by his feelings "for the little state of Florida." He had been impressed, he declared, by "the felicity of its climate, the fertility of its soil," and its "high destiny." [47] These differences did not impair the friendly personal relations between the two commissioners, but as the only non-Georgian in the group he found himself frequently opposed by every other member of the party. Tom, however, was inclined to place most of the blame for his situation on his superiors in Washington. The failure of federal officials to supply him with a copy of Ellicott's report, that "obligatory and final guide," had not ceased to exasperate him,[48] and its lack became increasingly embarrassing as the survey continued. He was also angered because he had received no communication from Secretary of War Barbour since late December, and he felt that he had been placed "on ground upon which the subordinate officer of the President of the United States ought not to stand." [49]

He was still seething over this bureaucratic neglect when on April 9 the survey party arrived on the banks of the Chattahoochee,[50] and discovered the expected error in their line. While they were there, Spalding received orders from Governor Troup to attempt a new

44 T. M. Randolph, Jr., to James Barbour, April 7, 1827, *ibid.*, 123–24.
45 Thomas Spalding to T. M. Randolph, Jr., April 4, 1827, *ibid.*, 133–34.
46 Randolph, Jr., to Spalding, April 4, 1827, *ibid.*, 135–36.
47 Randolph, Jr., to Spalding, April 26, 1827, *ibid.*, 141–43.
48 T. M. Randolph, Jr., to James Barbour, February 14, 1827, *ibid.*, 113–14.
49 Randolph, Jr., to Barbour, April 7, 1827, *ibid.*, 123–24.
50 Thomas Spalding to T. M. Randolph, Jr., April 9, 1827, *ibid.*, 136.

and more intensive search for the source of the St. Marys.[51] Randolph had by then convinced himself that the source was not only "indeterminate, but indeterminable by any geometrical or any physical process whatever," since the river rose in the midst of a swamp and was fed by innumerable springs, the volume of each of which varied from year to year. He argued therefore that he not only had no authority to make such a search but that since the commissioners of 1800 had been unable to locate the river's head, there was little chance that he and Spalding could do so.[52] Spalding agreed to carry out their alternate plan, and the party began to survey the line eastward.[53]

Two weeks and 93 miles later the commissioners reached the Withlacoochee River. Heavy rains had slowed them, and floods had necessitated a series of long offsets which had increased the margin of error. By this time, all hope of running an accurate line had vanished. With the Florida summer nearly upon them, it was not likely that a third attempt could be completed before the onset of hot weather made further work impossible.[54]

It was at this point that Spalding received orders from Troup to abandon the survey altogether.[55] With his colleague recalled, there was nothing for the Virginian to do but give up his work on the survey, which had already bogged down in failure.[56] He was careful to impute no blame to Spalding, and the two commissioners ended their joint labors with expressions of mutual regard and esteem.[57] On April 28 they turned northward into Georgia.[58]

Randolph's original instructions had included an order to investigate the claims of certain settlers for rations furnished the friendly Creek Indians,[59] and so he made a long detour through their country on his way to Milledgeville. He soon discovered that the semicivi-

51 George M. Troup to Spalding, March 15, 1827, *ibid.*, 130–33; Spalding to T. M. Randolph, Jr., February 9, 1827, *ibid.*, 136.

52 T. M. Randolph, Jr., to Spalding, April 10, 1827, *ibid.*, 136–38.

53 Spalding to Randolph, Jr., *ibid.*, 138.

54 Randolph, Jr., to Spalding, April 26, 1827, *ibid.*, 141–43.

55 George M. Troup to Spalding, April 18, 1827, *ibid.*, 139–40.

56 T. M. Randolph, Jr., to Spalding, April 26, 1827, *ibid.*, 141–43.

57 Randolph, Jr., to Spalding, *ibid.;* Spalding to Randolph, Jr., April 27, 1827, *ibid.*, 143–44.

58 T. M. Randolph, Jr., to James Barbour, May 15, 1827, *ibid.*, 127–30.

59 Randolph, Jr., to Barbour, February 2, 1827 and May 15, 1827, *ibid.*, 117–18, 127–30.

lized Creeks in west Georgia were almost starving. Most of them were living, he reported, on the roots of the China brier, a plant "rendered esculent only by a tedious preparation" and without "nutritive virtue enough to save the lives of their children." His observations convinced him that most of the Indians, particularly the young children, would die of hunger "without immediate relief from the United States," and he vigorously recommended that the Secretary of War authorize "the issue of one peck of corn per head per week." He also expressed agreement with the proposal previously advanced by Barbour that all of the Southern tribes be relocated far beyond the frontier, and he advised his superior that "the whole Creek nation could be easily prevailed upon . . . to consent to move over to the Mississippi," if "a special mission from the President" was sent to them. But, "whatever is done with them," he urged, "—must be quickly done, and by a commanding influence. . . ."[60]

He had no way of knowing then that the Secretary, aware of troubled conditions among the Creeks and of their lack of confidence in Indian agent John Crowell, was entertaining "some thought" of appointing the Colonel as agent to that nation. On February 16 Barbour had mentioned such an assignment to President Adams, but nothing came of the suggestion at this time, since Barbour in the same interview referred pointedly to Randolph's "eccentricities."[61] The idea was not dropped entirely, however, and the President and his Secretary of War returned to it after Randolph's services as commissioner were discontinued.

Tom's report on the Creeks, which also contained his announcement of the collapse of the survey, reached Washington on May 19. That same day Barbour discussed the new development with his chief, and they decided to do the only thing they could have done: to recall Randolph and to learn from him, if they could, "the cause of the suspension of the work by the governor of Georgia." But, the Chief Executive gave no sign that he was disappointed in the failure to settle the boundary.[62] There, as far as the federal government was concerned, the matter rested. Meanwhile, John McBride, the Georgia surveyor, had returned into the swamps on his own to find the

60 Randolph, Jr., to Barbour, May 15, 1827, *ibid.*, 127–30.
61 Adams, *Memoirs*, VII, 227.
62 *Ibid.*, 273–74.

disputed source of the St. Marys. Emerging in July, he reported to Governor Troup that the south branch of the river was indubitably the principal one. No decisive action was taken, however, and the boundary remained unsettled until 1866, when both Georgia and Florida agreed to accept Ellicott's mound as the true head of the river.[63]

By June 2 Randolph was back in Albemarle.[64] There he prepared to draft a report of his activities, and he requested Barbour for suggestions as to the content. The Secretary, so Tom declared later, "answered in the most direct manner, that no report was expected, or wanted." This reply convinced him that he "had not given them satisfaction enough to be employed again on the line," and he tried to dismiss "the whole subject" from his mind.[65] His resentment, however, was not easily erased, and he soon made his displeasure known. On June 15 he wrote a letter to his congressman, William Cabell Rives of Castle Hill. Rives had never been a close friend, and he had opposed Randolph's election as governor in 1819. But Tom, although propertyless and thereby voteless, still considered himself one of Rives' "constituents." Appealing to Rives on this ground, he told how he had been relieved of his duties by Barbour.[66] While he did not suggest any definite action, he was probably motivated by a desire to make trouble for the Secretary of War.

Rives may have spoken to Barbour about the matter, for the Secretary of War saw President Adams on June 20 and again suggested that Randolph be named as the United States' agent to the Creeks. The Indians were "much dissatisfied" with agent John Crowell, and Adams had decided to replace him. After some discussion, Adams and Barbour agreed the matter "would deserve some further consideration." [67]

Whatever chances Tom might have had to secure this appointment were quickly spoiled by his own actions. Shortly after his complaint to Rives, he wrote an angry account of his experiences in Florida and published it in the Charlottesville *Central Gazette*. Therein he told of his futile efforts to obtain a copy of the Ellicott

63 Coulter, *Thomas Spalding*, 209–11.
64 T. M. Randolph, Jr., to William Cabell Rives, June 15, 1827, in Rives Papers.
65 *Ibid.*
66 *Ibid.*
67 Adams, *Memoirs*, VII, 294.

report [68] and attributed his failure to the negligence—or worse—of Secretary of State Henry Clay. He charged also that he had received no satisfactory instructions from his superiors and, somewhat garbling the record, declared that he, Troup, and Spalding had agreed to abandon all efforts to mark the boundary until the Ellicott report could be found. While he explicitly exempted the President from criticism, he made serious imputations concerning two members of the President's official family. Furthermore, he spoke highly of the Georgia officials and showed a tendency to sympathize with their point of view. All of this, combined with the criticism of Clay which the article inspired in such a powerful antiadministration organ as the Richmond *Enquirer*, was not calculated to win him any approval in administration circles.[69] At any rate, no more was said in Washington of sending him among the high-strung Creeks.

After his recall, Randolph's public career came to an end. He had performed his duties energetically and conscientiously, and he had displayed what was for him an unusual amount of tact and consideration in his dealings with the Georgians. Both Troup and Spalding, although disagreeing with him on the procedure for running the line, made no complaints about his conduct. The Randolph who helped to run the Florida boundary seems an almost entirely different man from the bitter and violent bankrupt of North Milton or the vindictive council-baiting governor. While his personality, as his subsequent behavior demonstrated, had not undergone any substantial change, he had acquitted himself far more creditably than those who so casually sent him forth had any real right to expect, and the burden of his complaints against them was more or less justified. At any rate, the brief interlude of responsible behavior did not survive the shock of disappointment, and the black, depressing moods and the violent, unreasoning rages of the past returned with increased intensity.

In his interludes of rationality he devoted himself largely to a type of literary activity which he had formerly disdained [70] but which now, so he had decided, offered him "an employment for a

68 This document was still missing by March 21, 1828, although a special search had been made for it in the interim. See *Documents . . . 20th Congress.*

69 Abstract of Randolph's *Gazette* article in the Richmond *Enquirer*, July 6, 1827.

70 T. M. Randolph, Jr., to Nicholas P. Trist, June 5, 1820, in Trist Papers, University of North Carolina Library.

livelihood."[71] He had conceived earlier the idea of translating foreign agricultural works into "language such as will suit country people" and publishing them for sale to southern farmers.[72] Although he himself had a great "dislike to translations," he did not extend this "very old & noted prejudice"[73] to books and articles which were intended for the perusal of readers less learned than himself. After his return from Florida, he devoted a great deal of his time to this task, which he probably had begun late in 1826, and by the middle of June he had more than five hundred manuscript pages ready for the press. One of the items which he rendered into his own language was a French treatise by Raibaud-L'Ange on the effect of cold weather on olive trees,[74] and this sample he submitted to Congressman William Cabell Rives for a "sincere judgement" and an opinion on the general plan of which it was a part. The author also desired Rives' help in obtaining the "patronage" of "southern gentlemen" for the project,[75] but this appeal met with practically no encouragement. Nonetheless, Tom continued to work more or less consistently on his "favorite literary employment" until the last month of his life.[76]

He had resumed his former solitary habits, and although he took part in a Fourth of July celebration in Charlottesville,[77] such appearances were rare. As might have been expected, he kept out of the way of the family at Monticello, but he must have been aware of the difficulties they had encountered in his absence. Martha was still living in Boston with her married daughter, Ellen Coolidge, and was "forced to receive assistance from any one that can give it to her."[78] Partial aid for the impoverished family had been obtained in the

71 T. M. Randolph, Jr., to William Cabell Rives, June 15, 1827, in Rives Papers.

72 T. M. Randolph, Jr., to Nicholas P. Trist, November 3, 1827, in Trist Papers, Library of Congress.

73 Randolph, Jr. to Trist, June 5, 1820, *ibid.*

74 The work probably was Henri Raibaud-L'Ange, *Notice sur les Oliviers Frappés de la Gelée* (Paris, 1823).

75 T. M. Randolph, Jr., to William Cabell Rives, June 15, 1827, in Rives Papers.

76 T. M. Randolph, Jr., to Nicholas P. Trist, November 3, 1827, in Trist Papers, Library of Congress; Randolph, Jr., to Monroe, May 1, 1828, in Monroe Papers, Library of Congress; Randolph, Jr., to William Cabell Rives, May 3, 1828, in Rives Papers.

77 Richmond *Enquirer*, July 13, 1827.

78 Sidney Nicholas Carr to Jane Hollins Randolph, January 19, 1827, in Edgehill-Randolph Papers.

form of gifts by South Carolina and by the citizens of Philadelphia,[79] and Jefferson Randolph had spent the winter and spring in various fund-raising activities designed primarily for her benefit. He had proved himself, she said, what his "dear grandfather" had once called him, "a god send." But, although she had been refreshed by the peaceful life she was leading in Boston, her "nerves" were "still in a miserable state," and she suffered so much from "excessive languor and sadness" that she was no longer able, so she declared, to "comprehend the possibility of better days." [80]

Such being her state of mind, she was in no emotional condition to face a reunion with her husband. Randolph had never abandoned his claims to be recognized as the head of the family, and that summer he expressed his intention of following Martha to Massachusetts and persuading her to return to Albemarle, bringing the young children with her. Jefferson Randolph, fearing the effect of such a move on his mother, warned his brother-in-law of his father's plans and requested his aid in thwarting them. So did Virginia Trist.[81]

Coolidge, who was not ashamed to admit fears that his father-in-law might "come here to make himself and us the subject of remark," willingly gave the desired assurances. Should Tom come to Massachusetts, the Bostonian promised that he would be "received kindly," but he also pledged that Randolph would not be allowed to "compel" the return of the fugitives. More could be accomplished, he believed, "by judicious management than from an open defiance of his wishes." He viewed a legal separation "as altogether improbable" and a divorce as unthinkable, and he rested his hopes in the prospect that Randolph could be induced to take employment with the government "or even absent himself and go to a distance." Should he attempt to possess himself of the children, they would be "placed with some friend . . . where he cannot discover them." And if he persisted in his efforts, or if his conduct was less than "decent," his New England son-in-law was resolved "to close [his] doors upon him." [82]

Martha, however, was not entirely willing to cut the remaining bonds between herself and her husband of thirty-seven years. She

79 Ellen Nicholas to Jane Hollins Randolph, January 12, 1827, in Edgehill-Randolph Papers; T. J. Randolph to Citizens of Philadelphia, January 20, 1827, *ibid.*

80 Martha Randolph to T. J. Randolph, March 2, 1827, *ibid.*

81 Joseph Coolidge to T. J. Randolph, August 13, 1827, *ibid.*

82 *Ibid.*

had reached the point where she could no longer endure the constant quarrels and tirades which had "worn [her] life away," [83] but she still retained some feeling for him. Against her family's wishes, she was willing to pledge that he would be received at Monticello again "at a future day," and she even expressed a wish "to contribute to his support." [84]

Tom made no effort at pursuit, and he was probably soothed by the prospect she held out of a reconciliation at a future time. He did not even write to her, but she magnanimously attributed this silence to her own forgetfulness and expressed the fear that he may have been "hurt at what must have appeared an unfeeling neglect of his want." [85]

Meanwhile, Randolph had thrust himself into a national political controversy and proceeded to make it even more acrimonious and bad tempered than it already was. The presidential election of 1828 was a scant fifteen months away, and partisans of the major candidates were seeking all the support they could get, not only from living voters but from the distinguished dead. Thomas Jefferson, in his grave for barely a year, already had become transfigured into a political oracle, and his writings were being quoted sometimes to praise, sometimes to damn, both measures or individuals. The supporters of John Quincy Adams, a man toward whom the living Jefferson had held mixed feelings, invoked the spirit of Monticello on behalf of their candidate, and similar efforts were made by the champions of General Andrew Jackson on behalf of their hero.

Jefferson had left enough verbal ammunition behind him to supply both protagonists, but the volleys he had directed at Jackson came earlier and more readily to the hands of those disposed to use them. According to Daniel Webster, who visited Monticello late in 1824, Jefferson had been "much alarmed at the prospect of seeing General Jackson President," feeling, so he told his visitor, that the Tennesseean had "very little respect" for either the laws or the constitution and that he was "one of the most unfit men I know of for such a place." [86] The correctness of this version of Jefferson's remarks was later hotly disputed, but Webster and other anti-Jacksonians made the most of it. Also quoted against the war hero's

83 Martha Randolph to T. J. Randolph, February 29, 1828, *ibid.*
84 Joseph Coolidge to T. J. Randolph, August 13, 1827, *ibid.*
85 Martha Randolph to T. J. Randolph, December 5, 1827, *ibid.*
86 Fletcher Webster (ed.), *The Private Correspondence of Daniel Webster* (Boston, 1875), I, 364 ff.

cause was a quip, made to a few neighbors in 1824 and reportedly delivered "with a tone of sportive, almost of contemptuous derision," that "one might as well make a sailor of a cock, or a soldier of a goose, as a president of Andrew Jackson." [87] But, the most popular and most cited authority for Jefferson's views on this subject was Governor Edward Coles of Illinois, who had spent his early years in Albemarle and who still had relatives there. Coles had visited Monticello in August, 1825, and had heard his host declare, so one of the many versions of this discourse had it, "that General Jackson's extraordinary run *was an evidence that the Republic would not stand long*." [88] Such statements were approvingly and even gleefully quoted and alluded to by newspapers opposed to Jackson's election.[89]

In this situation, Jacksonians (or, more precisely, anti-Adamsites) in Virginia came to realize that their best hope of refuting Coles and Webster was a counterstatement by someone intimately connected with Jefferson. Thomas Walker Gilmer, an editor of the Charlottesville *Virginia Advocate*, was familiar with Jefferson's opinions of Jackson, which to some degree he shared, but he was also able to recall that the former had "entertained opinions equally unfavorable of the fitness of John Q. Adams, as a statesman." [90] Seeking support for this view, he turned to Thomas Mann Randolph for an account of his father-in-law's views.[91]

Thomas gladly obliged, for he had been irritated by "some illiberal expressions applied to General Jackson" he had encountered in the newspapers. He therefore gave Gilmer a statement which contained an account of several conversations, held at different times during 1825, in which Jefferson had disparaged John Quincy Adams and praised Andrew Jackson. In July or August of that year, he recollected, his father-in-law had described the general as the only

87 Quoted by Thomas Walker Gilmer to Edward Coles, May 27, 1827, *Niles Weekly Register*, XXXIII (December 29, 1827), 282.

88 Richmond *Whig*, May 15, 1827; Edward Coles to George Farquer *et al.*, November 23, 1827, *Niles Weekly Register*, XXXIII (December 29, 1827), 281–82; Coles to Charlottesville *Virginia Advocate*, May 22, 1827; *Niles Weekly Register*, XXXIII (January 19, 1828), 335.

89 Richmond *Whig*, May 15, 1827.

90 T. W. Gilmer to Edward Coles, May 27, 1827, in *Niles Weekly Register*, XXXIII (December 29, 1827), 282.

91 T. M. Randolph, Jr., to *Virginia Advocate*, August 18, 1827; also in Richmond *Enquirer*, August 24, 1827, and *Virginia Advocate*, September 1, 1827.

bulwark against federal encroachments and had expressed his pleasure that the Tennesseean would be available in 1828; in December he had described the hero as "honest sincere firm clear-headed and strong-minded."

Not willing to leave the matter there, Tom went on to declare that he had also heard his father-in-law express "a repugnance" toward Henry Clay. Jefferson, so Randolph declared, had characterized the Kentuckian as "a splendid orator without any valuable knowledge . . . or any determined principles." These sentiments, which were similar in their tone to those Tom himself had expressed to Gilmer less than three years before,[92] reflected his own dislike of Clay, which had grown as a result of the Florida boundary episode. This animosity led him to close his letter on a note of defiance. Should the Secretary of State take exception to his opinions, Randolph announced, "I shall hold Mr. Clay, and him only, responsible to me." [93] The inference was plain: the son-in-law of Jefferson was prepared to engage in a duel with the Secretary of State.

Randolph's challenge aroused, as he perhaps expected, a storm of protest. John Hampden Pleasants, editor of the *Whig*, observed that Jefferson's views, even had they been correctly quoted, "could neither make Gen. Jackson better or worse." And Pleasants was not willing to accept the son-in-law's interpretation of those views. "We in Virginia know Col. Thomas M. Randolph well," he snapped. "We know him to be a very curious and eccentric gentleman, possessing many strong and chivalrous traits of character, and much under the influence of powerful prejudices and passions." [94] An even more strident retort emanated from the *National Journal*, an administration paper published in the national capital and edited by historian Peter Force. The colonel's statements were dismissed as "an electioneering fetch" on Jackson and Adams, and a pointed reference was made to the estrangement between Randolph and his father-in-law. There was, therefore, "at least some suspicion of the witness." But, the *Journal* devoted most of its indignation to the "voluntary, gratuitous, and wanton" attack on Clay, which was animated by "impotent malice and disgusting vanity." As for the "empty, vaporing menace" with which the letter had ended, the

92 See Randolph's own opinion on Clay in 1824, on page 150 of this book.
93 Richmond *Enquirer*, August 24, 1827.
94 Richmond *Whig*, August 25, 1827.

Journal issued a counterchallenge: "If he is satisfied, very well—if not, why let him come." [95]

Within two days a copy of the provocative rebuttal came to Randolph's attention, and his reaction was characteristic. He was "exceedingly exasperated" at the insinuations made upon his veracity, and he was positive that Clay himself was responsible. He therefore boarded the next stage coach to Richmond, intending to go thence to Washington, where he meant to seek out Clay, demand an explanation, and, if necessary, issue a challenge. Some member of his family, probably Thomas Jefferson Randolph, learned of his intentions and sent an urgent dispatch to Secretary of War James Barbour, then in residence at his Orange County estate, and asked him to warn Clay. "I should myself ride to Barboursville this morning," wrote the informant, "but for the certainty of this visit becoming known in the neighborhood, and thus bringing on consequences which would, in the present state of the family be deplorable to them, independently of any anxiety which I may, or may not entertain to avoid his ire on my own account." [96] Barbour forwarded this communication to Washington on August 30 but advised his colleague in the Cabinet to "treat this call with contempt." [97]

The angry Randolph reached Washington on September 1 and took lodgings at Wheaton's boardinghouse. Immediately upon arrival he sent a note to Clay, accusing him of "the use of expressions, insulting in their purport and injurious in their consequences." Besides accusing the Secretary of being "the author of the piece in the 'National Journal' . . ." he also charged that Clay had made "unjust representations" to the Department of War, "which defeated the object of my mission to Florida." [98] Clay drafted a cool but conciliatory disclaimer, denying that he had ever seen, much less written, the offensive editorial. This reply he sent immediately to Wheaton's by the hand of Philip R. Fendall, a clerk in the State Department.[99]

95 *National Journal* (Washington, D.C.), August 25, 1825.

96 T. J. Randolph to James Barbour, August 28, 1827, in Calvin Colton (ed.), *Works, Life, Correspondence, and Speeches of Henry Clay* (Federal Edition, New York, 1904), IV, 172*n*, 173–74.

97 James Barbour to Clay, August 30, 1827, in Clay Papers, Library of Congress.

98 T. M. Randolph, Jr., to Clay, September 1, 1827, in Colton (ed.), *Works, Life . . . of Henry Clay*, IV, 174.

99 Colton (ed.), *Works, Life . . . of Henry Clay*, IV, 174–75.

Tom received the messenger courteously and read the letter while Fendall waited. Apparently satisfied by Clay's explanation, he thanked his caller and dismissed him. Fendall departed, convinced that Randolph's "eye indicated insanity in the most unequivocal manner." [100] Randolph returned almost immediately to Albemarle, and four days later Force issued an apology in the *Journal* in which he withdrew the earlier charge of deliberate misrepresentation and admitted that the Colonel might have been honestly misled by partisan zeal.[101]

The escapade must have been widely known in his own community and elsewhere in Virginia, but it was not generally held against him. Indeed, the *Advocate* stoutly defended the original letter and sharply attacked the *Journal* as a "mouthpiece of the administration." The Charlottesville paper also published several of the letters which had passed between Jefferson and Randolph in 1825 and early in 1826 as a refutation of the charge that the latter had not enjoyed Jefferson's confidence in that period.[102] Similar documents appeared in the *Enquirer* and in the *National Journal* itself.[103] Jefferson Randolph's in-laws, of course, saw the whole affair only as an attempt by the father to injure his son, but they were grateful that no "dire consequences" had resulted and and glad that his effort to influence political opinion "had fallen harmlessly to the ground." [104]

Randolph continued to give Jackson his zealous, if not too decisive, support. That fall he published a letter in the *Chilicothean*, an Ohio paper which was supporting the general, and there reiterated his earlier statements that Jefferson's dying vote had been cast for Andrew Jackson. In December he met at Charlottesville with 171 other local supporters of the general and was named to the county committee of correspondence which was appointed at that time.[105] He continued to appear in town on court days, when he was seen "constantly with the crowd," discussing politics,[106] but his

100 Philip R. Fendall to Clay, September 1, 1827, in Clay Papers, Library of Congress.

101 *National Journal* (Washington), September 5, 1827.

102 *Virginia Advocate*, September 1, 1827.

103 Richmond *Enquirer*, September 14, 1827; *National Journal* (Washington), September 5, 1827.

104 Peggy Nicholas to Jane Hollins Randolph, July 27, 1827, in Edgehill-Randolph Papers.

105 Richmond *Enquirer*, November 20, December 13, 1827.

106 T. M. Randolph, Jr., to Nicholas P. Trist, March 11, 1828, in Trist Papers, Library of Congress, and Trist's note thereon.

influence was gone. Meanwhile he had continued to be an active member of the Agricultural Society of Albemarle, and in October, 1827, he was elected to the presidency of that body,[107] an office which he held until his death. His duties were nominal, but his neighbors, by conferring this honor on him, acknowledged their continuing respect for his agricultural achievements.

He spent most of his time that fall alone at North Milton, reading, working on his translations of foreign works on agriculture, and brooding over his wrongs, real and imaginary. Occasionally he interrupted his "favorite literary employment" long enough to "walk to and fro, like a sentry, or pursue game like a schoolboy," but he felt he was not getting enough exercise. He tried to find employment as the superintendent of some small farm in the vicinity, and he even considered renting a few acres of land at Carlton from Charles Bankhead.[108] He was unable, however, to work out a satisfactory arrangement with his onetime son-in-law and so continued in his state of enforced idleness.

Then on November 1 Nicholas Trist invited Randolph to return to Monticello.[109] The son-in-law was in active charge at the house, and the two had remained on friendly terms. Randolph was touched by this offer, which carried with it an opportunity to spent his "remaining days in recovering that classic ground from its present ruinous condition," but he nonetheless refused the invitation. "Desolate, destitute, isolated and aged" though he was, he was unwilling to do anything that might put him in the power of the "Executor," as he termed his son Jeff.[110] Since his twisted pride forbade him to throw himself on the family's charity, he remained in solitude at North Milton for another four months. But, by the following March he was ill with rheumatism of the stomach, and because his funds had become "to low for any tavern," he reconsidered Trist's offer. When he learned that Martha was planning to return from Massachusetts,[111] he decided at last to put his pride behind him and thereupon requested Trist for permission to come back to Monticello.

Even in admitting defeat, he did not surrender unconditionally.

107 True (ed.), "Minute Book of the Agricultural Society of Albemarle," 338.
108 T. M. Randolph, Jr., to Nicholas P. Trist, November 3, 1827, in Trist Papers, Library of Congress.
109 Nicholas P. Trist to Randolph, Jr., November 1, 1827, *ibid.*
110 Randolph, Jr., to Nicholas P. Trist, November 3, 1827, *ibid.*
111 Martha Randolph to T. J. Randolph, February 29, 1828, in Edgehill-Randolph Papers.

He stipulated that he would have to have complete privacy, "making no part of the family, & receiving nothing from it in any way whatever." He asked therefore that he be allowed to occupy the north pavilion and live there in "undisturbed solitude." Such an arrangement, he convinced himself, was absolutely necessary for his tranquility. He made it plain that he intended to live at his own charge and even to do his own cooking. He asked only for a place where he could stable his horse and keep his firewood and for a small plot of ground which he could work as a garden.[112] Trist somewhat regretfully accepted these conditions but expressed the hope that his father-in-law would eventually rejoin the family group.[113] By late March Randolph had returned to Monticello and had taken up his abode in the north pavilion where he passed the remainder of his days.

During these last months he kept himself apart from the family, and they, respecting his desire for privacy, left him alone. Virginia and Mary did disobey his instructions, but only to the extent of paying a brief visit every morning to inquire after his health. He was failing rapidly, he complained constantly of a pain in his stomach, and he was "thinner and more feeble" than his kin had ever seen him.[114] From the time of his return, he "ceased going off the mountain" [115] and spent his time reading and translating, for he had still not given up hope that southern farmers would buy—and read—the works of foreign agriculturist if only such "valuable publications" were rendered into English.[116] But this project, like so many others he had undertaken, came to nothing. Although he had completed several hundred pages of manuscript by his death, none of his work seems to have found its way into print.

Martha returned from the north early in May.[117] In spite of her children's fears that Tom would renew his demands to be restored as head of the house,[118] her reunion with him was amiable and friendly.

112 T. M. Randolph, Jr., to Nicholas P. Trist, March 10, 1828, in Trist Papers, Library of Congress.

113 Nicholas P. Trist to Randolph, Jr., March 11, 1828, *ibid.*

114 Virginia Trist to Ellen Coolidge, March 19, 1828, in Jefferson Papers, Alderman Library, University of Virginia.

115 T. M. Randolph, Jr., to Monroe, May 1, 1828, in Monroe Papers, Library of Congress.

116 T. M. Randolph, Jr., to William Rives, May 3, 1828, in Rives Papers.

117 Nicholas P. Trist to Madison, May 8, 1828, in Trist Papers, Library of Congress.

118 Virginia Trist to Ellen Coolidge, March 19, 1828, in Jefferson Papers, Alderman Library, University of Virginia.

The joy of reconciliation was marred, however, by an awareness of their financial plight. Despite the energetic efforts of Jefferson Randolph to clear his grandfather's estate, it seemed inevitable by the spring of 1828 that Monticello would have to be sold.[119] Randolph faced the prospect that he, like the warrior of whom Tyrtaeus had sung, would have to leave his home and "go a-begging," but he was spared that last humiliation. On June 20, 1828, in the sixtieth year of his age "he died in peace and love with all his family and old friends and neighbors. . . ." [120] In his last days, he had even become reconciled with his oldest son, Jefferson, "on whom he bestowed . . . the most fervent blessing." [121]

They buried him in the graveyard at Monticello, at the feet of Jefferson. A few yards away, near her father's head, Martha was placed eight years later. The inscription on Randolph's tombstone bears only his name and the dates of his birth, marriage, and death, but the obituary which editor Thomas Ritchie printed in the Richmond *Enquirer* might well have served for an epitaph:

> He enjoyed every advantage which education could confer . . . . The Chevalier Bayard was not more chivalrous than he was . . . . *Danger* and *fear* seemed to be words unknown in his vocabulary . . . . And had he possessed less irritability of temper and a larger acquaintance with the volume of men and things, he would have stood foremost.[122]

Far from standing foremost, Thomas Mann Randolph experienced frustration and failure in nearly everything he attempted. For all of his talents and abilities, he achieved little or nothing of significance as a politician, as a soldier, or as a planter. Even his perfection of horizontal plowing, important as that innovation was to his own section of Piedmont Virginia, was not a contribution of major importance.

His "irritability of temper" and his limited understanding of "the volume of men and things" certainly contributed to his failure, as did the burden of debt which harassed him throughout most of his adult life. Randolph's distress, however, was aggravated by the domestic

119 Nicholas P. Trist to Madison, May 8, 1828, in Trist Papers, Library of Congress.

120 Martha Randolph to George Wythe Randolph, June 30, 1828, in Jefferson Papers, Alderman Library, University of Virginia.

121 Nicholas P. Trist, Obituary of Thomas Mann Randolph, manuscript copy by Martha Trist Burke, in Edgehill-Randolph Papers.

122 Richmond *Enquirer*, July 4, 1828, reprinted from the *Virginia Advocate*.

atmosphere in which he lived. His moody and irritable temperament would have made him a difficult husband and an indifferent father in any family, but as the husband of Martha Jefferson and as a member of the domestic circle at Monticello, his defects of temperament brought on tragedy. Placed by marriage in intimate association with a man of such near genius as Jefferson, he became morbidly conscious of the gap in talents which separated them, and he came to consider those around him as "swans" and of himself as a "silly bird." From this feeling of inadequacy and unworthiness came deterioration and ruin for himself, and deep sorrow for all of those around him.

It was, however, not only his tragedy but his fulfilment that he played out his life's role on a stage which was dominated by Thomas Jefferson, where he was continually conscious of Jefferson's superiority, and continually challenged by Jefferson's example. It was that very example, and Randolph's efforts to follow it, which gave his life significance and which commends him to our attention.

In politics, as in most other things, he was his father-in-law's pupil and partisan, and he continued to work and fight for Jefferson's policies and principles, even after their personal relations grew cool. In his outlook on national affairs, he adopted a defensive stance that was essentially conservative; in his approach to Virginia's internal problems, he was constructive and progressive.

Like Jefferson he supported the rights of the states against every federal challenge, but also, like his mentor, he realized that strict construction and states' rights were not enough. In this respect, Thomas Mann Randolph stood in sharp contrast to his cousin of Roanoke, who was so much like him in so many other ways. The two men saw Virginia's problems in the Union alike, but they viewed the Commonwealth's internal difficulties with totally different eyes. One was opposed to any change in the Constitution of 1776; the other supported thorough revision of that instrument. One fought to preserve the privileged position of the planter class; the other championed the westerners and the small farmers who challenged that position.

Thus Thomas Mann Randolph, while holding many of the sentiments and prejudices of the class to which he was born, was far from being typical of it. In political outlook, if not in temperament, he remained a child of the enlightenment, more in accord with the rationalist optimism of his father-in-law's generation than with the aristocratic pessimism of his own. In a day when many Virginia planters were dismissing Jefferson's principles as glittering generalities, he continued to support those principles and to accept their implications. As a son-in-law and as a husband, the aristocrat of Tuckahoe proved a source of disappointment and sorrow; as a Jeffersonian, he did everything that could have been expected of him.

Critical Essay on Authorities

MANUSCRIPT CORRESPONDENCE

There is no single sizeable group of Thomas Mann Randolph papers and Randolph's correspondence is scattered through the papers of his contemporaries, especially those of his celebrated father-in-law. A particularly rich source is the Jefferson Papers in the Massachusetts Historical Society, which comprise the major part of Jefferson's private correspondence. Also included in this group are many letters written by others to Thomas Mann Randolph and to other members of the Monticello circle. Additional letters of Randolph are in the other major Jefferson collections in the Library of Congress and the Alderman Library of the University of Virginia.

The Edgehill–Randolph Papers and the Carr–Cary Papers, both in the Alderman Library, are extremely rich, as are the two groups of the papers of Randolph's son-in-law Nicholas P. Trist, one of which is in the Library of Congress, the other in the Southern History Collection of the University of North Carolina. Also useful were the papers of such contemporaries as Joseph C. Cabell (Alderman Library), David Campbell (Duke University Library), Henry Clay (Library of Congress), John R. Cocke, Francis Walker Gilmer, Harry Heth (all in Alderman Library), James Madison (Library of Congress), James Monroe (New York Public Library and Library of Congress), and William C. Rives (Library of Congress).

Two small groups of letters from Randolph to Peachy R. Gilmer, in the Archives Division of the Virginia State Library, and from Randolph to Joseph C. Cabell, in the Duke University Library, contain much interesting information. The Orderly Book of Captain

Benjamin Graves, in the Virginia Historical Society, Richmond, was useful for Randolph's military activities on the York River during the late summer of 1814.

ARCHIVES AND PRINTED DOCUMENTS

Information on Randolph family properties was found in the deed and will books of Albemarle and Goochland counties, microfilm copies of which are in the Archives Division of the Virginia State Library. Additional information of this nature was found in the tax books of Albemarle, Bedford, Goochland, and Henrico counties for the years 1782–1828, the originals of which are in the State Library. For the Randolph family's litigation over the Lidderdale debt, the records of the United States Circuit Court, on deposit in the State Library, were invaluable.

The resources of the Archives Division of the Virginia State Library were also used to reconstruct Randolph's three terms as governor. The Executive Papers for his governorship (1819–22) comprise sixteen boxes and include correspondence and other papers addressed to the executive during this period. The Executive Letter Books for 1816 to 1822 contain copies of letters, messages, and other communications issued under his official signature during those years, and the three manuscript Journals of the Council of State for the years 1819–22 throw additional light on the routine events of his years in office.

The official records of the Virginia General Assembly, for both the colonial and the Commonwealth periods, were extremely useful. The three volumes covering the *Journals of the House of Burgesses* for the years between 1766 and 1776, edited by John P. Kennedy (3 vols.; Richmond, 1905–1906), contain information on the part played by Thomas Mann Randolph, Sr., in the colonial Assembly. For Thomas Mann Randolph, Jr.'s, service in Congress, the *Annals of the Congress of the United States*, 8th and 9th Congress, 1803–1807 (Washington, 1852), give verbatim texts of debates and other proceedings. Material on his career as governor (1819–22) and as assemblyman (1823–25) may be found in the printed *Journals of* the Virginia House of Delegates for the six legislative sessions between 1819–20 and 1824–25 (Richmond, 1821–24). For Randolph's participation in the Florida boundary survey of 1827, see *House Executive Documents*, 20th Cong., 1st sess., Doc. 2, (K), 105–43. Also useful for various aspects of his career are *American*

State Papers; Military Affairs (Washington, 1832), and William P. Palmer, Sherwin McRae, and H. W. Flournoy (eds.) *Calendar of Virginia State Papers . . .* (11 vols.; Richmond, 1875–93); volumes IX and X of the *Calendar* are especially valuable.

An unofficial but extremely useful document is Rodney H. True (ed.) "Minute Book of the Agricultural Society of Albemarle," in American Historical Society, *Annual Report, 1919* (Washington, 1920).

PRINTED CORRESPONDENCE

The various published editions of Jefferson's writings, as might be surmised, were as indispensable to this study of Randolph as were the major manuscript collections of the third President's papers. For the period it covers, Julian P. Boyd (ed.), *The Papers of Thomas Jefferson* (17 vols. [to date]; Princeton, 1950–), is unsurpassed in its inclusiveness and in its extensive interpretation. Older editions of Jefferson's works are Paul L. Ford (ed.), *The Writings of Thomas Jefferson* (10 vols.; New York, 1892–99), and A. A. Lipscomb and A. E. Berg (eds.), *The Writings of Thomas Jefferson* (20 vols.; New York, 1903). The former is the most accurate and satisfactory.

Primary materials relating to Randolph also appear in Henry S. Randall, *The Life of Thomas Jefferson* (3 vols.; New York, 1858); in Sarah Nicholas Randolph, *The Domestic Life of Thomas Jefferson*, (New York, 1871, reprinted, with introduction by Dumas Malone, New York, 1958); and in the two works edited by the late Edwin M. Betts, dealing with Jefferson's agricultural and horticultural interests, *Thomas Jefferson's Garden Book, 1766–1824, with Relevant Extracts from his other Writings* (Philadelphia, 1944) and *Thomas Jefferson's Farm Book, with Commentary and Relevant Extracts from Other Writings* (Princeton, 1953).

Other useful letters and other documents were located in Armistead Churchill Gordon, *William Fitzhugh Gordon* (New York, 1909); John P. Kennedy, *Memoirs of the Life of William Wirt* (Philadelphia, 1849); and Harriet M. Salley (ed.), *Correspondence of John Milledge, Governor of Georgia* (Columbia, S.C., 1949). James Wilkinson's *Memoirs of My Own Times* (3 vols.; Philadelphia, 1816), although outrageously biased in favor of its reputed author, was helpful for Colonel Randolph's part in the ill-fated St. Lawrence campaign of 1813.

TRAVEL ACCOUNTS, DIARIES, AND MEMOIRS

Scattered references to Randolph are found in travel narratives and similar works by various foreign as well as American contemporaries. Particularly helpful were the revealing comments by the French émigre nobleman Francois-Alexandre-Frédéric, Duc de La Rochefoucauld-Liancourt in his *Voyages dans Les États-Unis d'Amérique fait en 1795, 1796 et 1797* (8 vols.; Paris, 1799) and by the British diplomat Augustus John Foster in his "Notes on America" (manuscript in the Library of Congress and the Henry E. Huntington Library). Foster's notes have been published as *Jeffersonian America: Notes on the United States of America Collected in the Years 1805–6–7 and 1811–12*, edited by Richard Beale Davis (San Marino, California, 1954). Also useful was Mrs. Samuel Harrison (Margaret Bayard) Smith, *The First Forty Years of Washington Society*, edited by Gaillard Hunt (New York, 1906).

Randolph is mentioned in the diaries of contemporaries. Senator William Plumer's *Memorandum of the Proceedings of the United States Senate, 1803–1807*, edited by Everett S. Brown (New York, 1925) throws light on the Colonel's congressional years, while Volume VII of the *Memoirs of John Quincy Adams, Comprising Portions of his Diary*, edited by Charles Francis Adams (12 vols.; Boston, 1874–77), deals with Randolph's participation in the Florida boundary survey of 1827. *Jefferson at Monticello*, edited by Hamilton W. Pierson (New York, 1862) which contains the reminiscences of Jefferson's overseer Edmund Bacon, was published more than a generation after the events it describes and thus should be used with caution. It is balanced, to some degree, by the broadside rebuttal to it made by Thomas Jefferson Randolph, in *The Last Days of Thomas Jefferson* (Charlottesville, 1873; copy in the Alderman Library).

In a somewhat different category is the work titled *Travels through the Interior Parts of America* (2 vols.; London, 1789), which was long attributed to Lieutenant Thomas Anburey of the British army. This work was subjected to a searching examination by Whitfield Bell, Jr., in his article "Thomas Anburey's 'Travels through America': A Note on Eighteenth Century Plagiarism," in *Papers of the Bibliographical Society of America*, XXXVIII (1943), 23–36. Despite Dr. Bell's well-founded skepticism about this work,

Anburey's account of the visit of the British officers to Tuckahoe in 1779 has the ring of validity.

The description of Edinburgh during the years when the Randolph boys were at the university is based largely on William Creech, "Letters . . . respecting the Mode of Living, Arts, Commerce, Literature, and Manners of Edinburgh," which appeared as part of Sir John Sinclair's *Statistical Account of Scotland* (21 vols.; Edinburgh, 1791–99).

BIOGRAPHIES

Of the many Jefferson biographies available, one of the most useful has been the authoritative work by Dumas Malone, *Jefferson and His Time* (3 vols. [to date]; Boston, 1948–), which carries the great statesman's story through his election to the presidency in 1800. Earlier but still useful works are Randall's *The Life of Thomas Jefferson*, Randolph's *The Domestic Life of Thomas Jefferson*, and James Parton, *The Life of Thomas Jefferson* (Boston, 1874).

Among the biographies of other important contemporaries used in the work were Irving Brant's six-volume life of Madison (Indianapolis, 1941–1961), notably the third and fourth volumes—*James Madison: Father of the Constitution, 1789–1800*, (Indianapolis, 1950) and *James Madison: Secretary of State, 1800–1809*, (Indianapolis, 1953); Richard Beale Davis, *Francis Walker Gilmer: Life and Learning in Jefferson's Virginia* (Richmond, 1938); William Cabell Bruce, *John Randolph of Roanoke* (New York, 1922); and E. Merton Coulter, *Thomas Spalding of Sapelo* (Baton Rouge, 1940).

BOOKS, MONOGRAPHS, AND DISSERTATIONS

Among the most useful general works consulted were Thomas P. Abernethy, *The South in the New Nation, 1789–1819* (Baton Rouge, 1961), and Charles S. Sydnor, *The Development of Southern Sectionalism, 1819–1848* (Baton Rouge, 1948). These books are Volume IV and Volume V of Wendell H. Stephenson and E. Merton Coulter (eds.), *A History of the South* (8 vols. [to date]; Baton Rouge, 1947–). Despite its bias and occasional errors of interpretation, Henry Adams, *History of the United States of America during the Administrations of Thomas Jefferson and James Madison* (9 vols.; New York, 1889–91), is still valuable for its narrative of political, military, and diplomatic events. Published too late to be consulted in connection with this work, but extremely revealing of political cleavages of the period, is Norman K. Risjord, *The Old Republicans: Southern Conservatism in the Age of Jefferson* (New York, 1965).

More specialized works include Philip Alexander Bruce, *History of the University of Virginia* (5 vols.; New York, 1920–22), Avery O. Craven, *Soil Exhaustion . . . in Virginia and Maryland, 1607–1860*, (Urbana, 1926); Wayland F. Dunaway, *History of the James River and Kanawha Company* (New York, 1922); Thomas T. Waterman, *The Mansions of Virginia* (Chapel Hill, 1945), and Edgar Woods, *Albemarle County in Virginia* (Charlottesville, 1901).

Theses and dissertations consulted include Harry Ammon, "The Republican Party in Virginia, 1789 to 1824" (Ph.D. dissertation, University of Virginia, 1948); James H. Bailey, "John Wayles Eppes, Planter and Politician" (M.A. thesis, University of Virginia, 1942); and Carol M. Tanner, "Joseph C. Cabell, 1778–1856" (Ph.D. dissertation, University of Virginia, 1948).

ARTICLES

Thomas J. Anderson, "Tuckahoe and the Tuckahoe Randolphs," in *Annual Report of the Monticello Association*, 1936, was valuable for genealogical information. Also useful were Joseph Vance, "Knives, Whips and Randolphs on the Court House Lawn" in Albemarle County Historical Society, *Papers* (1955–1956), 28–35, and Norma B. Cuthbert, "Poplar Forest: Jefferson's Legacy to his Grandson" in *Huntington Library Quarterly*, VI (1942), 333–38. Much of the material on Randolph's plowing innovations is based on the author's "Thomas Mann Randolph, Piedmont Plowman" which appeared in Albemarle County Historical Society, *Papers* (1950–51), 37–43.

NEWSPAPERS AND PERIODICALS

Two of the most influential newspapers in the nation during Randolph's lifetime were the Richmond *Enquirer* and the Washington *National Intelligencer*, and extensive use has been made of both of them in this study. Other papers consulted were the Charlottesville *Central Gazette*, the Charlottesville *Virginia Advocate*, the Richmond *Compiler*, and the Washington *National Journal*.

The *American Farmer* (First series, Baltimore, 1819–34) and The *Farmer's Register* (Shellbanks, Va. and Petersburg, Va., 1833–43) were most helpful for agricultural matters. The latter periodical should be used in connection with Earl G. Swem (comp.), "An Analysis of Ruffin's 'Farmer's Register'," in Virginia State Library *Bulletin*, XI (1918), 411–44, if only because of its identification of the various semi-anonymous contributors.

Long before the age of Luce and David Lawrence, the United States had such prototypes of modern news-magazines in *Niles' Weekly Register* (Baltimore, 1811–49). The *Register* was particularly useful for its coverage of the 1828 presidential campaign and for the attempts of various participants to enlist the support of the departed Jefferson on behalf of their candidates.

Index